The Absolute Best Play Days

From Airplanes to Zoos (and Everything in Between!)

by Pamela Waterman

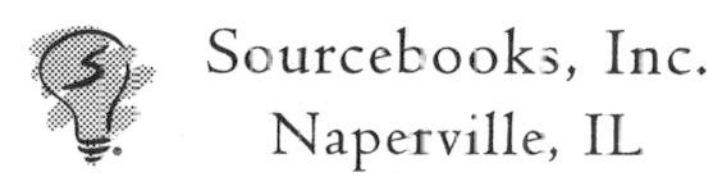

Cover design: Eric O'Malley, Sourcebooks, Inc.
Internal design: Kirsten Hansen, Sourcebooks, Inc.

Published by Sourcebooks, Inc.
P.O. Box 372
Naperville, IL 60566
Phone: (630) 961-3900
Fax: (630) 961-2168

ISBN: 1-57071-395-2

Printed and bound in the United States of America
10 9 8 7 6 5 4 3 2 1

Dedication

To my husband Jack, who encouraged me,
to my mother, who cheered me on,
and to Hilary, Gretchen, and Brenda, who inspired it all.

Acknowledgments

For all their ideas, time, and wisdom:

Lynda Zahm and Marilyn Romack, at New Morning School in Plymouth, Michigan, who continue to show the Primary class (and the co-op parents) how much fun it is to learn;

Laura Rush Stoabs and Gretchen Storck, babysitters extraordinaire;

Judy Teachworth, Patrick Persons, and the wonderfully helpful staff who make the Canton, Michigan, Public Library our favorite hangout;

the preschool teachers at Tender Learning Center in Burlington, Massachusetts, who first showed us the fun in creative play;

the preschool teachers at First United Methodist Church Early Childhood Center in Stillwater, Oklahoma, who have a lasting place in the hearts of our family;

Helen Pike, my author friend who kept me on track through the years of getting started;

Molly Keep, Shelly Arnold, Kaye Grubaugh, and Mercedes Williams, whose personal libraries of books and tapes proved to be a goldmine;

Robyn Greenberg, who kept insisting this would be good;

Todd Stocke and Jennifer Fusco, the editors who guided me through making it good;

Eric O'Malley and Kirsten Hansen for the beautiful design;

Shana Milke, whose strong and detailed indexing helped complete this project;

and to Emily Zahm, for all the Sunday afternoons of playing with our girls, so that this book could finally happen.

Table of Contents

52 Weeks of Theme Day Activities

How to Use This Book

Who hasn't had to help a six-year-old with a craft, read to a four-year-old, and play blocks with a two-year-old all at the same time?! Oh, and they need a snack, too! The reality of life is a frequent need to keep more than one child happy for more than one hour, and even the most creative parent, grandparent, teacher, or babysitter can run out of ideas. Younger ones want to feel they're doing just what the big kids are, and big kids get tired of toddler-limited play. Don't despair.

Children of all ages love Theme Days, where everything they do revolves around one idea, whether it's dinosaurs or detectives, school days or birthdays. I originally came up with these ideas so that my college-age sitter could keep my three children (then ages 6, 3, and 1) happy while I worked in my home office. All the books I'd seen either addressed many things for, say, just two-year-olds to do (not challenging for the older ones), or just one type of activity (e.g., crafts) for a range of ages (not enough for more than an hour's play). I decided to find lots of things for lots of ages to do together, and the idea grew into a family project. From there, friends who claim to be "creativity impaired" said it was just what they needed, and their children enjoyed helping with the testing.

You'll find that the themes in this book are designed to be non-gender-specific, and they offer different ways of doing the same thing to allow the full range of 2-to-6-year olds to join in. The activities and crafts use mostly everyday items, and the suggested books, cassettes, and videos are often available at public libraries or for rent/purchase at chain stores. Jump in anywhere, and enjoy this grab-bag of day-long possibilities.

What's Behind Each Theme

Each Theme Day section contains the following nine categories of information, with directions and notes for adapting the ideas for 2/3-year-olds, 4/6-year-olds, or your own situation. Sometimes the play activity makes use of the craft project, but otherwise you can do the activities in any order. You (and the children) may want to spend more time on one part than another, or skip a part entirely. Some outdoor activities can be adapted for indoors, and vice versa (especially considering the weather); similarly, the snack can be for morning or afternoon, or be made a part of lunch. Lastly, you can all decide when to snuggle in for the stories or to calm down with a videotape.

Art/Craft

Using paper, glue, tape, markers, cardboard, and all sorts of other simple supplies, the children will get to design artwork or put together crafts that illustrate some aspect of the day's theme. There are ideas for making things simply or more elaborately, depending on a child's skill level and interest, and the projects are designed for common sense and safety (generally meaning there is no use of balloons, marbles, beads, or other small objects). A materials list, instructions, and diagrams are on the third and fourth page of each theme's section. Also, feel free to adapt the ideas to what you can readily find (e.g., substitute wallpaper scraps for construction paper, or vice versa). Everyone will end up with a "thing" to keep, use, and display.

Indoor Activity

Every theme has one or more "active play" idea that can be done inside a house, whether the reason is a rainy day, a too-hot day, a too-cold day, or the need for a grown-up to get other things done indoors at the same time. A few of the ideas build upon the craft projects, but most are independent. The activities are generally designed for living and family rooms, but for fun and variety you may decide to set things up in a bedroom or even a not-too-fancy eating area. Children love it, too, when you move furniture around, to be different from the usual arrangement.

Outdoor Activity

Since children need the chance to run around, and caregivers need to let them burn off energy, there are activities designed to be done in the out-of-doors. The season and the weather will determine the possibilities (e.g., for Boat

Day, if it's hot, get out the wading pool; if it just rained, sail your new boats in a backyard puddle). You may find it fun to have a Snow Day in the middle of the summer, or play beach in the living room on a wintry Fish/Under the Sea Day. Other activities can be traded off for inside or outside, depending on everyone's mood.

Music

Activities with children just seem to go better when there is music playing in the background (if they want to get up and dance, that's great, too!), but don't feel you have to do the singing—just put on a cassette or CD and have everyone join in. The appendix lists many sources for music, plus you can look through your own collection of cassette tapes, CDs, and old records (if you still have a turntable). Check out what's available at the library. The children's section should have a variety of offerings divided by category, including some music combined with books-on-tape. Look, too, at the adult section for Broadway musical scores. You may only have one or two pieces that directly tie into the theme, but just keeping something going softly is a nice addition to the arts and crafts time, too. Lastly, take this chance to teach traditional children's songs such as "London Bridge is Falling Down," "I've Been Working on the Railroad," and standard nursery songs.

Book List

For each theme there is a list of ten children's books that tell related stories, often including an ABC, counting, or reference book. These have proven to be enjoyable to the full two-to-six-year-old range, but the symbols (2/3) and (4/6) indicate the simpler versus more verbal books. (However, many younger children will happily listen to the "older" books, so give them a try.) Check your city or school library for copies. Most public schools let adults take out books even if they don't yet have children in that school. Reserve purchasing books for special treats, unless you're really getting going on your own home collection. For more theme-related stories that are just as good but wouldn't fit elsewhere, see the Appendix: Even More Books.

Videotape List

There's nothing wrong with having everyone settle down to a commercial-free videotape when it's time to take a break. These days, there seems to be a video on every topic, whether it's a storybook read out-loud (such as from the Reading Rainbow or Children's Circle collections), a fairy-tale done in animation or with real people, a feature movie now on tape, or one of the ever-expanding number of non-fiction children's tapes that show and explain some aspect of the world around us. At least one tape is given per theme, and in some cases there is more than one version of the same story. Look for them in your library or local rental store, by title or subject; tapes with an asterisk (*) are listed in the appendix with the distributing company's name, address, and contact information for direct purchase.

Hints for Your Own Situation

For each theme, there is a sidebar that gives ideas you may use to better suit your specific children. Perhaps one or more of the children are four, five, or six years old, and can be trusted with smaller craft or food items (toothpicks, popcorn, or marshmallows). Or, you may have a very advanced (or enthusiastic) bunch of three-year-olds. For example, when building a castle, the two-year-olds will need Duplos or wooden blocks larger than their mouths, yet an older child may be quite capable of handling traditional Legos. If you are more ambitious and have the time, there are also ideas for more advanced projects, or projects that need work done ahead of time.

Snack-time

Everyone needs a snack sometime during a long day, and often lunch is a part of the plan. Don't leave eating-fun out of the day's theme—you will find ideas for munching that the children can help you to assemble, or that you may want to set up ahead of time. Very little cooking is involved, unless you choose to take it on. Adapt the food ideas for the children's tastes or dietary needs (consider food allergies or tolerance issues). One time-saver thought: when you're baking for a party, bake a second cake, leave it plain in round layers or as a sheet-cake, and freeze it. You can later decorate it with purchased canned frosting and decorating icing, to fit in with a day's theme. Also, keep canned frosting and tubes of different colored decorating icings on hand for quick "drawing."

A Little Something Extra

Each theme has an idea for a follow-up activity. It may be an address, phone number, or other resource to contact, which will let you find out a little bit more about the topic. It may also be a suggested field trip, a poem to learn, another good videotape idea, or in a few cases a recommended software package.

You can do the activities in any order, depending on the weather, the day's schedule, or just "going with the flow" of what the children feel like doing. When possible, let each game, project, or snack take as long as they want—you never know what will particularly inspire them, and who wants to stop that kind of fun?

Planning Ahead

Especially if you or someone else will be drawing upon these ideas on a regular basis (perhaps for a winter break or summer vacation), it really helps to plan ahead. See the next section for hints on "Stocking up on Supplies," including a check-list of ideas on art, craft, toy, and play/dress-up materials to discover, recycle, or buy. If a sitter is coming on a regular basis, get her or him in on the planning.

With enough notice, you can buy ahead some "special" related items (see the appendix); perhaps order a few catalog items to arrive throughout the months, spreading out the budget and creating some surprises. Maybe it's time to buy a new set of building blocks, wind-up fish, a set of plastic or wooden farm animals, or a book with a built-in "clock" to help teach about time. When possible, organize the materials, library books, and rental tapes a few days in advance, and pull out the next day's theme toys the night before or early in the morning. Use quiet coloring or reading time to set up for the next project, and get the older ones to help as much as possible. Don't forget to build in clean-up time, even for the little ones.

Change the order, change the age-level, and add your own touches. The children will love the variety, and you'll all be tickled it was so easy to fill those long days!

Note: Keep a camera handy—there'll be a lot of lively moments to capture for the future.

Stocking up on Supplies

Take stock of the toys, building things, dress-up clothes, books, tapes (music and video), and art/craft supplies already in your house. For each theme's craft, you may already have most of the "raw materials" on hand. For music and video tapes, look through your own collection and that of the local library, then consider asking your friends if you can swap off certain tapes (make a list of what you have, then copy the list to pass around). For toys in general, think about which things might be used in different ways than perhaps the original intention. Lastly look to see which items you still need or might want. Many of the art/craft supplies come in packages with enough to use for many different projects, and dress-up clothes may be found at yard sales and thrift shops throughout the year.

Prioritize your list to see what items you'll spend some "big" money on (a new tea set, "sliceable" plastic fruit and vegetables, a set of stencils—these items are on the order of $20 each), and where you can use items of lesser cost (new boxes of crayons, markers, and sidewalk chalk; pads of drawing paper, a package of construction paper, a new set of water colors or poster paint—on the order of $3 each.)

Art/Craft Supplies

What supplies do you already have?

	Have	Don't Have
Boxes of every shape and size–shoe boxes, cereal boxes, gift boxes, packing boxes (Store big boxes such as refrigerator or TV boxes by removing tape, collapsing them, and keeping them under beds, behind dressers, in the basement, etc.)		
Tubes from paper towels, toilet paper, shipping tubes		
Plastic baskets from strawberries or tomatoes		
Used white paper (for recycling back-sides)		

Have	Don't Have	
		Plastic baby wipe boxes
		Shoelaces
		Egg cartons
		Containers from frosting, yogurt, modeling dough, margarine
		Jars (plastic are best, but also glass; mayo, baby food); keep the lids
		Empty plastic bottles (shampoo, honey, dish liquid)
		Fronts from greeting cards
		Catalogs, particularly of children's items and flowers
		Plastic straws
		Wallpaper scraps
		Sandpaper
		Wire clothes hangers
		Empty thread spools
		Paint sample strips (great for collage snippets)

	Have	Don't Have
Cookie cutters (great for tracing on paper, & cutting modeling dough; nested sets of four may cost only $3)		
Cotton balls (in white and pastel colors)		
Yarn		
Ribbon (gift wrap, craft, or sewing types)		
Lids from cans of frozen juice		

Simple things to buy

	Have	Don't Have
Construction paper		
Tracing paper (Think you can't draw? Never underestimate the power of tracing paper.)		
Washable markers		
Yarn		
Rolls of white or brown paper (shelf-lining paper, butcher's paper, kraft paper, adding machine tape rolls)		
Chenille pipe cleaners		
Tape (regular, masking, and clear packing tape)		

Have	Don't Have	
		Glue and Tacky craft glue; also glue sticks (less messy than glue and works with most paper)
		Brass brads (fasteners)
		Sidewalk chalk
		Bubble blower liquid
		Modeling dough in different colors
		Stickers on sheets or rolls (watch for free ones in the mail with magazine offers)
		Crepe-paper streamers
		Velcro dots (adhesive backed)
		Sets of cookie cutters (hearts, stars, theme shapes)
		Thin poster board sheets (especially white); gold and neon colors cost more, but one sheet can go a long way
		Magnets (not too small, preferably with a hole in them)
		Water-color paint sets with chubby brushes
		Plastic spring-type clothes pins, and wooden craft ones
		Wooden craft sticks (⅜" by 4 ½" or ¾" x 6")

	Have	Don't Have
Wooden paint stirring sticks		
New coloring books that go with the day's theme		
Inexpensive plastic pails (buy a bunch in summertime)		
Facepaint sets		

More expensive supplies to consider buying

Washable crayons and markers

Stencil sets (large sturdy plastic ones)

Rubber stamps and washable ink pads

Bags of flat plastic "jewels"

Large bottles of washable poster paints (They cost several dollars each, but they last a long time and are worth it to get the washable type.) Build up a collection a bottle a week!

Paper hole punches in decorative cut-out shapes

Stick-EES plastic window-cling decorations

Have	Don't Have

Ways to organize the supplies

Some of these items you may have on hand, or you may consider buying:

Cardboard fold-them-yourself magazine holders (available at office supply stores for about $7 per four) are good for holding sheets of scrap paper, stencils, coloring books, construction paper, etc.

Brown gusset (accordion pleat) file holders will hold construction paper or white paper neatly on their edges.

Stacked metal or plastic letter trays can hold sheets of paper or any number of small boxes.

Boxes that new checks come in are a nice size for scissors, tape, and glue sticks.

Empty baby-wipe boxes are great for crayons, markers, rubber stamps, craft sticks, and cotton balls. They also keep upright the small bottles of bubble-blower liquid.

One strong box with a lid (copy paper-type) serves well for all the odds 'n ends.

Toys for Inside/Outside Play

Good toys you may already have

Wooden building blocks of assorted shapes and sizes
Duplo building blocks, maybe with some of the "themes" they offer (zoo animals, house furniture, etc.)
Puzzles of all kinds (cardboard, plastic, and wooden)
Puppets
Magnetic letters

Lower cost toys to buy

Have	Don't Have

Magnifying glasses
Butterfly nets
Wooden building block sets (on sale!)
Hula hoops (for circus acts, things that spin, and things that make noise)

"Special Treat" toys to buy

Plastic fruit and vegetables that "slice" apart and go back together with Velcro patches
A castle building set with little knights, horses, treasure chests, etc.
Real binoculars
Simple musical instruments (often sold in sets in catalogs)

Dress-Up Clothes/Props

Materials from around the house, yard sales, and thrift shops can all contribute to dress-up fun. An excellent costume idea book is *I Can Make Costumes* by Mary Wallace (Owl/Greey de Pencier Books 1996).

Dress-up materials on hand

Old lace or ruffle curtains (these make great bridal veils and shawls)
Hats and gloves
Old ballet/tap recital outfits
Vests
Suspenders
Scarves
Big old shirts, T-shirts, sweatshirts, and sweatpants
(Remember that ties and belts may not be good around the little ones.)

Have	Don't Have

Dress-up props to consider buying

Plastic hats (construction worker, race-car, police officer, firefighter)
Doctor's kit (plastic stethoscope, blood-pressure cuff, thermometer, etc.)
Carpentry tools (plastic hammer, screwdriver, wrench, pliers, toolbelt, etc.)
Cotton bandanas in all sorts of colors and patterns
Scarves (be careful younger children don't tie them around their necks)
Lengths of knit fabrics from the remnant tables at fabric stores (You can cut them to any size, and they won't ravel. Big squares make great instant capes, and long strips wrapped around arms or legs make everything from a cast to a ballet slipper.)

Several good ways to store dress-up clothes are in an old plastic hamper or in laundry baskets. Accessories can go in shoeboxes or small rectangular plastic baskets.

With children of these ages, you can usually get away with pulled-together outfits, so the more pieces you have the better—don't think you have to have a whole outfit that looks head to toe like it came together. Usually, the more colors and layers the better, and children don't seem to notice if a scarf or fabric scrap was never hemmed, or if the flea-market special is torn or spotted.

52 Weeks of Theme Day Activities

Airplanes

Art/Craft

- Make paper airplanes, simple or advanced. Decorate them with markers, crayons, rubber stamps, and stickers. Experiment with folding them in different ways. Add paperclips in different places to add weight, but tape them on so little ones won't pull them off (see directions).
- Make handkerchief or tissue parachutes, the old fashioned kind, by tying four strings or lengths of yarn to the corners. Bring the strings together in the middle at the free ends, and tie on a weight (paper clips, small black binder clips, or some pieces of cardboard with holes punched through for strings) (see directions).
- Make cardboard airplane models from a paper-towel tube, strips of thin cardboard (cereal-box type) and pipe cleaners or wide craft sticks (see directions).

Indoors

- Tape a drinking straw to the back of a paper airplane, then thread a string through the straw. Tie the string to furniture or knobs at opposite ends of a room, with one end lower than the other. Fly the airplanes inside by sliding them along the string (but make sure no one trips over the string).
- Have the children be airplanes themselves, zooming around a room (preferably a comfortable room without steps or breakables, to provide soft "landings!")
- Play your own version of either Red Light, Green Light or Simon Says, but call it Control Tower. Take turns letting each child be the Air Traffic Controller (do you have some kind of official-looking cap to wear?)
- Use masking tape to lay out a landing-strip on the living-room floor. Get out any toy airplanes you have, or the ones you've made, and take-off, land, and taxi around.

Music

Songs for traveling, or instrumentals that sound like soaring on wings

Hints for Your Own Situation...

An older child could work on a plastic kit that just snaps together, or a balsa wood kit with washable glue.

☆ ☆ ☆

Very young ones can enjoy the sticker and coloring part and then let you make all the paper airplane folds.

☆ ☆ ☆

Get more ideas from the book *Paper Airplanes* by Nick Robinson (Quintet/Chartwell 1991)

Snack-time

Long and thin pieces laid across each other make good "airplanes." Try celery sticks, strips of carrots, quarter-sections of graham crackers, strips of toast, or hotdogs sliced lengthwise (leave one half long, cut the other in half again across the middle). Tail pieces and a rudder could be from Bugles snacks. Depending on your choice of ingredients, you can "draw" windows and a windshield with salad dressing, squeezable jelly, or ketchup.

☆ ☆ ☆

A one-quart juice carton in the middle of the table can be the control tower.

Outdoors

- Fly the paper, plastic, or balsa planes and see whose goes highest, farthest, fastest (and which one survives the longest). Mark where they land and have the children pace off the distance and count the number of shoe-lengths.
- Watch birds flying and see how they use their wings to soar, float, slow down, and land.
- Watch for planes going overhead. Do any of them leave condensation trails? Can you see any propellor planes?
- Run around with "wings" out as planes, but mark a rectangle as the runway: only one child there at a time.

Books

The Airplane Book by Edith Kunhardt
(Golden/Western 1987) (4/6)

Flying by Donald Crews
(Greenwillow Books 1986) (2/3)

Planes by Richard Scarry
(Western/Golden 1992) (4/6)

A First Airplane Ride by Carol North
(Golden/Western 1986) (4/6)

Airplanes: A First Discovery Book by Pascale De Bourgoing
(Scholastic 1992) (4/6)

Plane Song by Diane Siebert
(Harper Collins 1993) (2/3)

Planes by Anne Rockwell
(E.P. Dutton 1985) (2/3)

Planes: See How It Works by Tony Potter
(Aladdin/Macmillan 1989) (4/6)

Mr. Little's Noisy Plane by Richard Fowler
(Grosset & Dunlap 1988) (4/6)

Little Red Plane by Ken Wilson-Max
(Scholastic Cartwheel 1996) (2/3)

Videos

Cleared for Takeoff (Fred Levine)*; The Big Plane Trip*
Angela at the Airport*; Walk, Ride, Fly!*
At the Airport! (Papillon Productions)*
The Magic Schoolbus: Taking Flight

Art/Craft Materials

white or construction paper
thread
tape, scissors
facial tissue
paperclips or a binder clip
paper towel tube
small paper cup or yogurt cup
posterboard or thin cardboard
pipe cleaners
wide (¾") craft sticks

Art/Craft Directions

Paper Airplane

1) Start with a piece of white paper. Fold it in half lengthwise

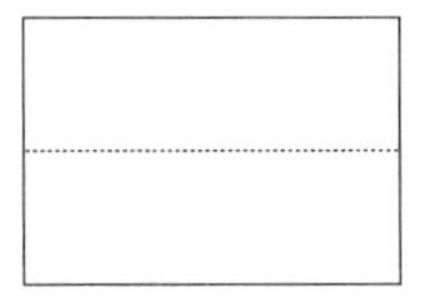

2) Fold corners back.

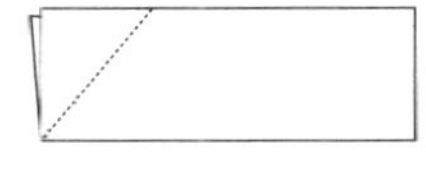

3) Fold edges back again.

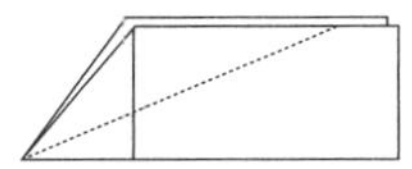

4) Fold 2 edges back again.

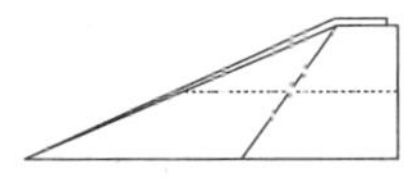

5) Fold both sides down halfway, then lift them up as wings.

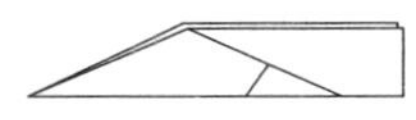

6) Tape together at top front edge, and bend up rear edges slightly. Try other bends, lengths, and cut-out bits.

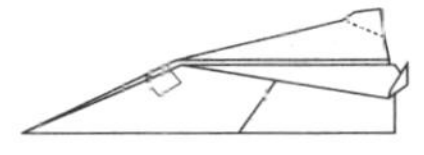

For a Little Something Extra...

Visit a nearby airport, even just to park nearby and watch the planes take off and land. If you can see lots of planes go over your house, note the time that the planes appear, and see if they fly over at the same time again the next day.

Tissue Parachute

1) Cut 4 pieces of thread, each about 12" long. Tape one to each corner of the tissue. Tie the free ends together.

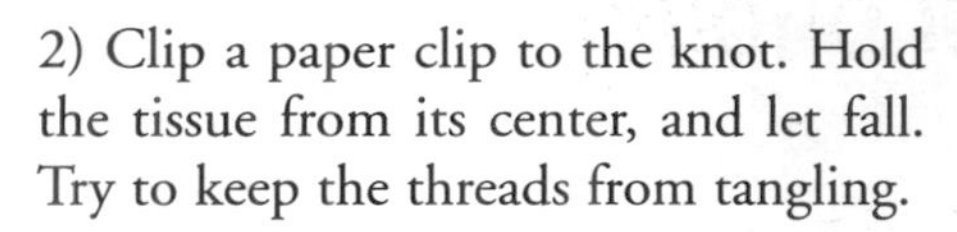

2) Clip a paper clip to the knot. Hold the tissue from its center, and let fall. Try to keep the threads from tangling.

Cardboard Airplane

1) Cut 4 slits in a paper towel tube, 2 on opposite sides.

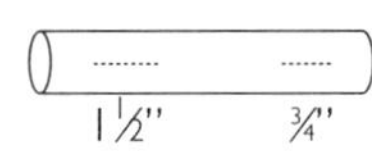

2) Cut a strip of cardboard to fit through the larger slits. Push through and tape.

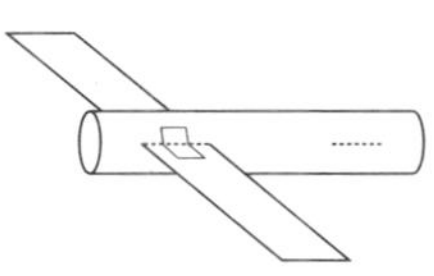

3) Push a wide craft stick through the smaller slot and tape. Cut and tape a cardboard rudder on top.

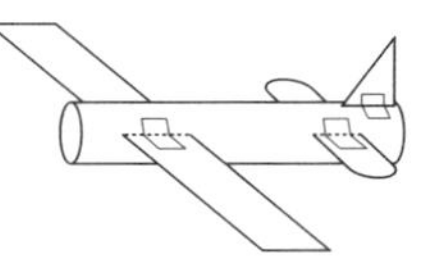

4) Tape a paper cup or yogurt cup on the front end.

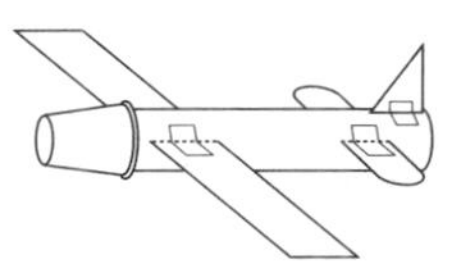

5) Cut a pipecleaner in half. On each, fold ends into middles to make loops, and twist together. Tape one over the other on the cup, for a propellor. Decorate with markers and stickers.

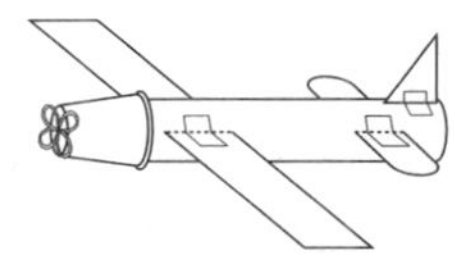

Astronomy

Art/Craft

- Make small rockets with paper towel tubes, toilet paper tubes, and construction paper (see directions).
- Get an empty refrigerator box from a store, and lay it on its side. Cut and decorate it to look like the space shuttle, adding other cardboard pieces for wings. (This could be a special place for reading.)
- Draw what outer space looks like to you, using white chalk (or other colors) on black construction paper.
- Make space helmets by covering a box with foil, cutting out a face-opening. Punch holes with a pencil, then thread some coiled pipe cleaners partially inside (tape down the inner ends) as antennae, or push through knobs, dials, and any hardware that you can safely secure on the backside without having any rough parts stick out (see directions).
- Make a pair of googly alien eyes you can wear like glasses, using an empty egg carton and pipe cleaners (see directions).

Indoors

- If everyone can't fit in your cardboard Space Shuttle at one time, line up chairs to be seats in a bigger Space Shuttle. Can you count numbers down for liftoff? Have them tell what they would see out the window as they go through the clouds, above the earth, and into space.
- Have a star show by projecting constellations on a wall or ceiling in a dark room or closet. Punch holes into sheets of cardboard in patterns (Big Dipper, Orion, Casseopia, etc.) and shine a flashlight from behind them.
- Dress up as astronauts; explore the house for life forms!
- Read *Little Bear* by E.H. Minarik (he goes to the moon).

Music

Hello Sun, Goodnight Moon (SongSisters);* "Twinkle, Twinkle Little Star";
Sailor Moon;* "Adventures in Space" (On the Move w/Greg & Steve)*

Hints for Your Own Situation…

Older children can make launchable rockets: inflate a balloon (oblongs are best) but don't tie it off. Tape a plastic straw along one side, then let the balloon deflate. Run a long string through the straw. Tie one end of the string to a doorknob or a tree branch. Tie the other end across the room or yard. Carefully inflate the balloon again, pinching it closed, then let it go. Watch it speed across the room, guided on the string!

☆ ☆ ☆

On a nice day, use the power of the sun to make sun-tea. Get a big glass jar, fill it with water, and put in tea bags as desired. Set it in the sun for the day. Bring inside, pour into ice-filled glasses, and enjoy.

Outdoors

- Try walking and jumping as if you were on the moon, where gravity is not as strong, and on Jupiter (as if you could walk on it!) where gravity would really pull you down and make you walk s-l-o-w-l-y.
- Astronauts must exercise. Have children run, stretch to reach for the stars, and bend to collect moon rocks.
- Play tag with shooting stars and comets! Cut out star shapes plus one big circle (comet). Tape the comet with a length of crepe-paper streamer to one person; tape stars to everyone else. As the "comet" runs, the stars try to catch up and grab the tail. The catcher becomes the next comet.

Books

Goodnight Moon by Margaret Wise Brown (Harper & Row 1982) (2/3)
Tinker and Tom and the Star Baby by David McPhail (Little, Brown and Co. 1998) (4/6)
Zenon, Girl of the 21st Century by Marilyn Sadler (Simon & Schuster 1996) (4/6)
Night Goes By by Kate Spohn (Macmillan 1995) (2/3)
Grandpa Takes Me to the Moon by Timothy R. Gaffney (Tambourine Books 1996) (4/6)
Beyond the Milky Way by Cecile Schoberle (Crown 1986) (2/3)
Arrow to the Sun by Gerald McDermott (Puffin/Penguin 1974) (4/6)
Min-Yo and the Moon Dragon by Elizabeth Hillman (Harcourt Brace Jovanovich 1992) (4/6)
Why the Sky is Far Away by Mary-Joan Gerson (Little Brown & Co. 1992) (4/6)
Nora's Stars by Satomi Ichikawa (Philomel Books 1989) (4/6)

Snack-time

Cut stars of bread, sliced cheese, or sandwiches, using a set of nested cookie cutters.

☆ ☆ ☆

Make a rocket ship dessert from peeled bananas. Cut one in half across the middle, then again lengthwise. Place each of the four pieces on a plate. Cut two chocolate bars in half, then each in half diagonally. Put a triangle on either side of one banana's lower edge to make "fins." Write USA on the banana with a tube of icing, and use canned whipped cream to squirt some "exhaust" coming out the base.

☆ ☆ ☆

For a special treat, serve miniature Milky Way candy bars.

Videos

The Magic School Bus: Out of this World/ In Outer Space;
Richard Scarry's A Trip to the Moon;
Star Scouts Discover NASA #1*; Walk, Ride, Fly!*

Art/Craft Materials

paper towel tube
2 toilet paper tubes
white paper
markers
scissors, tape, glue
box big enough to go over child's head
foil
pipe cleaners
knobs, dials, tubing (not too small)
egg carton

Art/Craft Directions

Rocket Ship

1) Cover 2 toilet paper tubes and 1 paper towel tube with white paper. If you don't have a paper towel tube, tape 2 more toilet paper tubes together end to end.

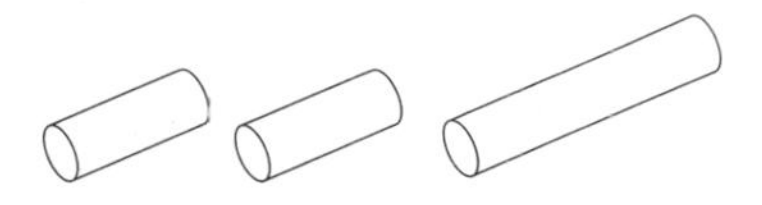

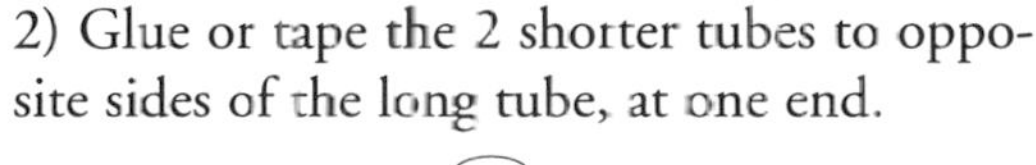

2) Glue or tape the 2 shorter tubes to opposite sides of the long tube, at one end.

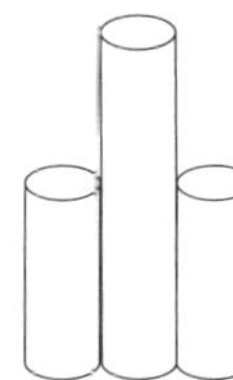

3) Cut half of a 6" circle out of a piece of white paper. Curl it into a cone until it makes a good fit over the top of the tall tube. Secure it with a little glue and tape.

4) Use markers to draw on stars, write USA down the side, and add an American flag.

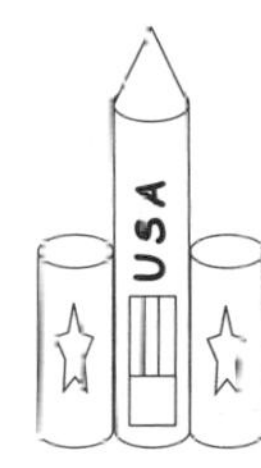

For a Little Something Extra...

Stay up late one night and watch the stars come out. Get a book on constellations, and see if you can find the Big and Little Dippers, Orion, Gemini, Casseopia, etc.

☆ ☆ ☆

Buy freeze-dried astronaut ice-cream from Edmund Scientific: (800) 728-6999

Space Helmet

1) Cut away any flaps from the box, and cut out an oval for the face hole. If it's a bit long, cut away arches to make room for the shoulders.

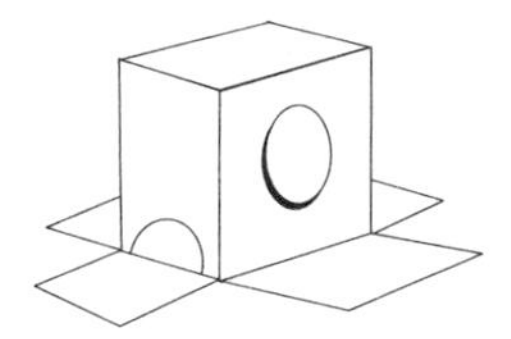

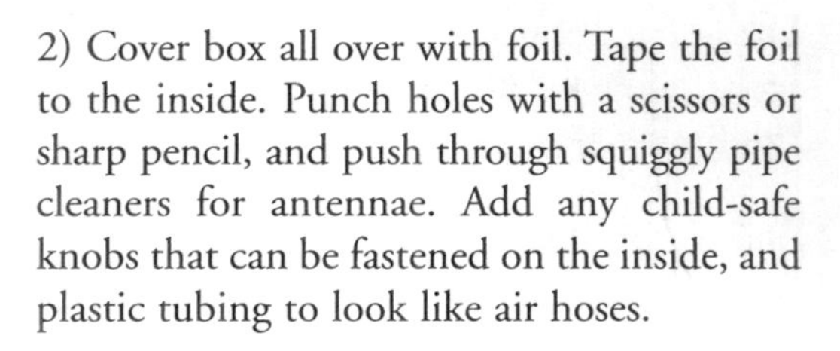

2) Cover box all over with foil. Tape the foil to the inside. Punch holes with a scissors or sharp pencil, and push through squiggly pipe cleaners for antennae. Add any child-safe knobs that can be fastened on the inside, and plastic tubing to look like air hoses.

3) Be careful how/when you play, since the helmet can limit your side vision. You may want to cut extra slots and holes for better visability.

Alien Eyes

1) Cut out 2 attached cups from an egg carton. Cut or poke holes in each center.

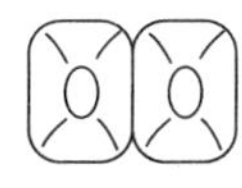

2) Decorate the cups with markers, or cover them both with foil. Poke holes on either side. Push a pipe cleaner through each hole and twist it to stay on. Add more pipe cleaners for antennae; add paper eyebrows or lashes.

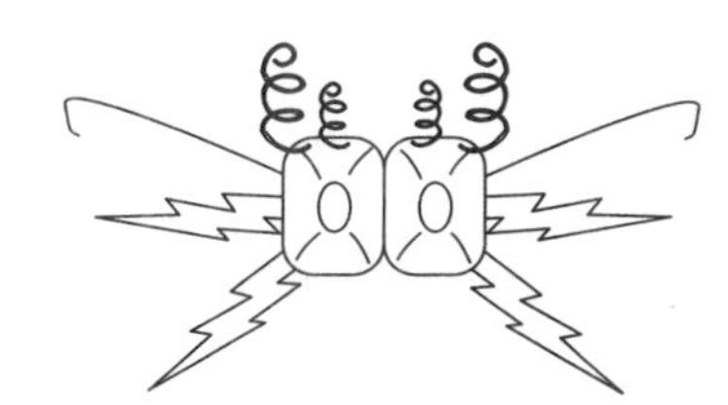

Balls

Art/Craft

- Roll balls out of modeling dough. See how small and how big a ball you can make. Can you stack them? Flatten them? Stick them together to make funny critters?
- Buy a tube of cake-decorating silver sugar balls (very small). Pour some in a flat tray. Put a book on top and see how easy it is to move the book around. Try again without the balls.
- Make sock balls for indoor tossing. Take old socks (use baby socks, children's socks, adult socks and tube socks) and, starting at the toe section, measure out roughly just before the heel starts, and cut it in two pieces. Children can stuff the long part into the toe section, and a grown-up can whip-stitch the opening closed (see directions).

Indoors

- Collect all your indoor balls (big rubber balls, foam balls, "koosh" balls, wiffle balls). Set up a laundry basket, stand back, and toss them in. Or, take a big box, draw a face or a flower on one side, cut out the mouth or center, and let children aim to toss soft balls inside.
- Take one ball, have everyone sit in a circle, and play hot potato, passing it around as fast as you can.
- Use stacks of books and folded board-games to lay out paths, walls, archways, and ramps. Have each child try rolling a small ball through the path without having it bounce or roll out of bounds.
- Collect 10 empty 1-liter soda bottles (or flavored water bottles). Line them up bowling-pin style (rows of 1, 2, 3, and 4), and take turns rolling a big ball at them. If they keep falling over, fill them part-way with water, screw on the lids, and try again.

Music

"Take Me Out to the Ballgame"
Play Ball! (Cincinnati Pops)*

Hints for Your Own Situation…

For older children, bake peanut-butter cookies that start out as balls of dough.

☆ ☆ ☆

Make "bubble" wrapping paper by blowing colored bubble-blowing liquid onto sheets of white paper. They will pop and leave a colored circle. You can use the dry paper as wrapping paper or notepaper (see directions).

☆ ☆ ☆

A tightly rolled-up pair of socks will also work for quite a while as a sock ball!

Snack-time

Depending on the age of the children, serve a bowl of round corn-puff cereal, make melon balls from cantelope or watermelon, serve the peanut-butter cookies that started out as balls, or make traditional popcorn balls.

☆ ☆ ☆

Try Hostess Sno-Ball snacks for a special treat.

Outdoors

- If you don't have a low basketball hoop, set up a bucket or laundry basket for tossing balls of all sizes. If you have a slide, roll different size balls down the slide to see if you can get them in the baskets. Which ones go faster?
- Have each child run across the yard while holding a ball, then drop it in a basket and run back; maybe make it a relay race. Play tag by tossing a beachball at someone.
- Inflate a beach ball, toss it up, and see if you can all keep hitting it to keep it in the air. Count how many times you can hit it before it falls. Tape a quarter to it, toss it again, and see how oddly it "flies."
- Huge rolling/climbing balls (handles or not) are great.

Books

Beach Ball by Peter Sis
(Greenwillow Books 1990) (2/3)
The Mystery of the Green Ball by Steven Kellogg
(Dial Press 1978) (4/6)
The Ball Bounced by Nancy Tafuri
(Greenwillow 1989) (2/3)
Play Ball, Zachary! by Muriel Blaustein
(Harper & Row 1988) (4/6)
Albert's Ballgame by Leslie Tryon
(Atheneum/Simon & Schuster 1996) (4/6)
Little Pig's Bouncy Ball by Alan Baron
(Candlewick Press 1996) (2/3)
Play Ball, Amelia Bedelia by Peggy Parish
(Harper Trophy 1972) (4/6)
Kenny and the Little Kickers by Claudio Marzollo
(Scholastic Cartwheel 1992) (2/3)
The Ball Book by Margaret Hillert
(Follett Publishing 1982) (4/6)
Playing Marbles by Julie Brinckloe
(Morrow Junior Books 1988) (4/6)

Videos

The Magic School Bus Plays Ball
The Huggabug Club: You Can't Win 'Em All!*

Art/Craft Materials

old socks, any size
needle, thread
scissors
blubble-blower liquid
food coloring
white paper (big rolls, if possible)

Art/Craft Directions

Sock Ball

1) Cut sock in two pieces, cutting roughly halfway between the heel and the toe.

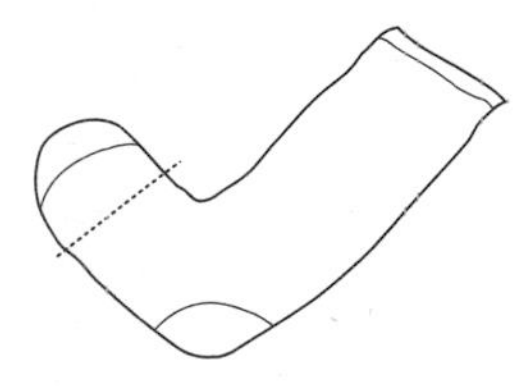

2) Open up the toe section. Roll up the remaining part and stuff it into the toe.

3) Pull edges together and bend them over to make a neat seam at the opening.

4) Stitch the overlapped edges closed with a whip stitch; don't worry that stitches show.

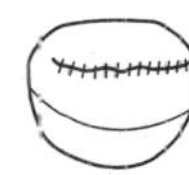

For a Little Something Extra...

The software package called *Thinkin' Things* (Edmark Corp.) includes five programs, one of which is called "Flying Sphere." It allows you to toss, catch, and move any number of different colored spheres. When they "hit," the colors mix!

☆ ☆ ☆

Buy colorful striped Zebra Beach Balls ($3.95 each from ActiveMinds Catalog). They come with a free sheet of ideas for different ways to use the stripes in games and activities.

Bubble Note/Wrapping Paper

1) Tape one piece, or part of a roll of white paper to a plastic-covered table. Or, do this project outside and weight the paper down with rocks.

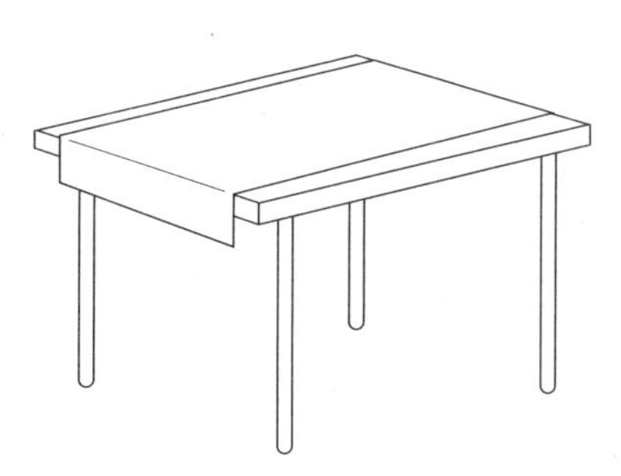

2) Pour small amounts of bubble blower liquid into individual plastic bowls (tubs from soft margarine are good). Add 6 drops or so of food coloring of each color desired, mixing in the different bowls. Stir.

3) Using a separate blower wand for each color, gently blow bubbles, aiming down toward the papers. When the bubbles pop, they will leave colored circles. Experiment with layers of different colors on one sheet of paper. Let the papers dry, then fold them or cut them to use as notepaper or wrapping paper.

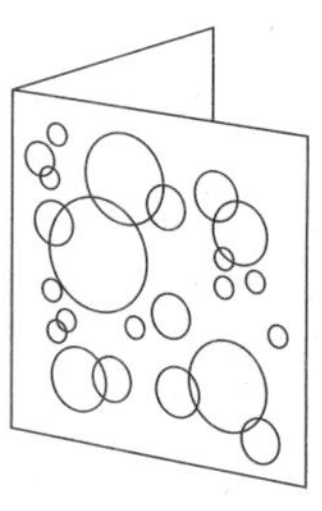

Bears

Art/Craft

- Make slightly stuffed bears by cutting brown paper bags or brown felt into two bear shapes. Decorate the fronts of the paper ones with crayons, markers, stickers, etc., or the felt ones by gluing on bits of colored felt for eyes, nose, etc. Glue the two pieces together at the edges, almost all the way around. After it's dry, stuff some tissues inside to puff it out a bit, then finish gluing. (You could use tape, too, or staples with tape over the backsides so they don't scratch.) (See directions.)
- Make paper or felt outfits to tape or press on your bear, like paper doll clothes.
- Make bear-ear paper headbands (see directions).

Indoors

- Collect all the teddy bears in the house. Get a blanket or tablecloth to spread on the floor, or a small table and chairs. Set out a tea set and have a teddy bear tea or picnic (just pretend, or make it part of snack-time).
- Not all bears are teddies. Do you have stuffed polar bears, pandas, or koalas? Use wooden blocks, shoe-boxes, books, etc. to set up the walls for a zoo. Use blue Legos or blue construction paper to make a pond for the polar bear, and an upside down bowl to be a snowy hill. Use a paper towel tube to make a tree for the koalas, then straws or craft sticks with green construction paper leaves will make bamboo shoots for the pandas (tape them together to make a fence).
- Cut out bear pawprint shapes from brown construction paper or paper bags, and tape them around the house. Make up stories about the invisible bear, where he is going, and what games he plays in each room he enters.

Music

"Teddy Bears' Picnic"
Totally Teddy (Derrie Frost)*
Unbearable Bears*

Hints for Your Own Situation…

Older children can use big embroidery needles to try sewing the felt bears together, or make the brown paper bears by punching holes around the edges and threading them together with yarn or shoelaces.

☆ ☆ ☆

Buy inexpensive bandanas or cut up fabric scraps to make outfits for the various teddy bears in the house. Help older children use safety pins to fasten together squares, triangles, and lengths of ribbon. Make capes, diapers, and silly hats. A circle of poster-board with the middle cut out will serve as a hat brim with a ribbon tied around it. A strip of cardboard, decorated and taped together into a band can be a crown or, together with a sheer fabric scarf, the headband of an Arabian bear.

Snack-time

Serve honey or jam on bread or muffins.

☆ ☆ ☆

Buy Teddy Grahams crackers.

☆ ☆ ☆

Cut wheat bread with several sizes of round cookie cutters, then assemble a head with ears, to make a bear that you can spread with honey, peanut butter or cut-up meat (see directions).

☆ ☆ ☆

Depending on your own bears' tastes and ages, serve berries, nuts, and sliced hard-boiled eggs —all good bear food!

☆ ☆ ☆

Serve "Three Bears" porridge—instant oatmeal!

Outdoors

- Pretend to be bears, and get down on all fours. How would bears explore your yard? Crawl, climb, stretch, and paw at the dirt for bugs!
- Bear cubs like to roll around on the ground, by themselves or with each other. Can you roll down a slope?
- Bears love to sniff. What can you sniff in your yard—flowers, trees, fresh dirt, a dog?

Books

Winnie the Pooh books by A.A. Milne
(the originals are 4/6; other versions 2/3)

Old Bear series by Jane Hissey
(Philomel Books) (4/6)

Corduroy by Don Freeman
(Viking Press 1968) (2/3)

Little Bear by Else Holmelund Minarik
(Harper Trophy 1957) (4/6)

Alphabears: An ABC Book by Kathleen Hague
(Scholastic/Henry Holt 1984) (2/3)

The Teddy Bear ABC by Clair Watts
(DK Publishing 1995) (2/3)

Bears: A First Discovery Book by Jeunesse/Bourgoing
(Scholastic) (4/6)

Hi Bears, Bye Bears by Niki Yektai
(Orchard Books 1990) (2/3)

Brown Bear, Brown Bear by Bill Martin Jr.
(Henry Holt 1992) (2/3)

Goldilocks and the Three Bears by Jan Brett
(G.P. Putnam's Sons 1987) (4/6)

Videos

Winnie the Pooh series; Paddington series*

Old Bear series*; GeoKids: Bear Cubs, Baby Ducks, etc.*
Little Bear: Meet Little Bear (E. Minarik/M. Sendak)
Get Your Teddy Ready (Shari Lewis)*; Corduroy and Other Bear Stories*
The Teddy Bear Factory*

Art/Craft Materials

brown grocery bags or
brown felt squares
tracing paper
markers, stickers, pencil, crayons
scissors, tape, glue, stapler
facial tissue

Art/Craft Directions

Brown Paper Bag/Felt Bear

1) Trace this bear, or enlarge it, or draw your own bear shape. Cut out two shapes from the brown grocery bags or felt. Decorate one side of one piece (markers and stickers for the paper ones, scraps of felt for the felt ones).

2) Glue together the edges of the bear, leaving several inches open for slight stuffing.

3) Stuff with shredded bits of tissue, poking them in with a pencil. Glue the opening closed. If the edges don't want to stay shut, add some tape, or staple the edges and tape over the backsides so the staples won't feel rough.

For a Little Something Extra...

Check out how many different kinds of bears you can see on your next trip to a zoo, or just sort out all the bears in your house by color, size, or fabric.

☆ ☆ ☆

Visit a National Park and find out about Smokey the Bear.

Bear-Ear Headband

1) Cut a brown paper bag into a strip about 20” long and 1½” wide. For each band, also cut out 2 paper squares about 3” on a side.

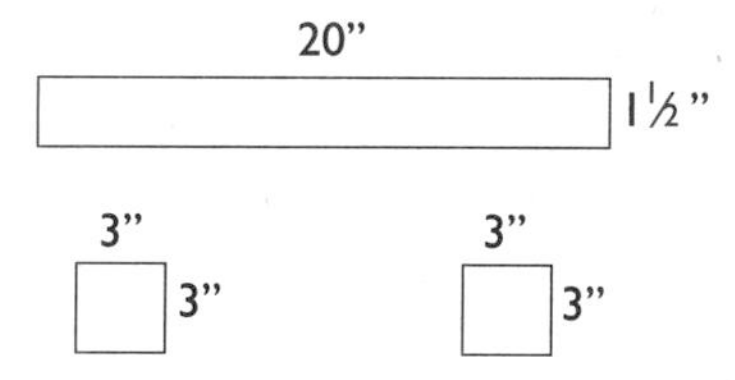

2) Overlap the ends of the band and fit the band to the child’s head. Staple the edges together, then cover the staples with tape.

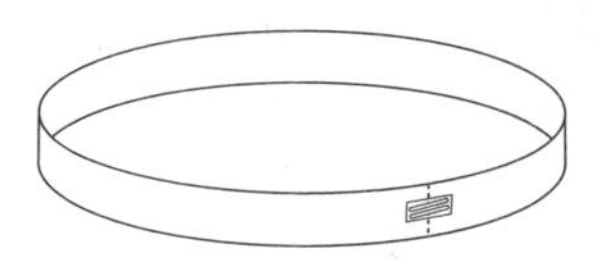

3) Use the scissors to round off the corners of the squares to make ears, and color the middles with red or pink markers.

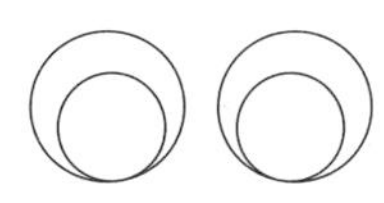

4) Fit the band on the child, and let her decide where she wants the ears. Staple the ears in place, and cover the staples with tape.

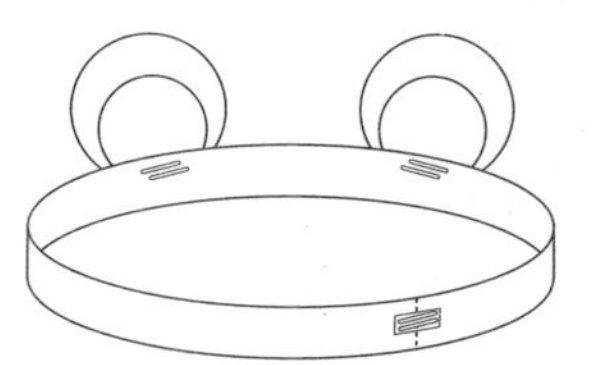

Teddy Bear Sandwiches

1) Cut slices of brown (wheat) bread into large and tiny circles, using cookie cutters or just a knife.

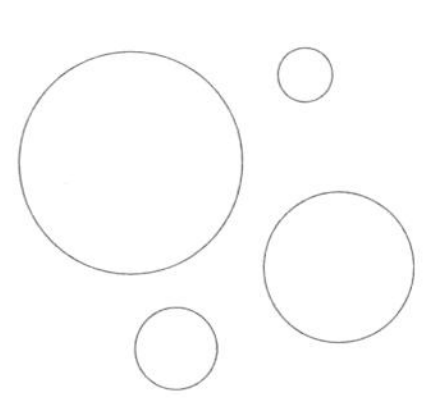

2) Lay the circles on a plate to make a bear head, or a whole bear. Decorate with honey, jam, fruit slices, or bits of cut-up meat.

Birds

Art/Craft

- Make binoculars from two toilet paper tubes by decorating them and taping them side by side. For older children, add a yarn or ribbon strap (see directions).
- Make snacks for the birds. Peel and core an apple. Cut it in cross-sections so you have flat circles. Soak them in lemon juice for a few minutes. Tie a string through the hole, and loop it over a bush.
- Make birds from folded paper and cardboard to hang from the ceiling or in front of a window (see directions).
- Make bird or "beak" masks from paper plates, string, construction paper, and posterboard (see directions).

Indoors

- How many different kinds of birds can you think of? Show how these birds would sing, walk, and fly (waddle like a duck or a penguin, peep like a chick, squawk like a parrot, caw like a crow, swoop like a hawk, honk like a goose).
- Play Blue Bird, Blue Bird Through My Window.
- Dance with pieces of crepe paper streamers in your hands to feel like a bird flying.
- Play "Bird Call" hide-and-go-seek. One child hides, then makes any sound that they think a bird would make. See who can follow the sound to find the hider, then take turns.
- At snack time, everyone can be "fed" as baby birds.

Music

"Kuckaburra;" "Little White Duck"
"Six Little Ducklings"
"The Ugly Duckling" (Danny Kaye)
"Feed the Birds" (Mary Poppins)

Hints for Your Own Situation...

Older children can make a pinecone bird snack (it's messy!) Wrap a length of yarn around the upper part of the cone, and tie, leaving about a foot for hanging. Use butter knives to spread peanut butter over as much of the surface as you can. Roll the cone in birdseed, then hang it on a tree. (Remember, once you start feeding birds, you must continue all that season—they will become dependent on it.) Remind them not to eat birdseed themselves.

Outdoors

- Take your binoculars out bird-watching. Are there any birds flying, sitting, walking, or drinking from a puddle?
- Listen for birds. Can you tell where they are sitting from the sound? Can you imitate their calls?
- Run around flapping your "wings" for good exercise: try little flaps for baby birds, big flaps for pigeons and bluejays, and huge flaps for eagles. How long can you stand on one leg like a flamingo? "Soar" like a hawk?
- Swing on swings to feel like you're flying.

Books

The Kingdom of Singing Birds by Miriam Aroher & Shelly O. Haas
(Kar-Ben Copies Inc. 1993) (4/6))

Seasons of Swans by Monica Wellington
(Dutton Children's Books 1990) (4/6)

Our Yard is Full of Birds by Anne Rockwell
(MacMillan 1992) (2/3)

Birds: A First Discovery Book by Claude Delafosse
(Scholastic Cartwheel 1993) (4/6)

Little Penguin's Tale by Audrey Wood
(Scholastic 1989) (4/6)

Feathers for Lunch by Lois Ehlert
(Harcourt Brace Jovanovich 1990) (2/3)

Round Robin by Jack Kent
(Simon & Schuster 1982) (2/3)

Make Way for Ducklings by Robert McCloskey
(Viking Press 1969) (2/3)

Grandmother's Pigeon by Louise Erdrich
(Hyperion 1996) (4/6)

Simon Finds a Feather by Gilles Tibo
(Tundra Books 1994) (4/6)

Snack-time

Serve separate bowls of "bird seed" (crispy rice cereal), "worms" (three-minute ramen noodles), and water; perhaps let them drink the water with a straw and pretend it's their beaks.

☆ ☆ ☆

Older children may enjoy eating toasted sunflower seeds.

☆ ☆ ☆

Make "nests" from shredded wheat biscuits. Crumble up two to four large biscuits in a bowl. If you'd like, sprinkle in some sugar. Drizzle in melted margarine, then mix. Press into muffin tins sprayed with non-stick spray, and bake 8 minutes at 325 degrees. Remove and fill with "eggs:" melon balls, blueberries, grapes (cut in half), or a spoonful of yogurt.

Videos

The Emperor and the Nightingale
GeoKids: Flying, Trying and Honking Around*
GeoKids: Bear Cubs, Baby Ducks, and Kooky Kookaburras*;
Mr. Popper's Penguins
Shamu & You: Exploring the World of Birds*

Art/Craft Materials

2 toilet paper tubes
construction paper
tape or masking tape
markers, stickers, crayons
hole puncher
yarn or thin ribbon
white paper
posterboard or thin cardboard
paper plates
feathers (optional)

Art/Craft Directions

Binoculars

1) Cover 2 toilet paper tubes with construction paper. Decorate with markers, stickers, etc. Write child's name on one side. Tape the 2 tubes side by side, wrapping the tape all the way around. If using masking tape, let the name show, then decorate the tape.

2) If you want, punch 2 holes near one end, one on each outer edge. String a length of yarn or ribbon through to make a neckstrap. Knot the ends through the holes.

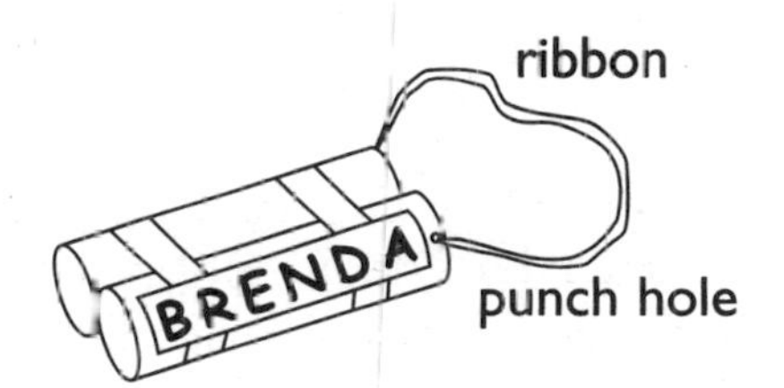

Bird Decoration

1) Trace this bird, or draw one of your own, onto posterboard, and cut it out. Decorate. Cut holes and slots as shown.

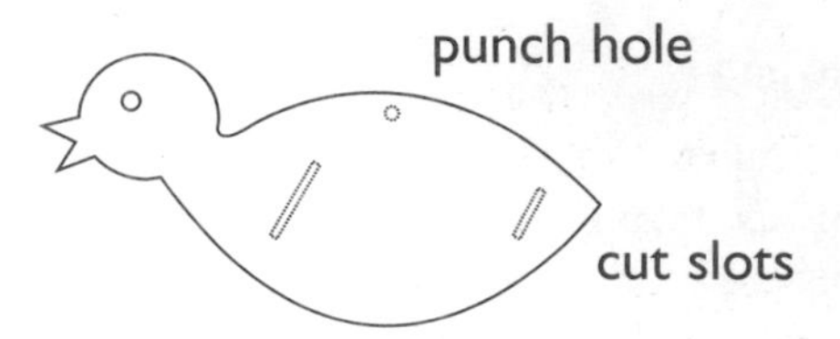

2) Fold two pieces of white paper in pleats. Cut one to about 5 inches. Slide them through the slots, with the longer one as wings, and the shorter one as a tail. Hang the bird from a piece of yarn.

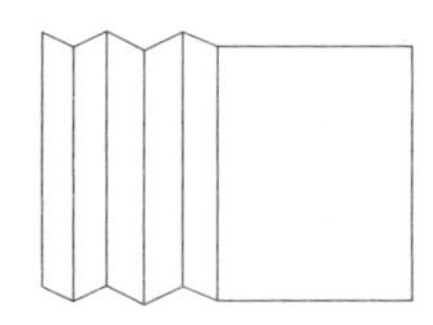

For a Little Something Extra...

If you have a video camera, leave it running (inside) while pointed out the window at a spot where you have left birdseed or bread-crumbs. (Try early morning to start it.) After two hours, rewind the tape and see if you've "caught" any birds on film! What kind of visitors did you have?

Bird Mask

1) Cut 2 round and 1 diamond-shaped holes in a paper plate, for eyes and a mouth. Use a hole punch and place 2 small holes on either side of the plate.

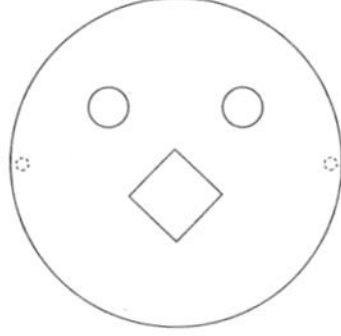

2) Cut 2 pieces of yellow or orange construction paper into 2 triangles.

3) Fold the triangles in half, and tape them around the diamond openings to form the top and bottom beaks. Tie lengths of yarn through the punched holes to make mask ties. Decorate with markers and feathers. (Feathers can be real, or made out of construction paper and decorated with markers.)

Birthdays

Art/Craft

- Draw the outlines of party hats on construction paper or wrapping paper. (Try some different and crazy shapes). Have everyone decorate their hats, then cut them out, assemble them with yarn or string ties, and wear them throughout the day (see directions).
- Buy a plain paper tablecloth for a dining table or cardtable. Have everyone use markers, crayons, stickers, etc. to decorate a part of it (you may want to draw dividing lines so children can identify their sections).
- Using a piece of posterboard, draw a variation of Pin the Tail on the Donkey: Horn on the Unicorn, Leg on the Flamingo, Beak on the Parrot, Arrow on the Bullseye (see directions).
- Celebrate someone's "half-birthday" (ex: a half-birthday for August 28 is February 28). Take a round cake, or cupcakes, cut them in half, frost, and celebrate!

Indoors

- Say that every day is someone's birthday somewhere, and today can be all of their "unbirthdays," so you always have an excuse for a party. Decorate with streamers.
- Wrap everyday items (a measuring cup, the lid to a plastic bowl, a comb, a plastic hangar, a crayon, a Lego, etc.) in gift wrap. Guess by the shape what's inside.
- If it's in the budget, wrap up small but real presents: a new coloring book, a box of favorite cookies, stickers that came free in the mail, even new socks!) Guess these too.
- Play Pin the Tail on the Donkey, Musical Chairs, beanbag toss, Drop the Clothespin in the Bottle.

Music

"A Very Merry Unbirthday" (Alice in Wonderland)
Happy Birthday (Sharon, Lois & Bram)*
Happy Birthday (Oscar Brand and Friends)*
Shining Time Station: Birthday Party Singsongs*

Hints for Your Own Situation...

Older children may cooperate on drawing one big picture all over a paper tablecloth. Each does part of the agreed-upon scene—pick a "place" such as a park, or a theme from one of the ideas in this book: under-the-sea, pirates, a zoo, favorite teddy bears, etc. Draw a centerpiece and a "platter" for setting out your snack.

☆ ☆ ☆

List the birthdays of everyone you can think of (friends, cousins, playmates, school chums); see if you know someone for every month, any holiday babies, or any birthday twins.

☆ ☆ ☆

Fold paper and design invitations for a party.

Snack-time

Make or buy cupcakes. Decorate them with more ready-made frosting, sprinkles, chocolate chips, M&Ms, etc. Add one candle each, and sing Happy Unbirthday!

☆ ☆ ☆

Make a pan of Jello Jigglers. Cut them in squares and rectangles. Use tubes of pre-made icing to draw on "ribbons" and "bows" to make them look like wrapped packages.

Outdoors

- Have a sack race using old pillow cases (or trash bags for older children).
- Set up an obstacle course: crawl through the legs of a row of plastic chairs (a tunnel); walk a path of two jump ropes or hoses laid side-by-side in squiggles; pick up a ball and carry it to a laundry basket; stack four blocks on top of each other; run around a tree; jump over buckets; walk a board laid flat; let a picnic cooler be the finish line, etc. (Reward each completion with a popscicle!)
- If you were an animal, what would be your favorite birthday present?

Books

The Birthday Thing by SuAnn and Kevin Kiser
(Greenwillow Books 1989) (4/6)

Too Much Birthday by Stan & Jan Berenstain
(Random House 1986) (4/6)

Birthday Wishes by Ann Schweninger
(Viking Kestrel 1986) (2/3)

Birthday Blizzard by Bonnie Pryor
(Morrow Junior Books 1993) (4/6)

Arthur's Birthday by Marc Brown
(Little Brown & Co. 1989) (4/6)

The Baseball Birthday Party by Annabelle Prager
(Random House 1995) (4/6)

Surprise! by Sally Noll
(Greenwillow 1997) (2/3)

The World's Birthday by Barbara Diamond Goldin
(Harcourt Brace Jovanovich 1990) (4/6)

The Half-Birthday Party by Charlotte Pomerantz
(Clarion Books/Houghton Mifflin 1984) (4/6)

Moira's Birthday by Robert Munsch
(Annick Press Ltd. 1987) (4/6)

Videos

Happy Birthday Old Bear*; Happy Snappy Birthdays*
Paddington's Birthday Bonanza*
Barney's Birthday

Art/Craft Materials

construction paper
wrapping paper
crayons, markers, stickers
scissors, tape
yarn for ties
posterboard

Art/Craft Directions

Party Hats

1) **Triangle hat:** cut one sheet of construction paper in half diagonally. Lay the two pieces next to each other, matching the shapes. Decorate.

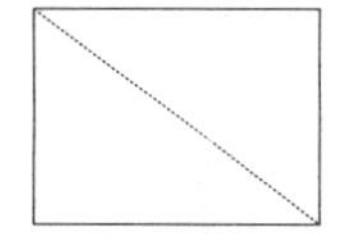

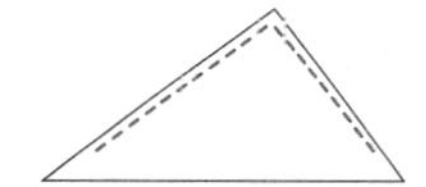

2) Staple the 2 top edges together, almost to the bottom, then bend up the the bottom edges to either side. Staple the ends together. Punch 2 holes on either side for chin ties.

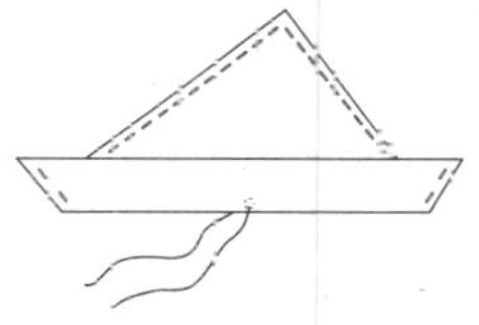

3) Tie yarn through side holes and tie hat on. (If you need bigger hats, use newspaper).

1) **Crown hat:** Cut strips of construction paper or posterboard (gold metallic is extra special), cutting a pointed, shaped, or scalloped edge.

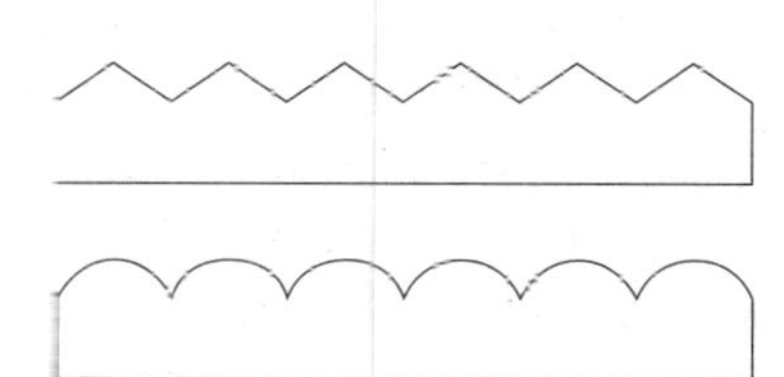

2) Bend strips into a circle, and fit to child's head. Staple, then tape the band edges together.

3) Decorate crowns with stickers or cut-out "jewels" from construction paper.

Pin the Tail on the Donkey Posters

Here are ideas for variations on Pin the Tail on the Donkey.

Cut horns for the unicorn.

Cut legs for the flamingo.

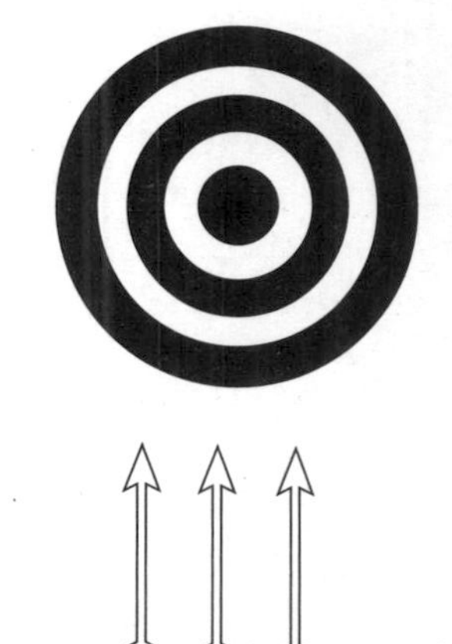

Cut arrows for the bullseye.

For a Little Something Extra...

A video that offers lots of ideas for hosting parties is "Happy Snappy Birthdays" from Kaplan Video Productions, Inc. (distributed by Big Kids Productions, Inc. (800) 477-7811).

☆ ☆ ☆

A great catalog of theme-based party supplies (pinatas, table settings, craft projects, favor ideas, etc.) is Birthday Express (800) 424-7843.

☆ ☆ ☆

Just before children's birthdays, help them choose some toys they no longer play with, and take the child with you to donate the toys to a charitable group.

Boats

Art/Craft

- Fold paper boats out of newspaper, white paper, or construction paper (see directions).
- Cut boats out of the bottoms (or length-wise) from waxed-paper milk or juice cartons; tape on a plastic straw mast, then add a cut-out paper sail and colored banner.
- Construct boats out of Legos. Draw a lake or the ocean on paper for them to sail on.
- Make fairy boats from walnut or pecan shell halves, with tiny drinking-straw masts stuck into a bit of modeling dough and holding a paper sail (see directions).
- Make a raft from craft sticks glued side-by-side onto two more sticks laid across the ends (see directions).
- Use markers or paint to draw different types of boats (tiny sailboats, big clipper ships, a tugboat, a rowboat, a canoe, a submarine, a steamship). Look in books, outdoor supply catalogs, and travel magazines for pictures to copy.

Indoors

- Gather any boats you have, and those you have made, then sail them in a plastic tub set into the sink or bathtub (keep towels around for overflow, and never leave little ones unattended). Can you be the wind and blow on them to make them move? What happens when a wave hits?
- See what else you have that might float (or sink): plastic stacking cups, shells, a keychain, a piece of paper, plastic bowls, a wooden spoon, margarine tubs, different kinds of bars of soap (take care not to get soap in eyes). Talk about which ones float and which ones sink; what happens if you fill a floating cup with water?
- Get two or three laundry baskets. Sit in them and pretend to sail away to distant shores.

Music

"Where Go the Boats?"
Little Mermaid (Disney); Muppet Treasure Island

Hints for Your Own Situation...

An older child can carve boats out of Ivory soap bars with a butter knife or thick plastic knife. It may help to draw an outline of the ship first, with a pencil or a pen.

☆ ☆ ☆

Help children cut flat kitchen sponges into boat shapes (sailboat, submarine, tugboat) and use them to sponge-paint notecards, a tote-bag, or a T-shirt.

Snack-time

Have an adult bake potatoes. After they've cooled, cut them in half, scoop out the insides (save for mashing) and use the microwave oven to melt cheese into each "boat."

☆ ☆ ☆

Make a banana boat: spoon yogurt onto a plate for the "sea," and place a peeled banana on that. Use jam to stick o-shaped cereal to sides for portholes. Use short sections of straws (or toothpicks) to attach strawberry halves as "jib" sails or slices of American cheese as square-rigger sails.

Outdoors

- Sail your boats or do floating experiments in plastic dish-tubs set on a patio. If it's hot, use a wading pool, but decide if the children go in, too, or if you all sit around the edge. Blow on the boats, fan them, race them, pull them with a string (for older children).
- After a rain, if you have puddles in a safe place, have everyone put on rain boots (if it's cool) or watershoes (if it's hot) and wade to make waves while they sail their boats. Watch leaves or pine needles floating as they form their own kind of boats.

Books

Four Brave Sailors by Mirra Ginsburg (Greenwillow Books 1987) (2/3)

Richard Scarry's Boats by Richard Scarry (Golden Books 1992) (2/3)

Ship of Dreams by Dean Morrissey (Harry N. Abrams, Inc. 1994) (4/6)

Sail Away by Donald Crews (Greenwillow Books 1995) (2/3)

I Love Boats by Flora McDonnell (Candlewick Press 1995) (2/3)

The Boats on the River by Marjorie Flack (The Viking Press 1946) (2/3)

Shipwreck Saturday by Bill Cosby (Scholastic Cartwheel 1998) (4/6)

Scuffy the Tugboat by Gertrude Crampton (Golden/Western 1974) (4/6)

The Little Boat by Kathy Henderson (Candlewick Press 1995) (4/6)

Who Sank the Boat? by Pamela Allen (Putnam & Grosset 1996) (2/3)

Videos

There Goes a Boat (Kid Vision 1994)*
All About Boats*

Art/Craft Materials

construction paper
scissors, tape
stapler, packing tape (optional)
milk or juice cartons
plastic straws, toothpicks
string, ribbons
walnut or pecan shell halves
modeling dough
craft sticks, glue
plastic bowls, cups

Art/Craft Directions

Folded Paper Boat

1) Take one sheet of construction paper, and fold it in half lengthwise to about 9" x 6".

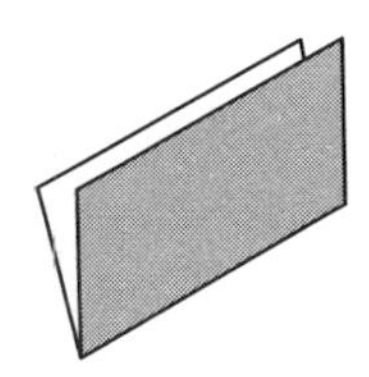

2) Unfold the paper, and fold it again one inch away from the first fold, on both sides of the center. Unfold again, but let the two sides stand up.

3) Fold the side edges down toward the outside, about one inch each.

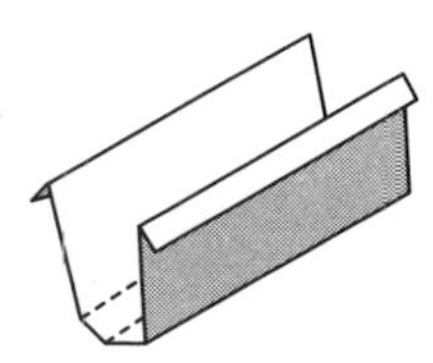

4) Cut in along the two off-center folds, going in just about two inches. Bend these "flaps" straight up.

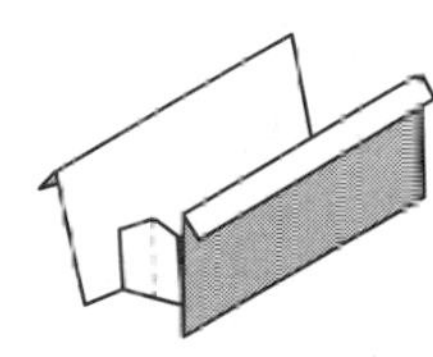

For a Little Something Extra...

Write to a Harbormaster or Ship's Captain, in care of your local Navy Base or Coast Guard Station. Tell him or her about your paper boat or raft, and perhaps include a drawing or photo of it. Ask about their favorite place to sail, if it's an exciting job, and what you'd need to do to be a sailor. Maybe they'll send a picture of their own boat!

5) Bend two sides in toward each other, crossing over the flap, just until the top corners meet to form a point and the bottom edges almost completely overlap.

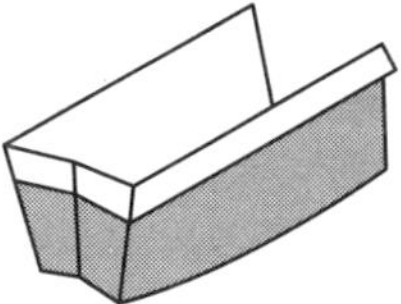

6) Tape the point together, then reach down with a stapler and staple the flap twice. Repeat at the other end of the boat.

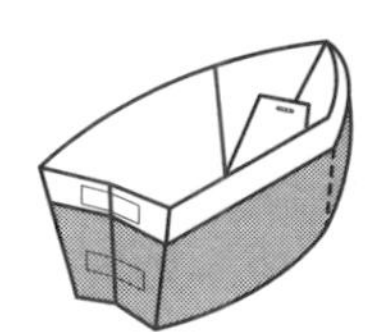

7) Put tape over the cut edges. For a longer lasting boat, tape the entire bottom and sides with clear packing tape.

Fairy Boat and Raft

For the Fairy Boat, stick a bit of modeling dough in the bottom of a walnut shell. Cut a plastic straw to make a mast, and a paper sail. Cut two holes in the sail, and slide it on the mast.

For a raft, lay craft sticks (small or large) across two more craft sticks, and glue them all in place. Stick a piece of plastic straw in a bit of modeling dough, to make a flag-pole. Tape on a tiny paper pennant.

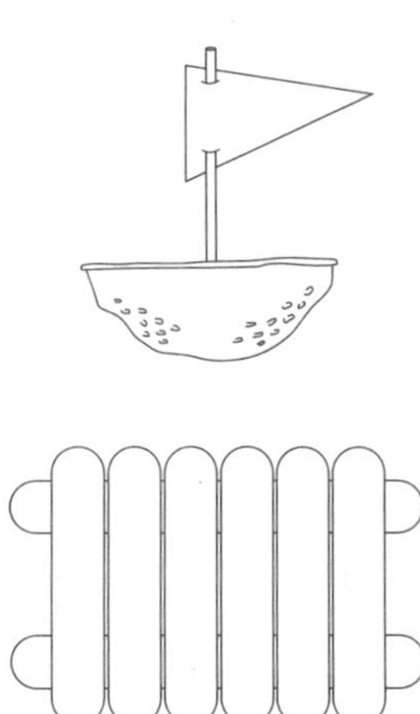

Bugs/Butterflies

Art/Craft

- Color and cut out butterflies with lacy wings. Cover the openings with inserts of colored tissue paper or cellophane; hang them together to make a mobile, or hang them over a window (see directions).
- Make a bug-collecting jar (clear plastic peanut butter jars are good—punch a few air-holes in the lid with a nail).
- Design spiderwebs with white chalk or crayon on black construction paper.
- Make spiders and ladybugs out of modeling dough and pipecleaners (they don't have to be just black and red!)
- Make a caterpillar from construction paper loops or an egg carton (see directions).
- Make a dragonfly by slightly criss-crossing two craft sticks, and gluing them across a third one. Draw on eyes, and decorate them with markers or stickers.

Indoors

- Get some exercising in by pretending to be inch-worms wiggling on their tummies on the floor; fireflies or bees zooming around the room; and butterflies slowly fluttering their wings (lie down on floor, put arms and legs out to side or up in air—together and apart).
- Get a bug's perspective on the house by saying, "For the next fifteen minutes, no walking—everyone crawl!" Do things look different from down there?
- If you could be a bug or insect, which kind would you be? Where would you like to make your home? What would you like to eat?

Music

Insects, Bugs & Squiggly Things (Jane Murphy)*

Try slow music for being inch-worms, fast music for being fireflies/bees, happy music for being a butterfly.

"Itsy Bitsy Spider;" "Flight of the Bumblebee"

Hints for Your Own Situation...

The paper butterflies can be more elaborate for older children, with several colors of tissue paper used; younger ones can simply use markers to color a butterfly shape that you draw.

☆ ☆ ☆

Who can find the longest insect (most colorful, loudest, fastest?) Why are praying mantis and ladybugs helpful?

☆ ☆ ☆

Look up butterflies versus moths in an encyclopedia.

☆ ☆ ☆

Start an ant farm with a kit from a catalog or nature store.

Snack-time

Serve gummy worms in ground up chocolate-cream wafer cookie "dirt" or chocolate pudding "mud."

☆ ☆ ☆

Slices of apple or orange, placed back to back, make butterfly wings with half a grape for a head and peelings from a mozzarella cheese-stick for antennae.

☆ ☆ ☆

Make ladybug open-face sandwiches: a slice of balogna, raisins pressed on top, straight thin pretzels for legs and also for feelers on a half black olive head.

☆ ☆ ☆

Use canned frosting to decorate vanilla wafers as different kinds of bugs.

☆ ☆ ☆

Make ants-on-a-log: celery sticks filled with peanut butter and topped with raisins.

Outdoors

- Take a tour of the yard in search of "wildlife," regardless of the season; what signs do you see that bugs have been around? (Look for webs, cocoons, casings, ant-hills, wings, or holes eaten in leaves.)
- Collect some bugs in your collecting jar. Be sure to put in some leaves and grass, and drops of water. Use a magnifying glass to watch them over the course of the day, and then release them.
- Run around with short-handled butterfly nets—are there moths, too? (No luck? at least it's exercise).

Books

Amanda's Butterfly by Nick Butterworth
(Delacorte Press 1991) (no words, 2/3)

The Butterfly Alphabet by Kjell B. Sandved
(Scholastic Hardcover 1996) (2/3)

The Very Hungry Caterpillar by Eric Carle
(Philomel Books 1969) (2/3)

Look ... a Butterfly by David Cutts
(Troll Assoc. 1982) (2/3)

Herman and Marguerite—an Earth Story by Jay O'Callahan
(Peachtree Publishers Ltd. 1996) (2/3)

The Best Bug Parade by Stuart J. Murphy
(Harper Collins Children's Books 1996) (4/6)

The Great Monarch Butterfly Chase by R.W.N. Prior
(Bradbury/Macmillan 1993) (2/3)

Creepy, Crawly, Baby Bugs by Sandra Markle
(Scholastic 1996) (4/6)

Bees by Tancy Baran
(Wonderbooks/Grosset & Dunlap 1971) (2/3)

Miss Spider's Tea Party by David Kirk
(Callaway/Scholastic 1994) (2/3)

Videos

Charlotte's Web; A Cricket in Times Square
Bugs Don't Bug Us!*; Eyewitness: Insect*
See How They Grow: Insects & Spiders (DK/Sony)*

Art/Craft Materials

construction paper
colored cellophane (optional)
wire hanger
plastic straws
colored tissue paper
white chalk or crayon
yarn or string

Art/Craft Directions

Hanging Butterflies

Pattern #1

Trace this pattern or draw your own. Use as a pattern to cut out several butterflies from colored construction paper. Cut out the oval shapes. Tape pieces of cellophane or tissue paper over the holes. You can hang just this one, from a length of yarn, or, you can make 6 or 8 butterflies, and turn them into a mobile. Hang them from different lengths of yarn, and on either side of small sections of plastic straws.

For a Little Something Extra...

Check out the Web site for the Young Entomologists' Society (1915 Peggy Place, Lansing MI 48910-2553). http://members.aol.com/YESsales/minimall.html. They have an extensive on-line catalog for all things "bug-related," including T-shirts and caps.

☆ ☆ ☆

This one's a splurge ($21.95), but order a Butterfly Garden (which includes a mail-in certificate for painted lady caterpillars) from Insect Lore (800) LIVE BUG. Or look for a similar butterfly kit in a kid's specialty store or a nature store.

Pattern #2

Mobile

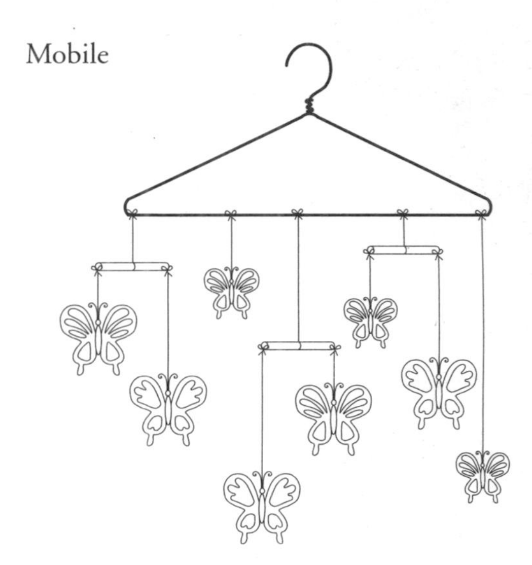

Paper Chain Caterpillar

Make a construction paper chain, like a holiday decoration, then glue a face shape and antennae to the front loop.

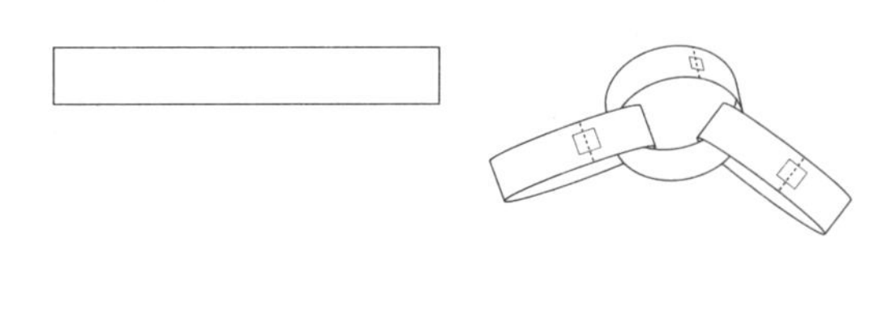

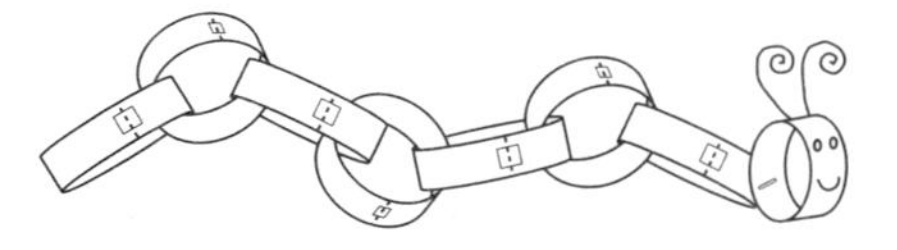

Egg Carton Caterpillar

Cut an egg carton in half length-wise. Stick pipe cleaners in the sides of 5 of the cups, tape them inside, and bend the ends up for 10 legs. Stick 2 more through the top of the first cup, and bend them up for antennae. Use markers to draw eyes, mouth, and spots.

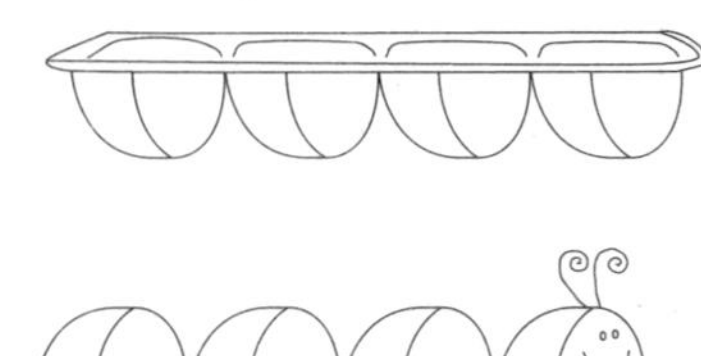

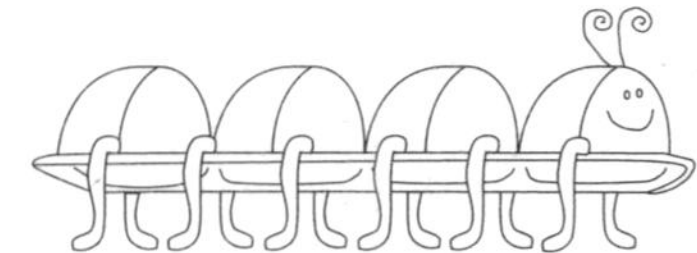

Camping

Art/Craft

- Put together a "mess kit": staple 2 paper plates, one cut in half, to a whole one. Fill with plastic fork and spoon and napkin. Take a plastic cup with a handle, or a paper cup with a small hole cut near rim, then tie a string through the hole or around the handle. Punch a hole in the rim of the plates; tie a short string from the cup to the plate rim. For younger children, use baby silverware (see directions).
- Make "trail mix" for later snacking. Combine one cup each of (your choice): raisins, rice/wheat/corn squares, tiny pretzel twists, chocolate chips, dried apricot bits, cereal, peanuts (if okay); divide into small bags.
- Decorate a paper lunch bag, with each child's name, to be their outdoor "hike" treasure-collecting bag. Add a handle to make it easy to carry (see directions).
- After a collecting walk, come inside and make a collage of the items by pushing them into a modeling-dough ball.

Indoors

- Spread a big blanket on the floor. Spread a sheet or another blanket over a rope strung between two chairs (or spread a tablecloth or blanket over a card table or several high-backed chairs). Get out the flashlights and the sleeping bags. Turn down the lights and tell stories.
- For a great night-time effect, buy a package of glow in the dark stars (about $3) that you can stick on any surface with a bit of sticky putty (included in star package). Stick them to the underside of the cardtable or blanket, and "charge" them up with the flashlights.

Music

Sing any Scout songs you know
Camping (Disney Children's Favorites #4)
Sing Around the Campfire (Sharon, Lois & Bram)*

Hints for Your Own Situation...

Older children can use a compass in the backyard to find out which way is north, which way the house faces, which way their room faces, etc.

☆ ☆ ☆

Braid plastic lacing (also known as gimp) into a holder (lanyard) for a whistle or keys (see directions).

☆ ☆ ☆

Can you find any animal tracks outside (could they belong to Fido or Fifi? a bird or a rabbit?)

☆ ☆ ☆

Younger children should not be given marshmallows.

☆ ☆ ☆

Use mirrors for sending sun signals (but not in others' eyes).

Outdoors

• You could just do the same as indoors, but there may be more options for tying a rope to a tree limb or a fence.

• If there are rocks or bricks around, put them in a ring with twigs inside, for a mock campfire pit. Sit around and share your lunch or snacks, and tell stories. Wear shorts, T-shirts, and caps; older ones can wear whistles.

• Go on a "hike" for as far as you can go, around trees, through bushes, to the far edge of the yard, to the mailbox, or to a garden's edge. Talk about all the things you see. Bring along paper bags for collecting nature's treasures.

Books

Arthur's Camp-Out by Lillian Hoban
(Harper Collins 1993) (4/6)

Bailey Goes Camping by Kevin Henkes
(Greenwillow 1992) (4/6)

The Berenstain Bears Go To Camp by Stan & Jan Berenstain
(Random House 1982) (4/6)

When I Go Camping With Grandma by Marion Dane Bauer
(BridgeWater Books 1995) (4/6)

Arthur Goes to Camp by Marc Brown
(Little Brown & Co. 1982) (4/6)

The Camping Trip by Robin Michal Koontz
(Cobblehill Books 1994) (4/6)

Pig Pig Goes to Camp by David McPhail
(E.P. Dutton 1983) (2/3)

Richard Scarry's Camping Out by Richard Scarry
(Aladdin/Simon & Schuster 1995) (2/3)

I Don't Want to Go to Camp by Eve Bunting
(Boyds Mill Press 1996) (4/6)

Camping Out by Richard Scarry
(Aladdin/Simon & Schuster 1995) (4/6)

Snack-time

Make microwave S'mores: take a square of graham cracker, topped with a half a chocolate bar, then a large marshmallow, then another square of graham cracker (for a sandwich.) Heat at about 70% power for 30 seconds (but check for your own microwave oven).

☆ ☆ ☆

Serve hotdogs, beans, bread and sliced apples for lunch, eaten with your mess kit utensils. Remember: don't leave litter at your campsite.

☆ ☆ ☆

Let children forage for snacks by clothes-pinning small plastic bags of cereal or trail mix to low tree branches. Have them run around to search.

Videos

Let's Go Camping (Vermont Story Works 1995)
There's No Camp Like Home (Winnie the Pooh)
Barney's Campfire Sing-Along

Art/Craft Materials

2 paper plates
paper napkins
hole punch
scissors, tape, staple
plastic spoons and forks
plastic handled cup, or paper cup
plastic lacing or string
key ring
brown paper lunch bag

Art/Craft Directions

Mess Kit

1) Cut one of the paper plates in half. Have the 2 plates face each other, and staple them together.

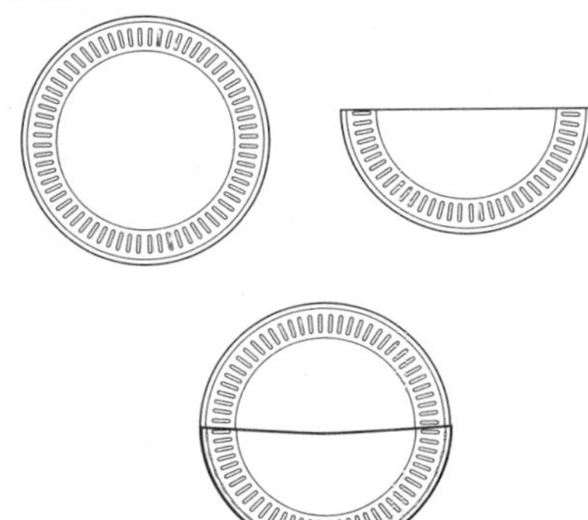

2) Punch a hole in the rim of the doubled plates. Tie a 1-foot length of string or yarn through the hole, and tie the other end to the handle of a plastic cup (or through a hole in the side of a paper cup).

3) Load up the mess kit with plastic silverware and a napkin.

For a Little Something Extra...

Buy each child a flashlight—they now come in wonderful colors.

☆ ☆ ☆

Write to a national park for brochures about their wonders.

Lanyard

1) Loop 3 strands of plastic lacing or yarn, 2 yards each, through the key ring and back through itself, so there are 6 lengths hanging.

2) Group the yarn into 3 groups of 2 strands each.

3) Braid the lacing to the desired length, then tie a knot and cut off any extra.

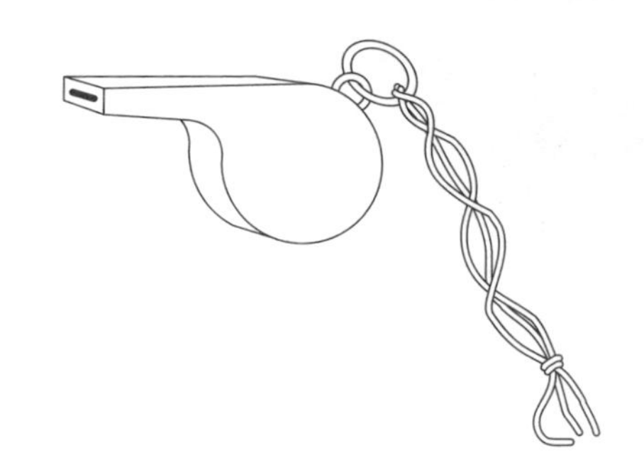

Collecting Bag

1) Cut the top 2" off a brown lunch bag and save. Decorate the bag with child's name and stickers.

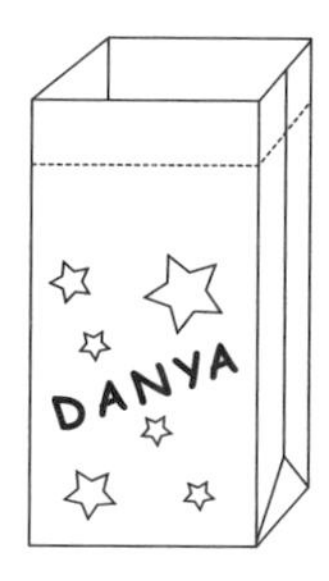

2) Turn down the new top edge to outside of bag. Flatten the remaining strip in half, then fold it in half lengthwise. Staple it to the bag as a handle.

Carpentry

Art/Craft

- Glue narrow craft sticks together around the outsides of a pint milk/juice carton to make a bird house or a log cabin (see directions).
- Make a toolbox out of a shoebox: cover it with plain paper, print the owner's name, and decorate if desired. Fill with any toy tools you have, plus a real (plastic) ruler and tape measure (see directions).
- Draw the "plans" for a birdhouse or treehouse; talk about using rulers, tape measures, and yardsticks to measure pieces of wood, lengths of fabric, and children's heights. Can you mark their heights on a wall somewhere?

Indoors

- Use building blocks, Legos, toy tools, and toolboxes to build a tower, a bridge, or a house. Use toy hammers or just a wooden block to "drill" and "nail" sections of plastic straws through holes cut into the bottoms of shoeboxes or babywipe boxes.
- Use a measuring tape to measure all the chairs or doors or cabinets or stuffed animals. Before you do, guess which ones will be bigger around. Use a yardstick to measure the size of a room, a bookcase, and their beds, and compare to their own heights. If you measure with hand-lengths, how many "hands" big are they?
- Turn a large cardboard box into a playhouse by decorating it with markers, then cutting out windows and doors. Paste on construction-paper shutters, and cut-out green bushes and colorful flowers.
- Go around the house and use your "tools" to pretend to fix a chair leg or a doorknob. Take turns running a "fix-it" shop and bringing in "broken" toys.

Music

"Whistle While You Work;" "If I Had a Hammer"
"London Bridge is Falling Down"

Hints for Your Own Situation...

Older children can roll sheets of plain paper into tubes (tape them to hold together), then see how they can be stacked or combined with flat sheets to make "skyscrapers." See if they'll hold the weight of several books.

☆ ☆ ☆

Measure inside house dimensions in footsteps or arm-spans.

☆ ☆ ☆

As the children measure lengths and widths, you can point out which things are "five times as big," or "half the length" of something else (it's never too early to start the concept of fractions).

Snack-time

Pack lunch boxes to take to the "work site;" fill with sandwiches, apples, cookies and thermos'; set an alarm clock to go off for "lunch break."

☆ ☆ ☆

Make a simple "gingerbread house" by sticking squares of graham crackers around the outside of a half-pint milk-carton using canned frosting as "glue;" two crackers across the top make the sloped roof; decorate with frosting, raisins, oyster crackers, chocolate bits, etc.

Outdoors

- Older children can collect non-pointy sticks, then use a block of wood to pound them into soft ground.
- Wear plastic hard-hats and overalls. Stuff your pockets with your plastic tools.
- Look around outside and inside the house; find five things made of wood, five of plastic, five of metal. Where can you find holes that were drilled? Can you see where nails or screws were used? What may have just been glued, or snapped together?
- Let children use sandpaper to smooth edges of wooden blocks.

Books

Albert's Alphabet by Leslie Tryon
(Atheneum/MacMillan Publishers 1991) (2/3)

Carla the Carpenter by Cathy East Dubowski
(Ladybird Books/Parachute Press 1992) (4/6)

The Mice Who Lived in a Shoe by Rodney Peppe
(Lothrop, Lee & Shepard Books 1981) (4/6)

The Big Concrete Lorry by Shirley Hughes
(Lothrop, Lee & Shepard 1989) (4/6)

Building a House by Byron Barton
(Scholastic/Greenwillow 1981) (2/3)

Once There Was A House by Greg Reyes/Judy Hindley
(Random House 1986) (4/6)

The Toolbox by Anne & Harlow Rockwell
(Macmillan Publishing 1971) (2/3)

Louise Builds a House by Louise Pfanner
(Orchard Books 1989) (4/6)

Snug House, Bug House by Susan Schade & Jon Buller
(Random House 1994) (2/3)

Frances Fix-It by Richard Scarry
(Golden Western 1988) (4/6)

Videos

Building Skyscrapers (David Alpert)*
I Can Build!*
House Construction Ahead (Fred Levine)*

Art/Craft Materials

narrow craft sticks
paper
construction paper
graph paper
shoebox
empty pint milk/juice cartons
cardboard
Velcro dot
tape, glue, scissors
ribbon (about 4", ½" to 1" wide)

Art/Craft Directions

Log Cabin

1) Cut and tape construction paper around the milk carton, to make a good surface to glue onto. Line up the craft sticks (snip them with scissors if you want them shorter).

2) Glue the craft sticks to the paper. Cut out and glue on paper windows and doors, and even a chimney along one end. Or, a long candy "chimney" taped in place could make a fun snack for later!

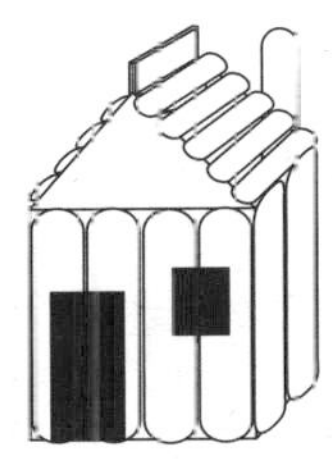

For a Little Something Extra...

Walk or drive to a construction site as big as an office building or as small as a neighbor's new garage or addition. From a safe distance, watch the heavy equipment dig and move dirt, and carpenters work with wood or steel beams.

Shoebox Toolbox

1) Cover with red construction paper. Tape a strip of bent cardboard as a handle on the lid.

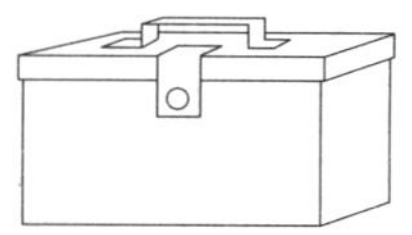

2) Make "hinges" along the back by stapling two strips of ribbon to the box and the lid. The "latch" is a piece of ribbon stapled to the lid. Velcro dots hold it to the box.

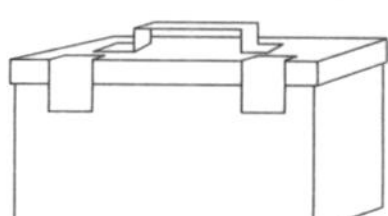

Birdhouse Blueprint

Draw the "plans" for a birdhouse (maybe you can do one using a computer graphics drawing package, but by hand is also fine). Do this ahead of time for them to see a sample, then let older children try their hand at their own. Tell how it's important to label everything, and to put in the measurements.

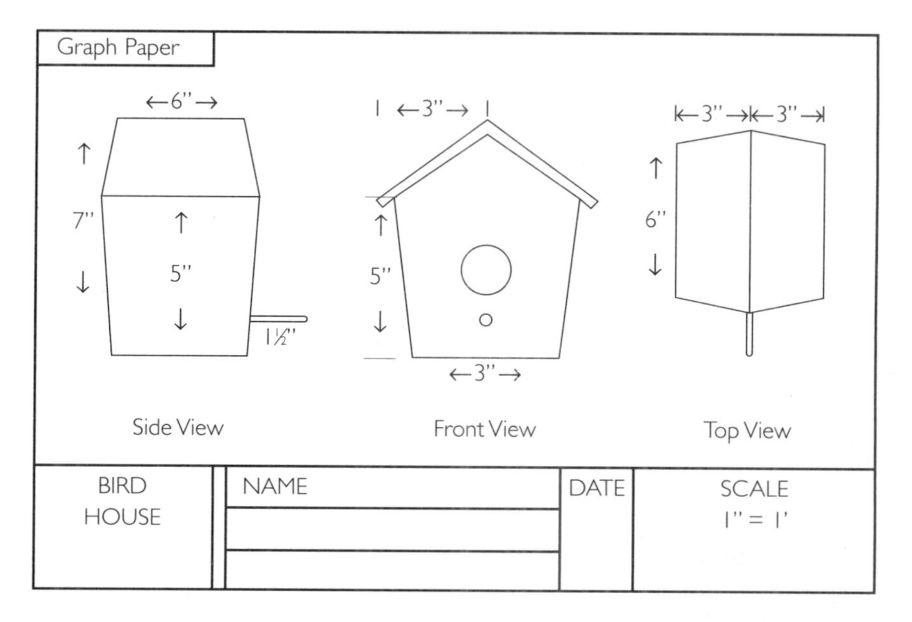

Cars/Trucks

Art/Craft

- Use car stencils to draw a basic car or truck, then customize it. Make it crazy colors, stripes, dots; put flames or tigers on it, or funny wheels.
- Make your town on a wide paper roll taped on a table or the floor. To cover a table, you may need two widths. Draw in basic street outlines, then fill in drawings of houses and trees, a fire station, pond, library, church, stores, theater, etc. You can build upwards by adding wooden-block structures, or small cardboard boxes, colored to have doors, windows, etc. (see directions).
- Turn a facial tissue box into a school bus: cover it with yellow paper, cut squares of blank white address labels (from rolls or printer sheets) to stick on as windows. Cut wheels out of cardboard, or use milk bottle or juice bottle tops, attached with brass fasteners (see directions).
- Collect any washable wheeled vehicles and dip them into paper-plates of poster paint. "Drive" them slowly across paper to create patterns and stripes, then rinse them off.

Indoors

- Collect all your little cars and trucks, and have them drive around your paper town. Did you include stop signs and signals in your town? Make sure you obey them!
- With bigger trucks, you can create a construction zone (get out those hard hats!) Put out pillows for hills to drive around, piles of blocks for dirt that needs to be moved, wooden blocks for logs to be hauled, and load up your dump trucks with anything that makes a good noise when you dump it out. Make "beep-beep" noises for backing up.
- Play Red Light, Green Light, taking turns who is the traffic director.

Music

Cars, Trucks & Trains (Jane Murphy)*
A Car Full of Song (Tom Paxton)*

Hints for Your Own Situation...

For older children, there are plastic model car kits that just snap together, and require no painting.

☆ ☆ ☆

Ahead of time, go to some car dealerships and pick up colorful new car and truck brochures (or save some ads from magazines). Have the children cut out cars they like, and paste them in a row onto a long roll of white paper. Mount this on a wall around a room or down a hall, like a parade—or a line of traffic!

Snack-time

Make a Volkswagen snack. Cut a round apple in half and remove the seeds. Lay it on a plate, round side up, and slice a bit off both sides. Make front and rear fenders from slices of the remaining apples. For wheels, attach four small round crackers (like Ritz Bits) with a bit of peanut butter or marshallow fluff. Headlights can be M&Ms or olives. Use a knife to trace the outlines of the windows, hood, and trunk.

☆ ☆ ☆

Make "checkered flag" racing sandwiches. Make any kind of half-sandwich from one slice of light bread, and another half from a slice of dark bread. Cut each half in half again, then make one whole checkerboard sandwich.

Outdoors

- Set up a car wash: tubs of soapy and plain water to wash all your plastic cars and trucks. Weather permitting, use a hose, dishpans, sponges, and plastic watering cans.
- Could you wash any real riding toys or tricycles?
- On a driveway or patio, use chalk to draw a road surrounded by buildings. Make the road wide enough for riding tricycles and ride-on toys. Make sure to put in intersections with stop signs, a pond, a library, a grocery store, a bank, a gas station, and a restaurant. Drive around, but watch out for each other!

Books

Cars and Trucks and Things That Go by Richard Scarry
(Golden Books 1974) (4/6)

Cars! Cars! Cars! by Grace Maccarone
(Cartwheel/Scholastic 1995) (2/3)

How Many Trucks Can a Tow Truck Tow? by Charlotte Pomerantz
(Random House 1987) (2/3)

ABC Drive! by Naomi Howland
(Clarion Books/Houghton Mifflin 1994) (2/3)

Truck Song by Diane Siebert
(Thomas Y. Crowell 1984) (2/3)

What Kind of Truck? by Margo Hover
(Golden/Western 1983) (2/3)

Cars and Trucks by Michael E. Goodman
(Goldern/Western 1989) (4/6)

The Little Black Truck by Libba Moore Gray
(Simon & Schuster 1994) (4/6)

Truck Talk by Bobbi Katz
(Scholastic/Cartwheel 1997) (2/3)

ABC of Cars and Trucks by Anne Alexander
(Doubleday & Co. 1956) (4/6)

Videos

Cars! Cars! Cars!*; Chitty Chitty Bang Bang
How a Car is Built (A Think Media Production)*
Road Construction Ahead (Fred Levine)*
Heavy Equipment Operator*; Walk, Ride, Fly!*

Art/Craft Materials

large roll of white paper
crayons, markers
scissors, tape
white adhesive address labels, (about 1" x 3")
various small cardboard boxes (for optional buildings)
facial tissue box
cardboard or 4 milk-jug lids
yellow construction paper
brass fasteners

Art/Craft Directions

Table Town

Here is one way to draw out a town for all your little cars, trucks, and action figures to move around in.

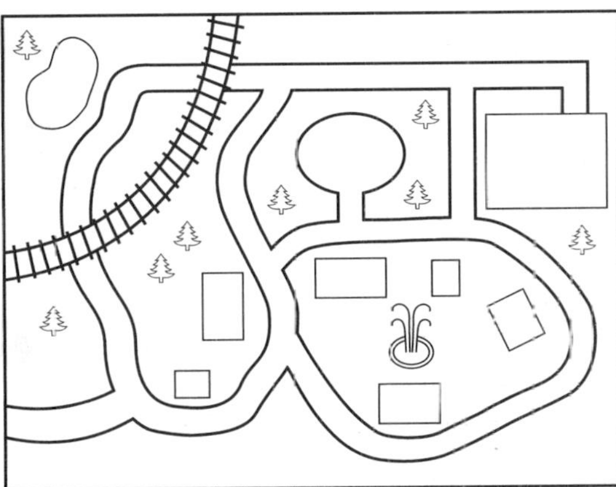

School Bus

1) Cut yellow construction paper to wrap around sides of an upside-down tissue box. Tape or glue paper on. Cut a rectangle to cover the top.

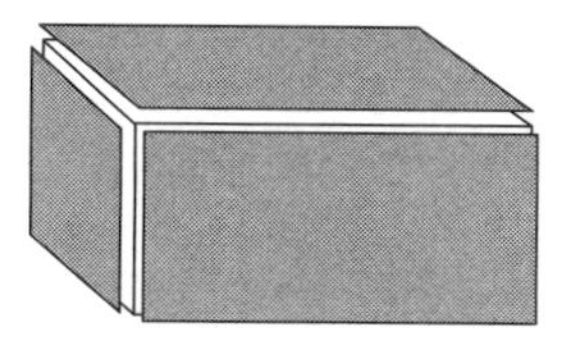

2) Draw the outlines of a bus windshield, driver's window, door that folds, windows, and "school bus" sign on front and sides.

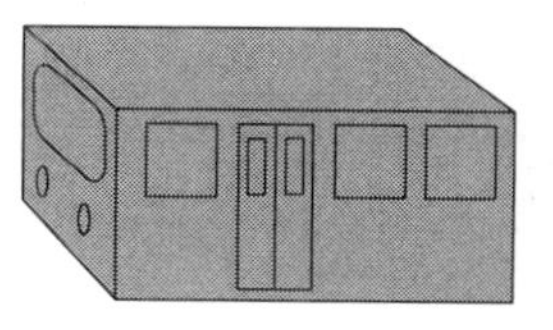

3) Cut address labels in half and paste them on to be the windows and windshield.

4) Cut out cardboard wheels. Poke holes into milk-jug lids. Put a brass fastener in each wheel, and poke it through to inside the box. Reach inside the slot in the bottom of the tissue box, to spread out the legs of the fasteners to make them stay.

For a Little Something Extra...

The software package Road Construction Ahead (Simon & Schuster Interactive) is based on the video of the same name from Fred Levine Productions. It allows children to build roads, get close-up views of earth-moving equipment, plan the path for a new road, and hunt for hidden hard-hats!

☆ ☆ ☆

Another fun video is "Encyclopedia Brown and The Case of the Amazing Race Car."

Castles/Royalty

Art/Craft

- Decorate many different-sized boxes to make a castle. Cover bigger boxes with white butcher's paper, stack and tape them alongside and on top of each other, and decorate with crayons or markers. Cut out a draw bridge and make large paper cone-shapes with paper flags on top for towers (see directions).
- Make princess "cone" hats (decorated paper cones with ribbons or crepe-paper streamers coming out of the tops) and knight's helmets (foil taped around sides of a box or rolled poster board, with wide slots in face area) (see directions).
- Make cardboard shields, covered with white paper. Decorate by creating your own "family crest" with your favorite things (see directions).
- Use decorated paper towel tubes for swords, with a margarine-tub "hand guard" (see directions).

Indoors

- Cover card tables with blankets or tablecloths to create rooms in a castle. To make "windows," cut them out of paper, with diamond windows drawn on, and pin them onto the blankets with safety pins. Securely pin on ribbons, and tie back part of the tablecloth for the look of heavy draperies.
- Get out your fanciest dress-up clothing pieces and crowns! Lace curtains and scarves can be pinned and tied for dresses, while an oversized shirt, belted in, makes a good knight's fancy tunic. Choose a title to call each other all day: such as Lady Hilary, Princess Gretchen, Queen Brenda, King Eric, Prince Alex, Sir Colin, Baroness Caitlin, or Lord Jeremy.
- Build Lego and block castles. Bring out toy horses.

Music

Soundtracks from Camelot, Cinderella, Sleeping Beauty

Outdoors

- On a blue-sky day, lie on your back and find castles in the clouds.

Hints for Your Own Situation...

From a deck of cards, take out a picture card. Tape it to the front of a strip of construction paper that will fit around the child's head as a headband. All day, each child can be "the Queen of Hearts" or "the Jack of Clubs."

☆ ☆ ☆

Bake jam tarts with older children. Mix ½ cup margarine, ½ cup sugar, ½ tsp. salt, 1 egg, and 1 tsp. vanilla until creamy. Add 1 ⅓ cups flour. Spoon onto a greased cookie sheet and top with a bit of jam (jelly gets too thin and runs). Bake at 350 degrees for 9 minutes.

☆ ☆ ☆

Look up "heraldry" in an encyclopedia (or the book *Knights* by Rachel Wright) to learn more about designs for a coat of arms.

- Pretend to be riding horseback around the yard (gallop by yourself, or use a hobby-horse or a small broom). Use your cardboard swords for a "jousting" match.
- Play the "Grand Old Duke of York." March everyone "up the hill and down again" (or from one end of the yard to the other) as they learn the song (see "For a Little Something Extra…").

Snack-time

Cut sandwiches into the shapes of the four card suits (perhaps with cookie cutters in those shapes).

☆ ☆ ☆

Pop-Tarts cut into diamond-shapes can be the Royal Tarts.

☆ ☆ ☆

Mix up your favorite instant pudding and call it the Royal Pudding.

☆ ☆ ☆

Make Royal Goblets. Tape small plastic cups to an empty toilet-paper tube, then to a circle of cardboard or a juice-can lid. Cover the "stem" with foil. (Or use plastic champagne glasses.)

Books

The Paper Bag Princess by Robert Munsch
(Annick Press Ltd. 1980) (4/6)
The Royal Nap by Charles C. Black
(Viking/Penguin 1995) (4/6)
The Tapestry Cats by Ann Turnbull
(Little Brown & Co. 1992) (4/6)
Her Majesty, Aunt Essie by Amy Schwartz
(Bradbury Press 1984) (2/3)
I Am Really A Princess by Carol Diggery Shields
(Dutton Children's Books 1993) (4/6)
The Prince & the Pink Blanket by Barbara Brenner
(Four Winds Press/Scholastic 1980) (4/6)
The Tough Princess by Martin Waddell
(Philomel Books 1986) (4/6)
The Queen's Holiday by Margaret Wild
(Orchard Books 1992) (2/3)
Conrad's Castle by Ben Schecter
(Harper & Row 1967) (2/3)
Into the Castle by June Crebbin
(Candlewick 1996) (4/6)

Videos

The Swan Princess; The Prince and the Pauper (Disney)
Cinderella (Disney or Rogers & Hammerstein)
Robin Hood (Disney)

Art/Craft Materials

thin poster board
crepe paper streamers
cardboard boxes (big and small)
scissors, tape, markers, yarn
roll of white paper
flat "jewels"/buttons
ribbon scraps
paper-towel tubes
margarine tubs
foil
posterboard
hot-glue gun

Art/Craft Directions

Cardboard Castle

1) Stack boxes of all shapes until you're satisfied with the arrangement as the walls and towers of a castle. Tape them together. Cover as much as you want with white paper, to make a good coloring surface.

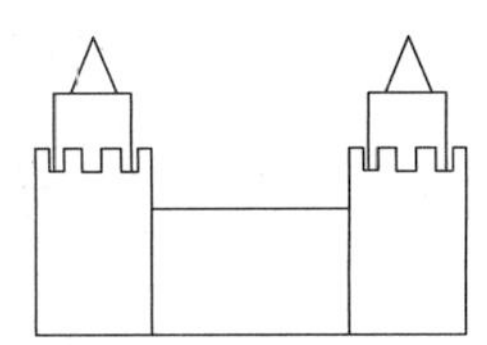

2) Use markers to draw "stonework" all over the white boxes. Roll up some pieces of white posterboard, and trim the edges to look like towers. Staple them in circles, and tape them to the box tops. Draw and cut out a drawbridge. Add yarn for "chains."

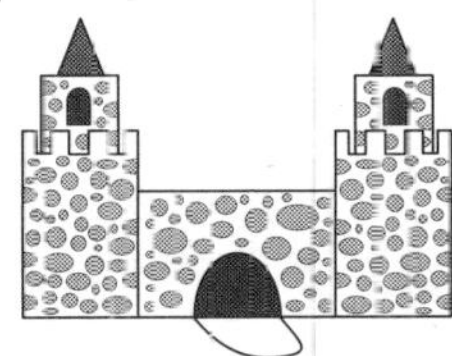

Princess Hat

1) Cut a wedge out of posterboard, and decorate it with markers, stickers, or glued jewels. Overlap edges and staple.

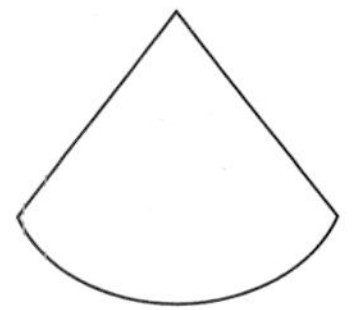

2) Staple ribbons to the sides to make chin ties. Cover staples with tape.

For a Little Something Extra...

Learn: "Oh, the Grand Old Duke of York, he had ten thousand men. He marched them up to the top of the hill, and he marched them down again. And when they were up, they were up, And when they were down, they were down, And when they were only half-way up, They were neither up nor down."

☆ ☆ ☆

Write to (or visit) the Higgins Armory Museum. They have Ancient, Medieval, and Renaissance armor!
100 Barber Ave.
Worcester, MA 01606
(508) 853-6015

Knight's Helmet

Roll thin posterboard into a can shape. Tape edges together. Mark where eye and mouth slots should be, then cut them out. Cover the helmet with foil, bending it into the slots, and taping it on the backside.

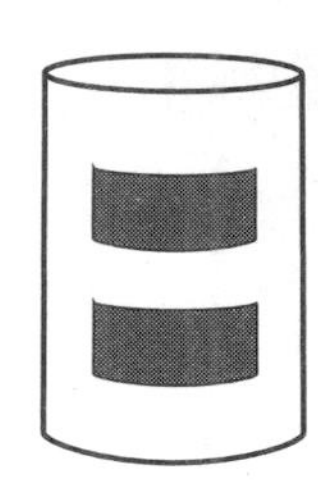

Shield

Design your own family crest. Cut out the basic shape from posterboard, then use marker to divide the shield in four sections. Draw your favorite things, shapes, and colors in each section. Cut and tape a strip of cardboard to the back to use as a handle.

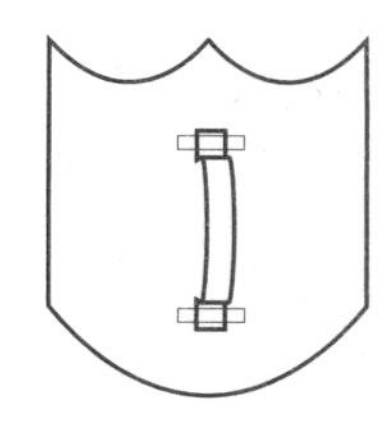

Sword

Cover a paper towel tube in foil; tape. Cut a hole out of the bottom of a margarine tub, large enough to slip the tube through. Slide the "sword" in and tape it to the tub inside and out.

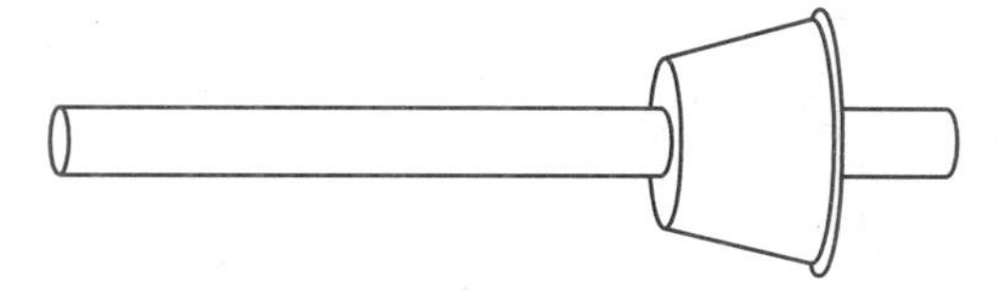

Circus

Art/Craft

- Make animal or clown masks for pretend play, or feather/paper tiaras for acrobat's crowns. Tie a bundle of red or orange rug yarn with loose ends to make a clown's wig. Make a black paper top hat and mustache for the ringmaster (see directions).
- Cut long strips of construction paper. Use a black marker or crayon to mark off "ticket" designs, then roll up the strips to use for playtime (see directions).
- Use face paints to make clown faces with red spot cheeks, a strong-man face with large mustache, or fancy eyelashes for a lion-tamer or bareback rider.
- Make a megaphone from posterboard (see directions).

Indoors

- Put on crazy clothes for clown costumes, and take turns making silly faces or doing crazy dances to make each other laugh. Put on bathing suits and pretend to be acrobats, doing somersaults on pillows on the floor.
- Use hula hoops laid on the floor to make a "three-ring circus." Make stuffed animals do tricks of jumping through the hoops, or dancing on their hind legs. Take turns being the ringmaster, announcing each daring trick.
- Tie ribbon or crepe-paper streamers onto hula hoops, to make a decorated hoop through which the children can jump as they pretend to be tigers or dancing poodles.
- Take turns tying a scarf over your head, sitting at a table, and being a Gypsy Fortune Teller. Spread out a deck of cards, "read" palms, and look into a ball. Make up crazy fortunes for each other.

Music

Under the Big Top (Stephen Fite)*
The Circus*

Hints for Your Own Situation…

For older children, splurge on some helium balloons. Tie three together and tape to a small table to mark the entrance to your circus.

☆ ☆ ☆

Serve lunchbags of popcorn to older children.

☆ ☆ ☆

Make a circus train to pull all the stuffed animals around the room. Use a variety of open-top shoe boxes (or bigger ones if needed), decorated to look like fancy cages on the sides.

Snack-time

Serve Animal Crackers in individual boxes, or just set each plate with a parade of animal crackers from a big box.

☆ ☆ ☆

Make ice-cream cone clowns. Put a cupcake paper upside down in a small bowl. Put a round scoop of ice-cream on it. Push a sugar cone (pointed end up) on top of that, tilted back a little. Use chocolate bits, butterscotch bits, raisins, M&Ms, or cut-up gum drops to make eyes, nose, mouth, and ears.

☆ ☆ ☆

Serve what the animals eat: carrots, thin pretzel sticks (hay), bananas, peanuts (if allowed), apples, and water!

Outdoors

- Take turns being wild animals and jumping through a hula hoop, while someone else can be the ringmaster.
- Is there a tent to use outdoors? If not, you could use clothespins to clip a tablecloth or two to some branches or lawn chairs, to set the mood of the circus tent.
- Have everyone be elephants walking in a circle. Bend over, with one arm dangling in front as a trunk and the other arm hanging in back as a tail. Use your "trunk" to hold onto the "tail" of the person in front of you.
- Practice walking along a 2x4 laid on the ground—you'll be a great tight-rope walker! Hold an umbrella for the full effect!

Books

Peter Spier's Circus by Peter Spier
(Doubleday/Delacorte 1991) (4/6)

Roncalli's Magnificent Circus by Gabriel Lisowski
(Doubleday & Co. 1980) (4/6)

Circus by Lois Ehlert
(Harper Collins 1992) (2/3)

Barnyard Big Top by Jill Kastner
(Simon & Schuster 1997) (4/6)

If I Ran the Circus by Dr. Seuss
(Random House 1956/1984) (4/6)

Mirette on the High Wire by Emily Arnold McCully
(G.P. Putnam's Sons 1992) (4/6)

The Toy Circus by Jan Wahl
(Harcourt Brace Jovanovich 1986) (4/6)

Zorina Ballerina by Enzo Giannini
(Simon & Schuster 1993) (4/6)

Circus Numbers by Rodney Peppe
(Delacorte Press 1969) (2/3)

Babar's Little Circus Star by Laurent de Brunhoff
(Random House 1988) (2/3)

Videos

Mr. Rogers' Neighborhood—Circus Fun
Madeline and the Gypsies; Dumbo

Art/Craft Materials

white posterboard
scissors, yarn
hole puncher
markers
red or orange yarn
black construction paper or posterboard
tape measure

Art/Craft Directions

Masks

1) Cut an animal or clown shape out of white posterboard, either as a full face or just the eye section.

2) Cut out eye and mouth holes, and decorate with markers. Punch holes on both sides, and tie lengths of yarn through them to make ties.

Wig/Mustache

1) For a wig, cut at least 30 pieces of red or yellow yarn into 24" lengths. Tie them together in the middle, and spread it over the child's head. You can make pigtails.

2) For a mustache, cut a long curly shape out of the black posterboard or paper. Tape it onto child's cheeks for a short time, so tape doesn't irritate skin.

For a Little Something Extra...

Call your Chamber of Commerce, or keep an eye on the newspaper to see if a circus will soon be coming to your area.

Top Hat

1) On black construction paper or posterboard, draw a 16" circle. Measure child's head with a tape measure, and draw an oval in the center, roughly the length around that you measured. Cut out the oval shape, and save it to use as the top of the hat.

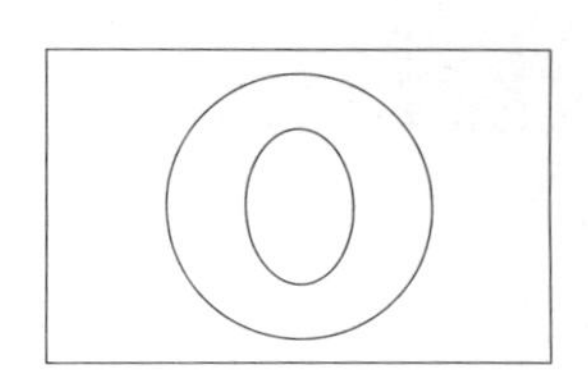

2) Cut a rectangle that is 10" high and one inch longer than the measured head size. Roll the rectangle into the oval, letting edges overlap. Tape edges together along the seam, and tape the tube shape to the brim. Tape the cut-out oval to the top of the tube.

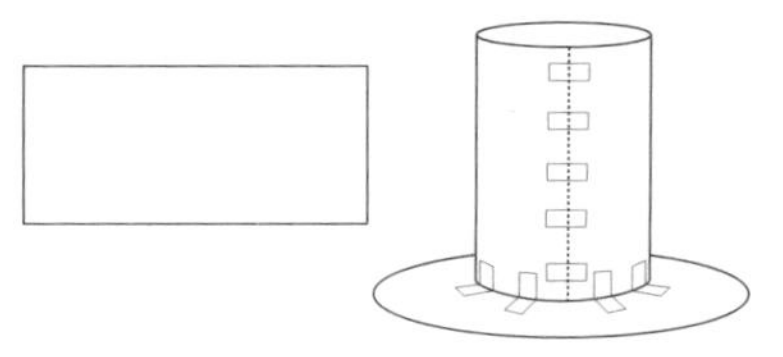

Tickets

Cut strips of red paper 1" wide by 12" long. Draw lines in black to divide the strip into a row of ticket-shaped rectangles. Write "ADMIT ONE" on each.

Megaphone

Cut a piece of posterboard into a wedge shape. Roll it up and staple or tape along the edges. Step right up!

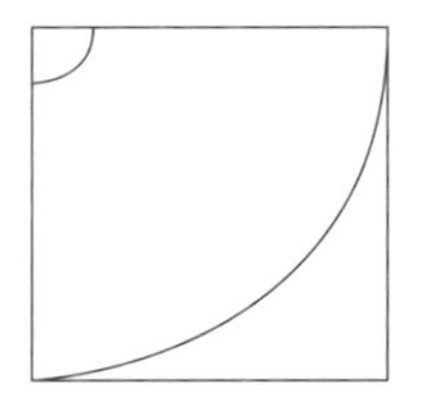

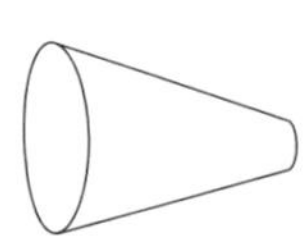

Clocks/Time

Art/Craft

- Using construction paper, cut out clock faces and mark the hours with markers. Cut out hour and minute hands; use a brass fastener to attach the hands to the clock face.
- Fold paper to make a cuckoo clock with opening doors; make a bird and attach inside to the end of a pleated strip of paper (see directions). You could mail this as a greeting card/get well card ("Hope you feel better soon!")
- Make an hourglass from two identical empty jam jars and a paper, putting one upside down on top of the other one, and filling it with some salt. Time how long it takes the salt to get from one side to the other (see directions).

Indoors

- Go around the house and see how many clocks there are. Have each child do his/her own count, and compare; did they get all the watches, the VCR, the microwave?
- Which clock runs fastest? slowest?
- Think of how many nursery rhymes and stories involve clocks (e.g., Hickory Dickory Dock), and act them out.
- Set up ramps made from boardgame boards and stacked books. Collect several sizes and types of balls, and roll two down at a time. Count how many seconds each one takes. Do they get to the bottom at the same time?
- Get a wind-up alarm clock and hide it somewhere in the house. Either play a simple game of finding it by its ticking noise, or see if someone can find it before the bell rings. A variation on this would be to hide a special toy or animal, set a kitchen timer for five minutes, and see if children can find it before the timer buzzes.
- Have children guess how long ten seconds really takes.

Music

"Rock Around the Clock;" "Hickory Dickory Dock"
"My Grandfather's Clock"

Hints for Your Own Situation...

Do you have an old broken alarm clock? Let an older child use a screw driver to take it apart, then talk about the mechanism inside.

☆ ☆ ☆

Use a timer or stopwatch to time each other tying a shoe, or doing silly things.

☆ ☆ ☆

Make a sundial out of cardboard (guess where to make the markings, or see reference book on next page, "Earth-Friendly Outdoor Fun.") If you can, leave it outside on a sunny day to see how well you judged the angles.

Snack-time

If ahead of time you can bake a round layer cake, decorate the frosted top to look like the face of a clock; or, a rectangular cake can be decked out with a grand-father clock design.

☆ ☆ ☆

Serve instant pudding, instant potatoes or rice, a three-minute egg, or a microwave pizza. Is this a day for a "fast food" treat?

Outdoors

- Get a stopwatch, or a watch with second-hand. Have the children run, hop, skip, or jump as long as they want to, and time how long they could do it. ("Wow, you hopped on one foot for seven seconds!")
- Draw a big clock face in chalk on a driveway or patio. Put in some of the hour numbers, one less than there are children. Use the circle to play a form of Musical Chairs (sing away!) or Duck, Duck, Goose. Older children can practice counting and tell you which hours are missing.
- If you made the sundial, put it outside. Check every half hour to see how accurate your markings were; add new ones. What happens when the sun goes behind a cloud?

Books

Sarah's Secret Plan by Linda Johns
(Whistlestop/Troll Assoc. 1995) (4/6)
The Great Kettles: A Tale of Time by Dean Morrissey
(Harry N. Abrams 1997) (4/6)
Sue Patch and the Crazy Clocks by Ann Tompert
(Dial Books/Penguin Books 1989) (4/6)
Tick-Tock by Eileen Browne
(Candlewick Press 1993) (4/6)
The Backwards Watch by Eric Houghton
(Orchard Books 1991) (4/6)
The Guy Who Was Five Minutes Late by Bill Grossman
(Harper & Row 1990) (4/6)
Tick Tock Tales by Margaret Mahy
(Margaret K. McElderry Books 1994) (4/6)
The Eleventh Hour: A Curious Mystery by Graeme Base
(Harry N. Abrams 1989) (4/6)
All About Time by Andre Verdet
(Scholastic Cartwheel 1995) (4/6)
Earth-Friendly Outdoor Fun by George Pfiffner (ref.)
(John Wiley & Sons 1996) (6+)

Videos

Best Birthday Present Ever (Richard Scarry)

Art/Craft Materials

construction paper
scissors, tape, glue
posterboard or paper
two identical empty jars, like jam jars or baby-food jars
salt (about ½ cup or less)

Art/Craft Directions

Cuckoo Clock Card

1) Draw a little cuckoo bird (make it silly if you want) on colored paper, about 2" tall.

2) Fold a piece of construction paper so the edges meet in the middle.

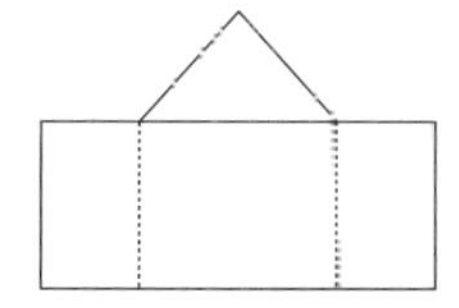

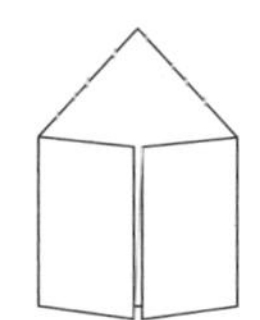

3) Cut away 3" from the top front edges, make the back edge look like a triangle. Use markers to decorate the top area as a clock. Color windows and window boxes on the lower flaps. Write a message partly on the outside, and partly inside.

4) Cut a 1" wide, 12" long strip of paper, and fan-fold the whole length. Tape one end to the back of the bird, and one end inside the card behind the doors. Open the doors to let the bird out, and read the message.

For a Little Something Extra...

Figure out how to set the clock on your VCR!

Listen to the radio to hear the exact time, then set the house clocks to be correct.

Hourglass

1) Trace the opening of one of the empty jars on the posterboard, and cut out the circle. Poke a small hole in the center of the board.

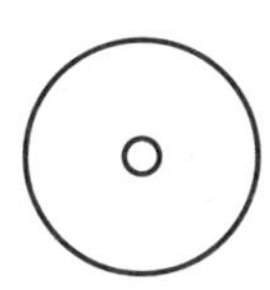

2) Fill one jar partway with salt (maybe one-half cup for a jam jar, or 2 tablespoons for a baby-food jar.)

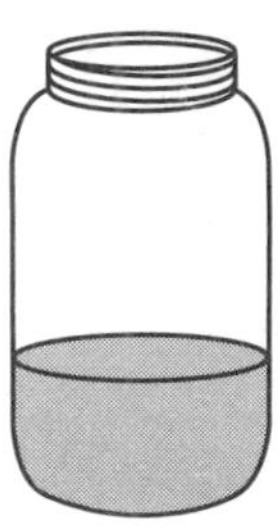

3) Tape the circle on top of the jar with the salt.

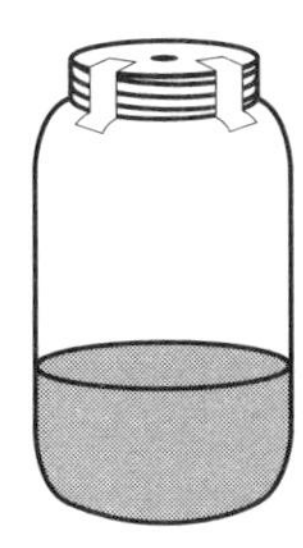

4) Turn the second, empty jar upside down and put it on top of the first jar. Tape it around the edges to make a seal.

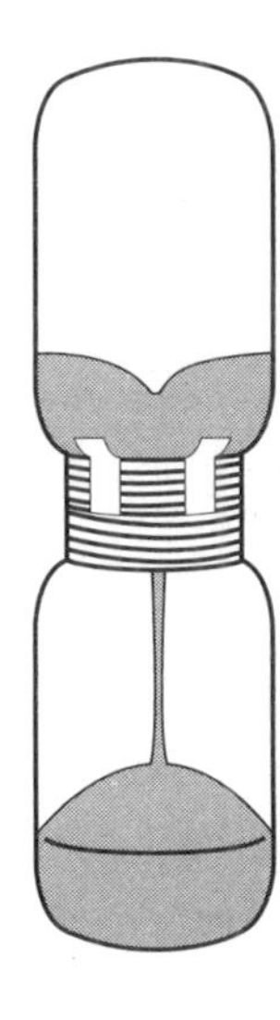

5) Turn the hour-glass over, and watch the salt begin to flow through the hole. Time how long it takes. If you want it to run faster, take it apart and make the hole bigger. If you want it to run slower, put in a new circle of posterboard with a smaller hole. You can also change the amount of salt inside.

Colors/Light

Art/Craft

- Create a simple color wheel: trace a large circle on a sheet of white paper. Divide it into six pie-shaped sections. Color the sections, in clockwise order, red, orange, yellow, green, blue, and purple (see directions).
- Tell children that red, yellow, and blue are called primary colors, then go all out with mixing and painting.
- Make an ever-changing color swirl bottle from water, food coloring, and vegetable oil (see directions).
- Make a cardboard lighthouse from a paper-towel tube and an empty yogurt/pudding container (see directions).
- Fill ice-cube trays with water. Squeeze a few drops of food coloring (red, yellow, and blue) into three of them. Use plastic eyedroppers or small spoons to mix a tiny bit of one color with another in a different section of the tray. What colors can they create?

Indoors

- Buy prisms from an old chandelier (most antique stores have boxes of them, for about $1 each). Go around the house and see what light sources will create a good rainbow through it (regular lamp, fluorescent light, flashlight, sunlight). Can you make the rainbow shine where you want?
- Hunt around the toy area to collect and sort colored blocks, stacking cups, tea sets, etc., by color. How many groups can you find? Do some fit in more than one group?
- Do you have any colored plastic you can place over a flashlight to make it shine red or green light. (Try colored plastic wrap, but don't let young children have it.) How does it make things look different?

Music

"Colors of the Wind" (Pocahantas)
Rainbow Palace*

Hints for Your Own Situation...

Buy a kit for making a kaleidoscope.

☆ ☆ ☆

Ask older children if they can name any animals that only come in black and white (zebra, orca whale, penguin, dalmation, panda).

☆ ☆ ☆

If children can use bubble-blowers, pour bubble liquid into six different plastic bowls. Add a few drops of food coloring to each, making primary and mixed colors. Using bubble wands, blow bubbles onto sheets of paper; the popped bubbles will leave neat colored circles when the paper dries. Use for making note-paper or wrapping paper.

☆ ☆ ☆

Look in an encyclopedia for the pictures that make up a colorblindness test.

Snack-time

Put together a yellow lunch (corn muffins, cheese, Golden Delicious apple, apple juice) or a red snack (red grapes, raspberry jam on toast, red fruit punch).

☆ ☆ ☆

What colors make brown? (Red and green mixed). Serve chocolate milk, wheat bread, peanut butter, and Oreo cookies.

☆ ☆ ☆

Make a rainbow cooler: mix cherry gingerale with raspberry sherbet. Serve topped with a scoop of lime sherbet.

Outdoors

- Draw with colored chalk, and experiment with adding water (either let the chalk stick get wet itself, or spray water from a spray bottle or squirt toy, to see the effect on the drawing).
- Can you find something outside that is one of each of the six colors on your color wheel?
- On a sunny day, play shadow games with your hands, your bodies (two children, in front of each other, waving arms or objects such as balls). Try funny combinations.
- When shadows are long, play shadow tag, where the tagger catches you if she or he can step on your shadow!

Books

The Art Lesson by Tomie de Paola
(G.P. Putnam's Sons 1989) (2/3)

The Color Wizard by Barbara Brenner
(Bantam Double Day 1989) (2/3)

How is a Crayon Made? by Oz Charles
(Scholastic/Simon & Schuster 1988) (4/6)

Color Dance by Ann Jonas
(Scholastic/Greenwillow 1989) (2/3)

Colors: A First Discovery Book by Jeunesse/ Bourgoing
(Scholastic 1989) (4/6)

My Many Colored Days by Dr. Seuss
(Alfred A. Knopf 1996) (2/3)

The Color Kittens by Margaret Wise Brown
(Golden/Western 1977) (4/6)

All the Colors of the Earth by Sheila Hamanaka
(Morrow Jr. Books 1994) (4/6)

A Rainbow of My Own by Don Freeman
(Viking 1966) (2/3)

Just One More Colour by Brenda Silsbe
(Annick Press 1991) (4/6)

Videos

GeoKids: Camouflage, Cuttlefish, and Chameleons Changing Color*
Hullabaloo: Colors!*

Art/Craft Materials

white posterboard or paper
a pot lid for tracing (6” to 12”)
markers, scissors, ruler
paper towel tube
red ribbon (about 24” inches long, ½” wide)
empty 16 oz. plastic bottle with cap
vegetable oil, food coloring, water
empty yogurt or pudding cup
empty margarine or whipped cream tub
modeling dough, small rocks (optional)

Art/Craft Directions

Color Wheel

1) Trace a circle, 6” to 12” in diameter, on a piece of white posterboard, and cut it out. Use a ruler to divide the circle into 6 pie-shaped wedges. Use markers to color each wedge red, orange, yellow, green, blue, and purple, in order.

2) Trace a second circle, the same way. Cut it out and divide it into 6 wedges again. This time, color 2 reds side by side, 2 yellows, then 2 blues. Use yellow again, but this time color over its neighboring red. Use red again, but this time color over its neighboring blue. Use blue again, but this time color over its neighboring yellow. Same results as #1!

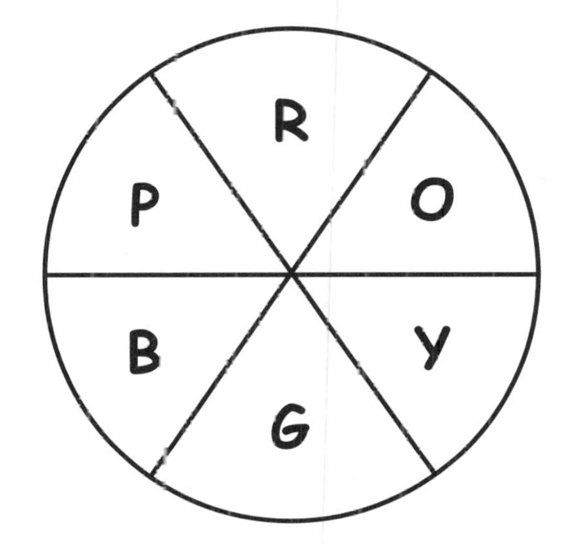

For a Little Something Extra...

Plant a "color garden" in a window box. Use what works best in your temperature region (e.g., red poppies, orange zinnias, yellow marigolds, blue bachelor buttons, and purple pansies). Water and watch!

Colored Water Mixer

1) Mix 1½ cups of water with red food coloring. Pour water into an empty plastic bottle.

2) Add 1 Tablespoon of vegetable oil. Screw top on tightly. Tip the bottle over and watch the oil drops race around, without mixing. Try again with different proportions.

Lighthouse

1) Cover the paper towel tube with white paper; glue or tape in place. Wrap the red ribbon in a spiral around the tube, and tape it in place.

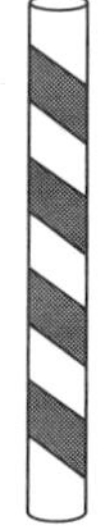

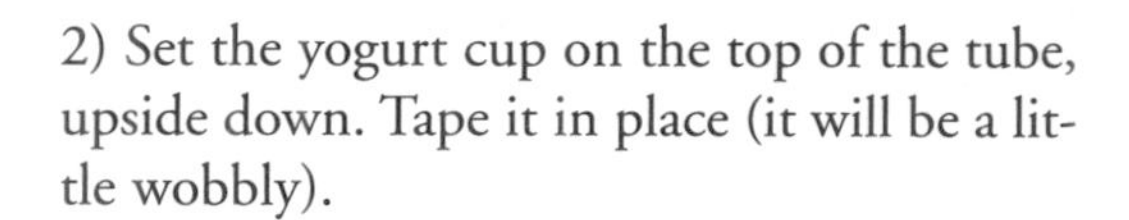

2) Set the yogurt cup on the top of the tube, upside down. Tape it in place (it will be a little wobbly).

3) Use the bottom of the tube to trace a circle on an upside-down margarine tub. Cut out the circle, and push the tube all the way down into it. This base can be the rock on which the lighthouse was built. If you have some small rocks, stick them to the base with modeling dough. Use black marker to draw big windows on the yogurt cup.

Dancing/Jumping/Hopping

Art/Craft

- Make hula "grass" skirts by folding and taping lengths of crepe paper streamers over a ribbon to be tied around the waist (see directions).
- Use markers, feathers, glitter and ribbons to decorate and cut out fancy masks for a masquerade ball (ladies and gentlemen wear these for Mardi Gras) (see directions).

Indoors

- Have fun trying to do these dances, but be creative! For a square dance, show children a do-si-do movement (walk in a square around each other, but keep your face looking at the same wall the whole time). Have them hook arms and swing around—let them take it from there!
- Put on Carribean music, place a yardstick or broomstick across two chairs, and try doing the limbo; change the stick height with stacks of books at either end.
- Any lively music with a beat is a candidate for the bunny hop (everyone needs to learn that!), leap-frog or kangaroo jumping (how far can you go?)
- On a hard floor, see if they can hear their shoes do a tap dance. Try different dress-up shoes and see which ones make the loudest sounds.
- Teach them the Hoky Poky song, and do it in a circle.
- Put on different kinds of music, and make up moves for a Highland fling (got any plaid skirts or scarves for wrap-around kilts?), a ballet dance (costume or not, get up on those tippy-toes!), or a waltz (teach bows and curtsies, then count 1-2-3, 1-2-3).
- Soft, dreamy music works for hula dancing (and calming down time). Tie on the grass skirts, and go for bare feet.

Music

Hop Like a Bunny, Waddle Like a Duck*
Raffi tapes, ballet music
Carribean songs
Broadway show tunes
Rhinoceros Tap (Boynton & Ford)*
Folk Dance Fun*

Hints for Your Own Situation...

Watch to make sure younger children don't chew on crepe paper—the ink comes off!

☆ ☆ ☆

Older children can try coming up with a dance step for everyone else to follow. Create a pattern: one slow tap, two fast taps, then turn in a circle. Can everyone else do it? Then another one says: touch your right foot, then your left foot, then jump with both feet, then clap your hands. Try different tempos of music.

☆ ☆ ☆

Even if you don't know the macarena or an official line dance, challenge older children to follow your lead with hand and foot motions, staying in a row, then turning.

Outdoors

- Get some exercise with hopping and jumping. Use chalk to draw a hopscotch path, or draw circles and call them stepping stones. Can you hop from stone to stone without missing—on one foot or two?
- Do a long bunny hop around the yard, or down the sidewalk. Then do it again, but make it a penguin walk, an elephant walk, a stretching panther walk, or any other animal they want to imitate.
- Bring a casette player outside and continue the fun!

Snack-time

Jello Jigglers cut in cubes make their own kind of dance when you nudge a bowlful!

☆ ☆ ☆

Serve up a macarena (macaroni), a square dance (American cheese squares), the Dance of the Sugar Plum Fairy (plums), and a tango (tangerines).

Books

The Bear Dance by Chris Riddell
(Simon & Schuster 1990) (4/6)

The Twelve Dancing Princesses by Marianna Mayer
(Morrow Junior Books 1989) (4/6)

Tabu and the Dancing Elephants by Rene Deetlefs
(Dutton Children's Books 1995) (4/6)

I Wear My Tutu Everywhere! by Wendy Cheyette Lewison
(Grosset & Dunlap 1996) (2/3)

Moondance by Frank Asch
(Scholastic 1993) (2/3)

Song and Dance Man by Karen Ackerman
(Alfred A. Knopf 1988) (4/6)

Barn Dance! by Bill Martin Jr. & John Archambault
(Henry Holt & Co. 1986) (4/6)

Cordelia, Dance! by Sarah Stapler
(Dial Penguin 1990) (4/6)

The Dancing Man by Ruth Bornstein
(Clarion/Seabury 1978) (4/6)

Aunt Elaine Does the Dance from Spain by Leah Komaiko
(Doubleday/Delacorte 1992) (4/6)

Videos

The Flower Ballet; Riverdance; The Nutcracker
Workout with Mommy & Me/Daddy & Me*
Miss Christy's Dance Adventure*
Dance Along! (Sesame Street)*
I Want to Be a Ballerina*

Art/Craft Materials

roll of green crepe-paper streamers
ribbon (1" wide, about 1 yd.)
stapler, tape, scissors, ruler
white posterboard
feathers, glitter glue, sequins
yarn, lace
markers, hole punch

Art/Craft Directions

Hula Grass Skirt

1) Cut 1 yd. of 1" wide ribbon. (For easiest assembling, tape each end of ribbon to a chair.)

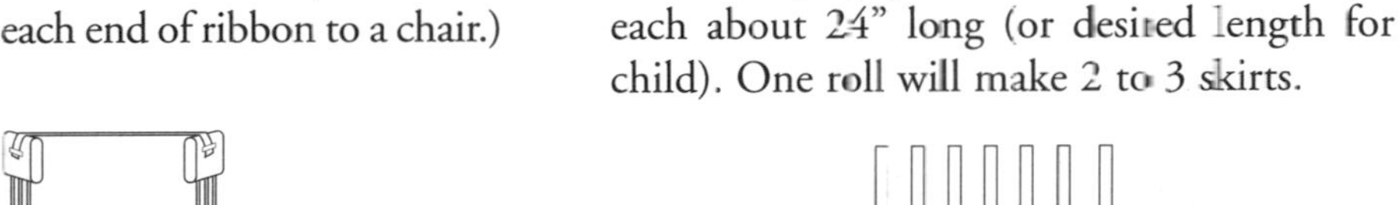

2) Cut crepe paper roll into 10 to 14 strips, each about 24" long (or desired length for child). One roll will make 2 to 3 skirts.

3) Leaving about 8" of ribbon free, bend each strip over the ribbon, over-lapping about 1½", and staple the streamer to the ribbon, through both sides of the crepe-paper. Continue adding strips, right next to each other, until enough strips are attached to wrap all the way around child's waist. Add or remove strips as desired. Tie skirt on with free ribbon ends.

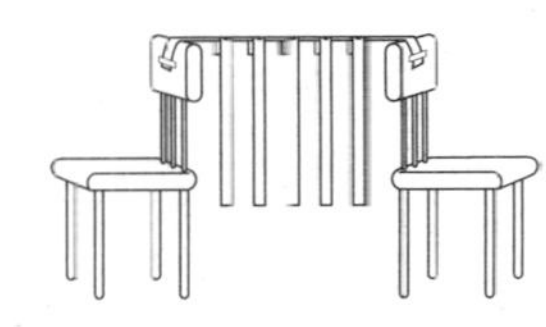

For a Little Something Extra...

Older children may enjoy a Fred Astaire or Gene Kelly movie; try the *That's Entertainment* video series.

☆ ☆ ☆

Go to a community square dance.

☆ ☆ ☆

Buy real ballet slippers just for fun (about $12 in shoe marts).

Masquerade Ball Masks

1) Enlarge this shape, then copy it onto white (or another color) posterboard.

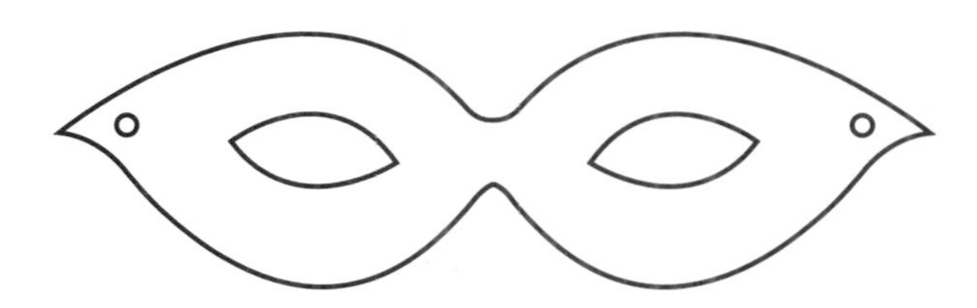

2) Punch holes in both sides and knot lengths of yarn through the holes to make ties or staple mask to the top of a plastic straw for a holder.

3) Decorate with glitter glue, feathers, lace, and markers, as creatively as you'd like.

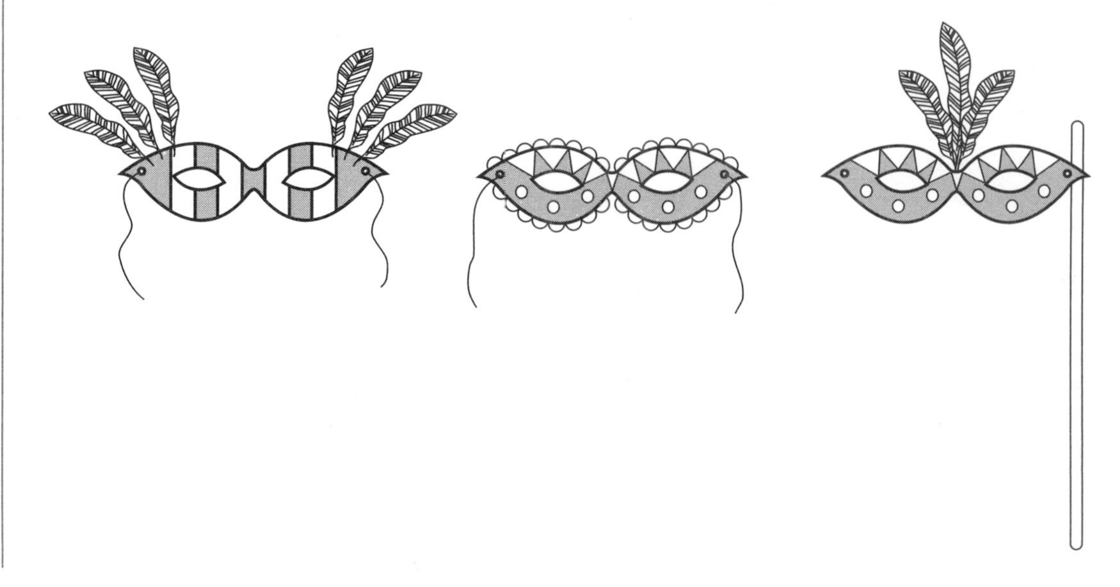

Detectives

Art/Craft

- Turn fingerprints into art. Press thumb and fingertips onto a washable inkpad, then press them onto paper. Use the prints as parts for drawing bugs, cars, and flowers, by giving them legs, wheels, stems, etc.
- Press fingers onto pieces of clear tape or the surface of a mirror. Lightly sprinkle baby powder over tape to make fingerprints show up. Can you see the differences?
- Assemble a detective's kit: get a magnifying glass, a flashlight, a can of baby powder, a clean paintbrush (for dusting for fingerprints), and an empty envelope for clues.
- Make detective badges out of foil, string, and cardboard, and a detective's hat (see directions).
- On a pad of paper, use a pen to heavily draw a simple picture. (Make sure your preschooler can handle a pen.) Tear off the top sheet. Rub lightly over the next sheet with the side of a pencil or a crayon—the same picture reappears!

Indoors

- Go on a mystery search: make up a scavenger list of household items, and give everyone a basket or shoebox to collect them in. For younger children, look for a wooden block, a toy car, a stacking cup, a headband, a piece of paper, a tiny book; older children can hunt for a measuring spoon, a blue marker, a red sock, a rubber stamper, a roll of tape, a necklace, a Lego block, a cracker.
- If you have carpet, gather different shoes for the children to wear. With everyone else in another room, have one child put on a pair and walk on the carpet, leaving patterned footprints, then take off the shoes. Have the others guess which shoes made the prints. Take turns.
- Fill a bag with odd items. Each child can reach in, feel the item, and try to guess what it is.

Music

Theme songs from detective shows
(Mannix, Hawaii 5-0)

Hints for Your Own Situation…

Older children (who know their letters) like figuring out codes. Make up a simple one by writing a "key" that makes a=1, b=2, etc., or uses symbols for letters (happy face=a, sun=b, etc.), then write a short message. Have them make up their own simple picture code, and see if they can figure each other's out.

☆ ☆ ☆

Figure out mystery sounds or smells. Let one child go in another room and make a noise (jump, open/close drawer, bang two plastic bowls—you can pre-select these items). Others can guess what made the noise. Or, fill empty film cans with scent samples (cinnamon, orange slice, peanut butter, baby powder, chocolate bits) and have them guess (no peeking).

Outdoors

- In the snow, leave bootprint trails for others to follow (Or use a shallow puddle or damp sand to create a trail.)
- Have each child pick up something to examine, without the others seeing it. Put the item in a paper bag; have other children close their eyes, reach in, feel it, and guess what it could be (maple leaf, twig, chalk, flower petal, etc.)
- Use a magnifying glass to get a close-up view of (depending on the season/weather): tiny wildflowers, one flower petal, different textures of leaves, different colors and types of rocks, grass, dirt (see any bugs?), a sidewalk, a puddle (anything in it?), a plastic swing, and house paint.

Books

Piet Potter's Hot Clue by Robert Quackenbush
(McGraw Hill Books 1982) (4/6)
My Dog and the Knock Knock Mystery by David A. Adler
(Holiday House 1985) (4/6)
The 13th Clue by Ann Jonas
(Greenwillow Books 1992) (4/6)
Rollo and Tweedy and the Ghost at Dougal Castle by Laura Jean Allen
(Harper Collins Publishers 1992) (4/6)
The Mystery of King Karfu by Doug Cushman
(Harper Collins 1996) (4/6)
Helpful Betty Solves a Mystery by Michaela Morgan
(Carolrhoda Books Inc. 1993) (4/6)
Richard Scarry's Find Your ABC's by Richard Scarry
(Random House 1973) (4/6)
Mystery at Camp Crump (Investigator) by Jerry Smath
(Troll Assoc. 1994) (4/6)
The ABC Mystery by Doug Cushman
(Harper Collins 1993) (4/6)
The Mud Flat Mystery by James Stevenson
(Greenwillow Books 1990) (4/6)

Snack-time

Write children's initials on a piece of light-colored bread using a clean, tiny paintbrush and either water or lemon juice. Be generous in wetting it. Pop the slice into the toaster set on dark. The mystery letters will appear! Serve with butter or jam.

☆ ☆ ☆

Feeling really ambitious? Mix up a batch of pancake batter. Drizzle initials (be sure to "write" backwards) on the griddle, wait about 15 seconds, then add more batter to cover and make a normal round pancake. When they're flipped over, children will see their initials come out of nowhere!

Videos

Encyclopedia Brown series; The Great Mouse Detective
Where in the World is Carmen SanDiego?
Detective Tigger (Winnie the Pooh Playtime)

Art/Craft Materials

foil
string or yarn
cardboard
scissors, glue stick
2 sheets of construction paper
safety pin

Art/Craft Directions

Detective Badge

1) Cut a badge shape from cardboard. Draw your initials on the front.

2) Rub all over the badge front with a glue stick. Cut bits of string long enough to go around your initials. Lay the string bits on the glued surface, covering the lines of the letters.

3) Cover the badge with foil, gently pressing around the string shapes to mold the foil and make the shapes show through as raised initials. Tape the foil to the back around the edges. Tape a safety pin to the backside.

For a Little Something Extra...

Try writing with a wax (unlit) candle on a piece of paper. Rub over the paper with side edge of a pencil, and the letters appear. Use to write secret message.

☆ ☆ ☆

Treat older children to an "Alex Undercover" activity kit, with different detective-type things to use and do (available at specialty children's stores such as Noodle Kidoodle).

Detective Hat

1) Cut a 9" x 12" sheet of construction paper as follows (approximately):

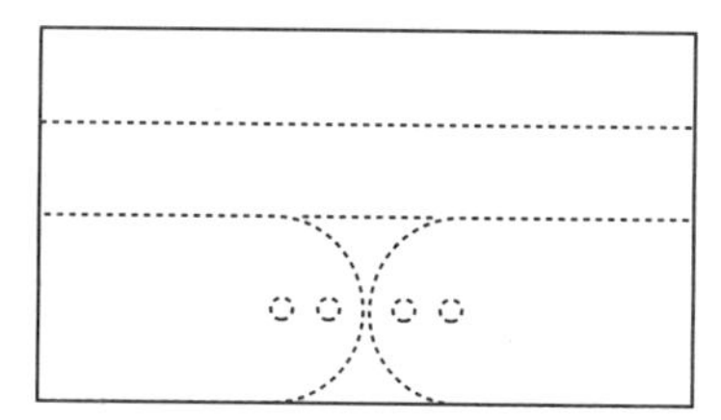

2) Staple the 2 long strips together, end to end, and fit band to child's head. Punch 2 holes in rounded edges of large pieces.

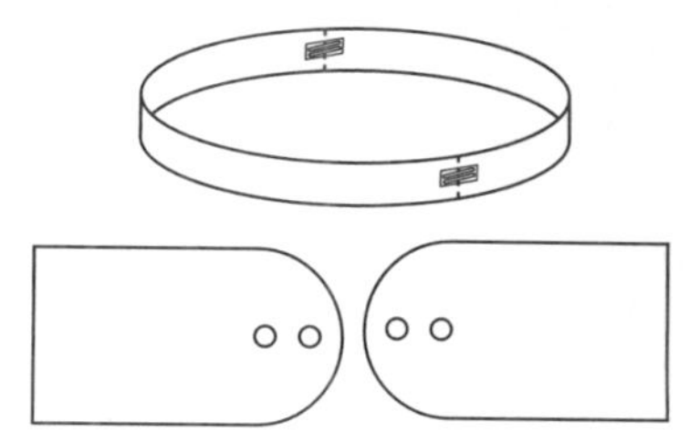

3) Staple wide pieces to opposite sides of band. Bend them up and over to overlap, so that the band tilts in a bit, and the two sets of holes line up. Tie the flaps together in a bow, with a piece of yarn.

4) Cut 2 brims from another piece of construction paper, or scrap paper, as shown.

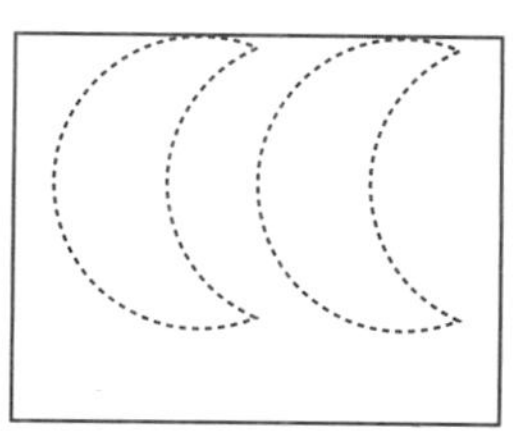

Tape the brims to the front and back of hat. Use black marker to draw on a plaid pattern all over hat.

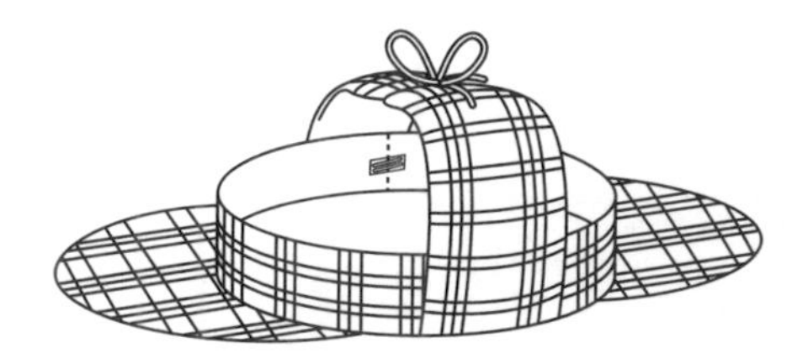

Dinosaurs

Art/Craft

- Cut apart large brown paper bags to make wide drawing paper for dinosaur scenes. Use stencils, markers, crayons, and rubber stamps to create dinosaur scenes.
- Make dinosaur puppets, either from paper lunchbags or socks. On paper bags, glue spikes, horns, teeth, legs, etc., cut from construction paper. On socks, glue will hold up (for at least a day's play!) for adding cut-out felt eyes, teeth, fangs, tails, etc. Folding a paper plate in half and cutting triangles on the round edge makes a great stegosaurus (see directions).
- Modeling dough in different colors is a great medium for making your own dinosaurs. Use cookie cutters to help make body-part shapes, then assemble a "heart-a-saurus," a "star-a-saurus," or a "tri-circle-a-saurus."

Indoors

- Gather any toy dinosaurs you have for a rocking, rolling dinosaur dance (make them fly through the air). Then, get everyone up and moving, growling and stomping as their own choice of dinosaur. Walk on "hind" legs as T. Rex, or clomp on all fours as a lumbering diplodaucus.
- Show children how to do a Conga Line dance, but pretend you're all dinosaurs. Watch out for tails swinging into furniture!
- Have everyone sit in a circle and play "Hot Potato," except that the ball is really a dinosaur egg that could hatch into something fierce at any minute!

Music

The Dinosaur Album*
Where are the Dinosaurs? (Diane Batchelor)*
Dinosaur Choir (Bonnie Phipps)*

Outdoors

- Make one big pile of leaves as a dinosaur nest!

Hints for Your Own Situation…

Older children who are comfortable with basic sewing could stitch the face pieces on the sock puppets by hand. Slip a piece of cardboard inside first, so they don't sew both sides of the sock together.

☆ ☆ ☆

If you can trust the children with buttons, let them build a dinosaur by sliding buttons along pipe cleaners (as "backbones with discs"), using more pipecleaners wrapped around as legs, and poking the neck portion into a small Dixie cup for a head (poke the end through to stick out as a tongue).

☆ ☆ ☆

Cut out cardboard dinosaur "footprints," and use them outside to trace with chalk. Make a trail of them down the sidewalk or across a patio to amaze the grown-ups!

Snack-time

Serve hot-dogs, ham slices or the favorite lunch meat to the meat-eating dinosaur children, and serve lettuce, cut-up fruit or canned fruit, and finely sliced raw vegetables to the plant-eating dinosaur children.

☆ ☆ ☆

Make a "Swamp of Hidden Surprises" for their dessert. Make instant pudding, preferably a dark chocolate, then stir in pieces of thin pretzels (logs) and chocolate bits (rocks).

☆ ☆ ☆

Of course, all dinosaurs need water to drink. Set small paper-cups nestled on cut green paper napkins (leaves), so little dinosaurs can drink the "dew."

- If you don't mind the mess, let the children dig for "fossils" in some soft ground or a sandbox. Old spoons or thick plastic spoons work well in dirt, and laundry scoops make good diggers in sand. What do they discover? (You may want to "bury" some plastic dinosaurs ahead of time.)
- Bring modeling dough outside. Roll a ball, then flatten it. Find different textures of rocks, twigs, or shells to press into the dough, making your own patterns of "fossils."

Books

Lizard's Song by George Shannon
(Greenwillow Books 1981) (4/6)
Good Night Dinosaurs by Judy Sierra
(Clarion Books/Houghton Mifflin 1996) (4/6)
Saturday Night at the Dinosaur Stomp by Carol Diggory Shields
(Candlewick Press 1997) (4/6)
Baby Dot: A Dinosaur Story by Margery Cuyler
(Clarion Books 1990) (4/6)
The Dinosaur Eggs by Francis Mosley
(Barron's Educational Series 1988) (4/6)
When Dinosaurs Go Visiting by Linda Martin
(Chronicle Books 1993) (4/6)
The Magic Schoolbus in the Time of the Dinosaurs by Joanna Cole
(Scholastic 1994) (4/6)
Dinosaurs, Dinosaurs by Byron Barton
(Scholastic/Thomas Y. Crowell 1989) (2/3)
Berenstain Bears and the Missing Dinosaur Bone by Stan and Jan Berenstain
(Random House 1980) (2/3)
Dinosaur Dress Up by Allen L. Sirois
(Tambourine Books 1992) (4/6)

Videos

The Land Before Time (Parts I-V)
Patrick's Dinosaurs/What Happened to Patrick's Dinosaurs?

Art/Craft Materials

paper lunch bags
markers, crayons, stickers
scissors, tape, glue
construction paper
felt
old sock
paper plate

Art/Craft Directions

Lunchbag Puppet

1) Draw eyes, nose, and mouth of your idea of a dinosaur, using the bag folded flat. Open the bag partway, and draw more teeth inside.

2) Cut ears, arms, legs, and spikes out of construction paper. Tape or glue them to the backside of the bag. Put your hand up inside the bag to move the mouth, and rrroar!

Sock Puppet

1) Cut out felt shapes for eyes, teeth, tails, horns, etc., to fit on the sock you've chosen.

2) Glue the pieces onto the sock using Tacky glue. Or, older children could try stitching them: put a piece of cardboard or a narrow book inside while you sew, so that you don't sew both sides together by mistake. You can add color with markers, too.

Paper Plate Stegosaurus

1) Cut a paper plate in half. Staple both halves together, facing each other. Cut out triangles along the rounded edge to make spikes.

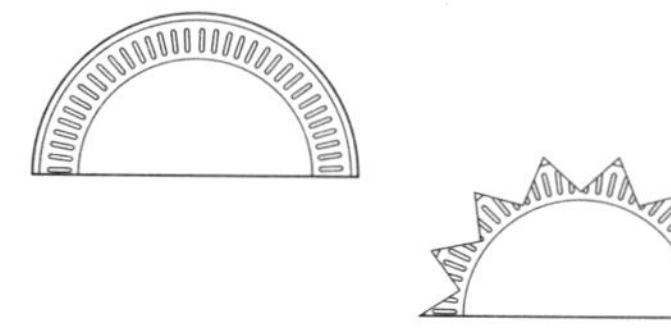

2) Cut out a paper head and neck, and four legs, from construction paper. Tape or staple these on. Color in the eyes and mouth. Slip your hand inside between the two lower edges.

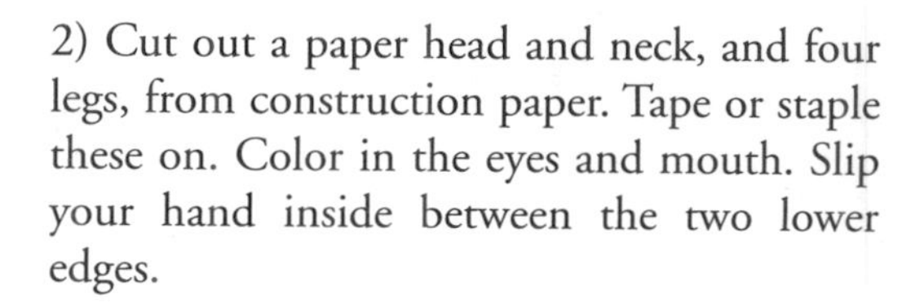

For a Little Something Extra...

Visit a natural history museum to see real dinosaur bones (or at least a model skeleton that was made by making a cast of a real one).

Doctor/Dentist/Vet

Art/Craft

- Make get-well cards to keep for when they're needed. Fold a piece of paper into four sections. On the front, trace around each child's hand and let them decorate it with a funny face, or add flowers. Write: "Just Waving a Little Hello." Let them "sign" their names.
- Make a nurse's cap from white paper and a red marker (or red construction paper) (see directions).
- Make a toy toothbrush for the stuffed animals. Fold a small square of white paper around one end of a craft stick and tape. Draw lines for bristles (see directions).
- Make nametags for everyone to wear during the day: Dr. Katie - Heart Helper, Dr. Niki - The Kitty's Friend, Dr. Marianna - Tooth Tickler, etc. (see directions).

Indoors

- Collect all the stuffed animals in the house. Set up either a hospital, a veterinary hospital, or a dentist's office: use little chairs or milk crates to set up a waiting room, a box for a desk, a toy phone, two chairs facing each other for an examining "table," and a box for holding supplies.
- Taking turns, one child can bring in the "sick" or "injured" patient or pet, and describe what's wrong; another child is the doctor, or nurse, or ambulance driver.
- Use scarves for slings (folded in a triangle and knotted over the shoulder), real band-aids, ribbons, strips of white cloth or crepe-paper streamers and tape (for making casts). A purchased toy medical kit with stethoscope is extra fun.
- Use the craft sticks, or new, inexpensive toothbrushes, to clean the "teeth" of all your stuffed animals.

Music

Sing: "This is the way we brush our teeth, brush our teeth, brush our teeth. This the way we brush our teeth, so early Monday morning." Make up versions for "make a cast, hear your heart, put on band-aids, check your ears," etc.

Hints for Your Own Situation...

Have older children lie down on a white roll of paper, and draw around them for an outline. Then let them draw what they think is inside themselves. Ask if they can draw a circle for their tummy show where lungs are for breathing (where does it "move" when you breathe?), and add a heart. They can also add toes and put circles where their elbows and knees are.

☆ ☆ ☆

Using flashlights, let children have the fun of sticking out their tongues and not getting in trouble! Use a clean spoon to hold down the tongue. Take turns seeing what's inside.

☆ ☆ ☆

Sing "Just a Spoonful of Sugar" from *Mary Poppins*

Snack-time

Use trays to serve snacks, the way they do in hospitals. (If you don't have any trays, make some by covering a piece of cardboard with construction paper.) Draw up a menu, or offer a choice of juice or milk, peanut-butter sandwich or toast, an apple or cookies (or maybe the classic, Jello!)

Outdoors

- Tour the yard and talk about outdoor safety: no running with sticks, watch out for roots or cracks in a sidewalk, wear your helmet when bike-riding, wear sunblock on tender skin, hold still when you see a bee, don't pet strange animals, etc.
- Have everyone run around for fifteen seconds, then show them how to hold onto the side of their necks to feel their pulse and "check" each other's. Is it different a bit later?
- Let two children help a third one (with a "hurt foot") by having the third child put one arm around the other's shoulders and hop. Or, hold a three-legged race.
- Play tag or do somersaults to get your heart exercising!

Books

Who's Sick Today? by Lynne Cherry
(E.P. Dutton 1988) (4/6)

Barney is Best by Nancy White Carlstrom
(Harper Collins 1994) (4/6)

A Visit to the Hospital (Sesame Street) by Deborah Hautzig
(Random House 1985) (4/6)

Going to the Hospital by Mr. Fred Rogers
(Putnam & Grosset 1988)

The Berenstain Bears go to the Doctor by Stan & Jan Berenstain
(Random House 1981) (4/6)

Island Baby by Holly Keller
(Greenwillow Books 1992) (4/6)

The Little Puppy by Judy Dunn
(Random House 1984) (4/6)

Arthur's Tooth by Marc Brown
(Little, Brown and Co. 1985) (4/6)

Dragon Tooth by Cathryn Falwell
(Clarion/Houghton Mifflin 1996) (4/6)

Rosie's Baby Tooth by Maryann Macdonald
(Atheneum/Macmillan 1991) (4/6)

Videos

My Visit to the Doctor (ages 2-4)*
Sesame Street Visits the Hospital*

Art/Craft Materials

white paper
craft sticks (wide are best)
red marker or red construction paper
black marker or pen
safety pins
scissors, tape, stapler

Art/Craft Directions

Nurse's Cap

1) Cut out two sections of white paper as shown. Staple the two pieces together just at the pointed corners.

2) Cut one strip of paper in a 5" x 6" rectangle.

3) Spread the stapled pieces apart, and staple the band between them, arching it up and over as shown.

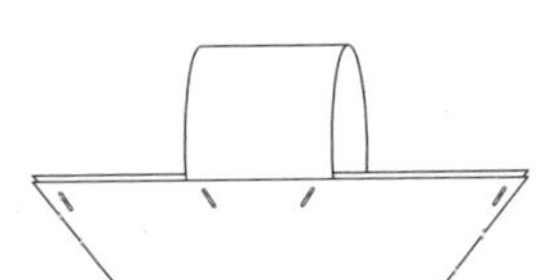

4) Cut a red construction paper cross and tape it to the front (or color a cross with a red marker).

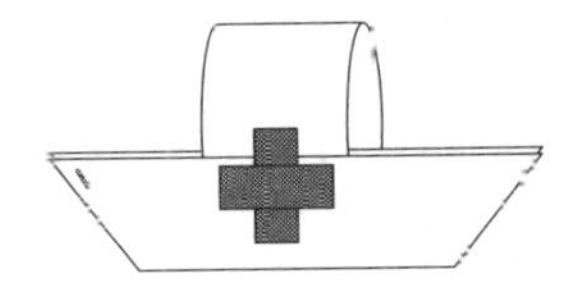

Toothbrush for Stuffed Animals

1) Cut a piece of white paper about 2” x 3”. Fold it in half to 2” x 1½”. Tape it over the end of a large craft stick. (If you have to use a small craft stick, cut the paper about 1½” x 2” to start.)

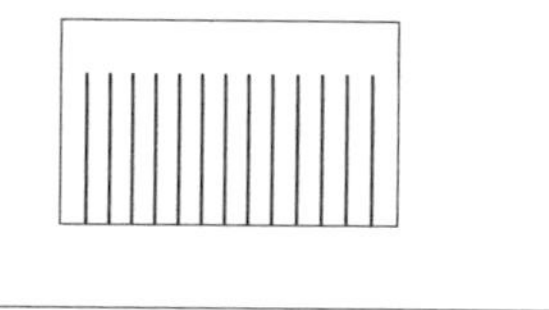

2) Draw black lines on the paper for bristles, then tape the lower edges together. (The tape will help stiffen the paper.)

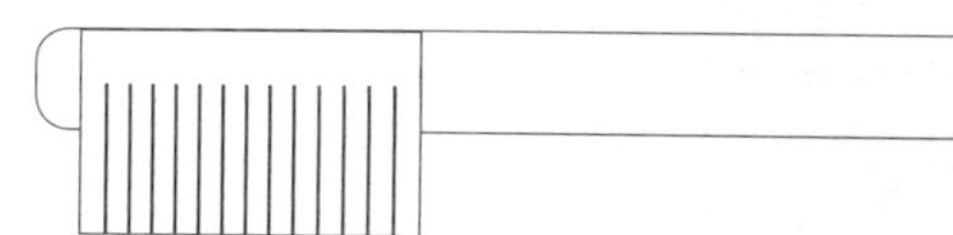

Medical Nametags

Cut posterboard into rectangles about 2” x 3”. Draw children’s names toward one side of them, and add a symbol that shows their medical specialty. Tape a safety pin to the backside.

For a Little Something Extra...

Call a local veterinarian and ask if you can tour her or his office.

☆ ☆ ☆

On your next visit to the doctor or dentist, ask about the different pieces of equipment or instruments you see—what they’re for, and how they work. Maybe you can feel the polisher’s tickle, or hear your heartbeat.

Dragons/Fairies

Art/Craft

- Make paper or poster-board dragon wings or fairy wings to wear for dress-up; staple ribbons to the edges to tie them on (see directions).
- Make magic fairy wands from cardboard, plastic straws, optional glitter glue, and ribbons (see directions).
- Make dragon masks by decorating white poster board or cut-apart brown paper bags; punch a hole on side edges and tie yarn pieces through holes (see directions).
- Make dragon windsocks from construction paper and crepe paper streamers or ribbons (see directions).

Indoors

- If you're in the mood to be fairies, everyone can dance around to ballet-type music, waving their wands and changing chairs into bears and clocks into socks (read *The Wizard, the Fairy, and the Magic Chicken* by Helen Lester for a really good laugh!)
- If it's more like a dragon-day, put on your wings and masks. Look around the house for "treasures" to collect (since most dragons in stories had caves full of gold and jewels they had stored away). Gnash teeth as desired.
- Take turns telling what you'd wish for if you could have three wishes.
- Act out Cinderella, taking turns after each scene so that everyone gets a chance to be the Fairy Godmother. See if the children can relate most of the story themselves.
- Sing Little Bunny FooFoo, since the Good Fairy plays a big role in that song.

Music

Dinosaurs, Dragons, and other children's songs (Kevin Roth)* (includes Puff the Magic Dragon)
Soundtrack from Cinderella (Rogers and Hammerstein)
Dance of the Sugar Plum Fairies (Nutcracker Suite)

Hints for Your Own Situation...

Make sugar cookie dough ahead of time; color most of it green, and a small amount red. Help children roll out and cut green circles and triangles, then let them assemble them into dragon shapes. Use red dough bits (or cinnamon red-hots) for eyes, "fire" coming out of the mouths, claws, and decorations. Sprinkle with sugar for sparkle, then bake according to recipe.

☆ ☆ ☆

On a sunny day, watch for a sunbeam streaming in a window. Look for the "fairy dust" dancing in the light.

Outdoors

- Run around and let your dragon windsocks blow behind you in the breeze.
- Fairy wings are a lot like butterfly wings; is it the right time and place for butterflies? Look around. You might at least see some other winged creatures (birds, moths, bees, flies). Any dragonflies?
- If there were dragons in your backyard, where do you think they'd hide, or like to live? Go on a search.
- Collect leaves and rocks and make a fairy circle on the ground, away from the main path, where "they" can dance.

Books

The Fairie's Nighttime Book by Beverly Manson (Doubleday & Co. 1983) (4/6)

The Wizard, the Fairy and the Magic Chicken by Helen Lester (Houghton Mifflin 1983) (2/3)

How Drufus the Dragon Lost His Head by Bill Peet (Houghton Mifflin 1971) (4/6)

The Dragon ABC Hunt by Loreen Leedy (Holiday House 1986) (2/3)

Emma's Dragon Hunt by Catherine Stock (Lothrop, Lee & Shepard 1984) (4/6)

There's No Such Thing as a Dragon by Jack Kent (Golden/Western 1975) (4/6)

Queen Mab: the Fairies of Cottlingley Glen by Cynthia Eng (Random House 1997) (4/6)

There's a Dragon About by Richard and Roni Schotter (Orchard Books 1994) (4/6)

The Popcorn Dragon by Jane Thayer (William Morrow & Co. 1953) (4/6)

The Flying Dragon Room by Audrey Wood (Scholastic/ Blue Sky 1996) (4/6)

Snack-time

Dragons are a symbol of the Chinese New Year, and red is a color of celebration. Serve fortune cookies and "tea" (apple juice) on red napkins or paper plates.

☆ ☆ ☆

Serve older children popcorn in honor of *The Popcorn Dragon* by Jane Thayer (his fiery breath came in handy!)

☆ ☆ ☆

Set a place for a fairy to come join you for snack. Tape a plastic juice-can lid on top of an empty spool or film can to make a fairy table (in the middle of your table). Set a thimble or marshmallow next to it for her chair. If you have a doll's tea set, put a saucer with a bit of cheese or cookie on the table.

☆ ☆ ☆

Serve tiny crustless "tea" sandwiches.

Videos

Peter Pan; The Gnomemobile; The Reluctant Dragon
Pete's Dragon; Puff the Magic Dragon
Cinderella; Sleeping Beauty, Mulan

Art/Craft Materials

posterboard
ribbons (sturdy; about 2 yds. per pair of wings)
stapler, scissors, markers
glitter glue
plastic straw
ribbons (thin; about 2 yds.)
yarn
construction paper
crepe-paper streamers
hole puncher

Art/Craft Directions

Dragon or Fairy Wings

1) Draw these wing shapes on poster-board and cut them out. Don't cut them apart—they need to have about 5 inches of poster-board connecting them.

2) Decorate them with markers, glitter glue, stickers, etc. Staple the center of the sturdy ribbon across the top of the center section. To put them on the child, hold them against his back, bring the ribbons over his shoulders, bring them down crossed across his chest, pull them around his waist to the back, cross them in the back, and bring them to the front to tie in a bow.

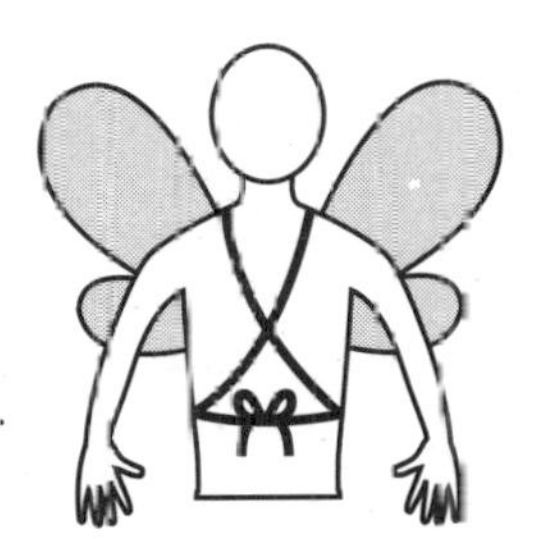

For a Little Something Extra...

Look up information on the Chinese New Year and the Dragon Festivals.

Fairy Wand

1) Trace two stars of the same size on cardboard (use a cookie cutter as a stencil). Decorate one side of each with stickers, markers, etc.

2) Tape the end of a drinking straw to the center of one, and tape or staple ribbons coming from the middle.

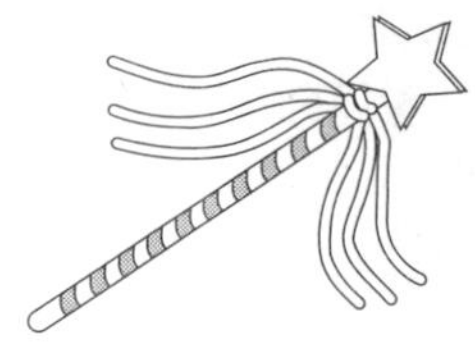

3) Glue, tape, or staple the other star on top, sandwiching the straw in between the two.

Dragon Mask

1) Draw a mask on white posterboard and color it in with markers (markers work best on the "dull" side of posterboard). Cut out eye and mouth holes.

2) Punch holes for knotting lengths of yarn to each side, to use as ties. If you want to make a bigger mask, just color on eyes, and cut nose holes to let them be used for seeing through.

Dragon Windsock

1) Cut a 9" x 12" piece of construction paper in half lengthwise. Decorate one of the 4 1½" x 12" pieces with a dragon design.

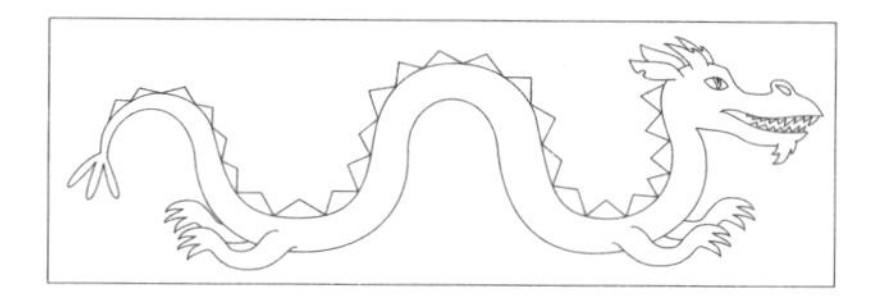

2) Bend the strip into a circle and staple the edges together. Cut 24" strips of crepe-paper streamers (about 8 strips per windsock). Staple them around one edge of the band. Punch 3 holes in the top edge. Cut 3 pieces of yarn 12" long each. Knot each one through a hole, then tie the three together at the top to make a hanger.

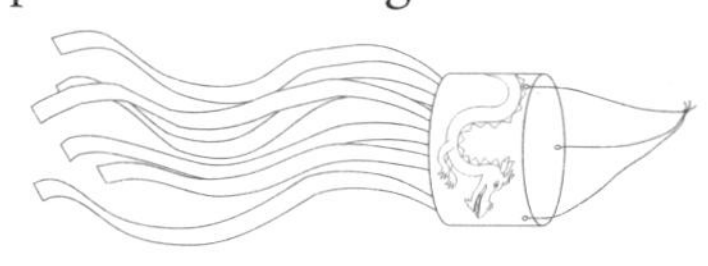

Farmlife

Art/Craft

- Take a big packing box (or box from a stove or TV) and turn it into a red barn. Draw the outlines for traditional barn windows. Cut out a double door to crawl through. Tape overlapping pieces of red construction paper on the sides, to look like boards. Staple two pieces of poster board together, then tape them to the box-top with strong packing tape, to make a roof shape.
- Make stables for various small animal toys. Stand shoeboxes on their sides. Cut out windows along the sides, then glue "fringed" green, yellow, and brown construction paper shapes inside and out for grass and hay on the ground. Make craft stick fences (see directions).
- Have any blue ribbon? Make county-fair awards by taping a length of ribbon to a circle of blue construction paper, with a gold star in the middle of it (see directions).

Indoors

- Gather all the stuffed animals you have that could live on a farm, including dogs and cats. Use your boxes, building blocks, and other toys to create a barnyard, stables, and fences. What do the animals need to eat? Where do they like to run and play? What are the baby animals' names?
- Do you have any toy tractors or trucks that will hold some of your animals? Use them to take everyone to a "county fair"—make the animals prance or trot and give them all blue ribbons for prizes (taped or safety-pinned).
- Take turns going into your box barn. When inside, make a noise from some farm animal, and have the other children guess what they're supposed to be. Take turns.
- Use child-sized rakes so everyone can clean up the "barn-yard;" gather rocks in plastic buckets for "eggs."

Music

"Old-MacDonald;" "Farmer in the Dell"

Hints for Your Own Situation...

Ahead of time, spray animal crackers with a polyurethane sealer, or brush with clear nail polish; let dry. Children can paint them with poster paints, then glue a pin-clasp on the back. (Have a grown-up use a hot glue-gun for best results.)

☆ ☆ ☆

The crowning touch for your big barn: make cardboard weather-vanes. Have older children draw or trace their favorite animal shape (from a book, stencils or cookie cutters), tape it to an 8" strip of cardboard, and mount them all on the barn roof—the more the merrier (see directions).

Snack-time

Build "haystacks" from two large shredded-wheat biscuits leaning against each other in a bowl (or a mound of bite-sized shredded wheat). Offer honey to dip them in, and serve cow's milk or apple-tree juice to drink.

☆ ☆ ☆

If you can find cookie cutters in farm-animal shapes, cut sliced balogna to look like a pig, and turkey and chicken slices to look like those birds.

☆ ☆ ☆

Think dairy farm: for those who like it, serve cottage cheese or cheddar cheese, buttered bread, or ice cream!

Outdoors

- Pretend that your whole yard is a barnyard. Could a corner with some tricycles be the "horse" corral? Set a bucket of raw oatmeal nearby. Gather some grass to feed the imaginary sheep and cows. Scatter crumbs or birdseed for "chickens." Can you make the noises for all of these animals, plus geese, pigs, mice, goats, and an owl?
- Play Duck, Duck, Goose.
- Draw a big cow on a white posterboard, and tape it to the side of the house (or a picnic table turned on its side). Have everyone color in black spots, but leave off the tail. Cut tails from paper, and play Pin the Tail on the Cow.

Books

Pig Surprise by Ute Krause
(Dial Books 1989) (4/6)

Early Morning in the Barn by Nancy Tafuri
(Greenwillow 1983) (2/3)

Sherman the Sheep by Kevin Kiser
(MacMillan 1994) (4/6)

Rock-A-Bye Farm by Diane Johnston Hamm
(Simon & Schuster Books 1992) (4/6)

Wake Up, Sun! by David Harrison
(Random House 1986) (4/6)

Animals A to Z by David McPhail
(Scholastic Inc. 1988) (4/6)

I Want to be a Farmer by Edith Kunhardt
(Grosset & Dunlap 1989) (2/3)

Farm Life by David McPhail
(Harcourt Brace Jovanovich 1985) (4/6)

Harvey Potter's Balloon Farm by Jerdine Nolen
(Scholastic 1994) (4/6)

Wake Up, Farm! by Alvin Tresselt
(Lothrop, Lee & Shepard 1991) (4/6)

Videos

Babe; Charlotte's Web; Let's Go to the Farm*
Fantastic Journey to the Farm*; Baby Animals*
See How They Grow: Farm Animals (DK/Sony)

Art/Craft Materials

shoeboxes
construction paper (green, yellow, and brown)
scissors, markers, tape
craft sticks, modeling dough
blue construction paper
gold star stickers, or gold posterboard
white posterboard
cookie cutters in animal shapes (optional)
pictures of animals to trace/copy

Art/Craft Directions

Box Stable

1) Depending on the size of your toy horses, use one box on its side, or two boxes side by side on end. Have the open side face you. With two, tape them together.

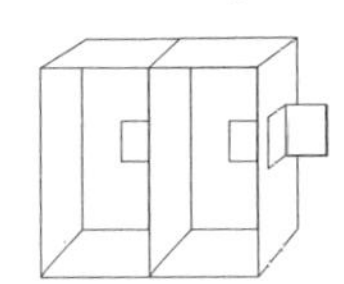

2) Draw windows on the sides, and cut along the top, one side, and the bottom of each window. This way, you can fold the window shape out, like a shutter, bending along the uncut side.

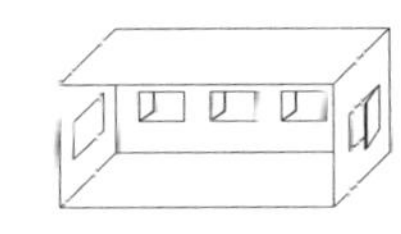

3) Cut strips of brown, yellow, and green paper, about 2" x 12". Use scissors to cut rough fringe along one long side, about 1" deep.

4) Bend the fringed paper around the bottom edges of the boxes on the outside and the inside and tape them in place. Cut shreds of yellow paper and glue them, scattered, on the stable floor, for hay.

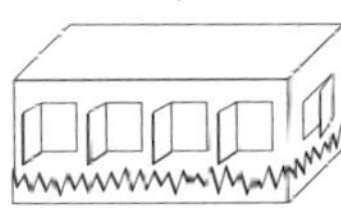

For a Little Something Extra...

Visit the animals at a county fair, tour a dairy farm, possibly at a university agricultural school, or see if the local zoo has a children's petting farm.

Craft Stick Fence

Glue narrow or wide craft sticks across each other, as shown, and stand them up in bits of modeling dough.

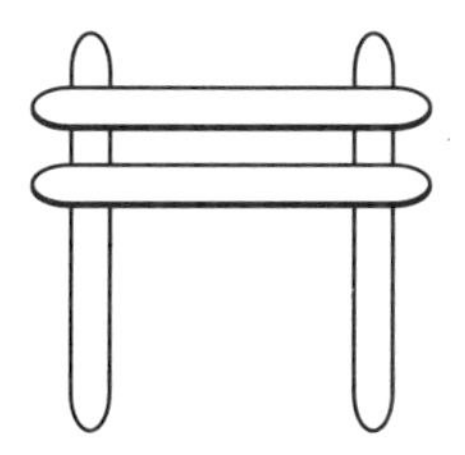

Blue Ribbon Award

Cut a circle of blue construction paper. Glue a big gold star in the middle, or lots of little gold stars around the edge. Cut a length of blue construction paper for a ribbon, and glue it to the back, hanging down. Print "First Place" or "Winner" on it.

Weathervane Animal

Trace an animal from a book, a stencil, or a cookie cutter. Cut it out from posterboard or construction paper. Cut two strips of posterboard 1" x 8". Tape them together all the way, except for the bottom inch. Tape the animal to the top. Spread the two bottom strips apart, and tape them over the peak of your box barn (or tape them to the bottom of an upside down shoebox, for a table decoration).

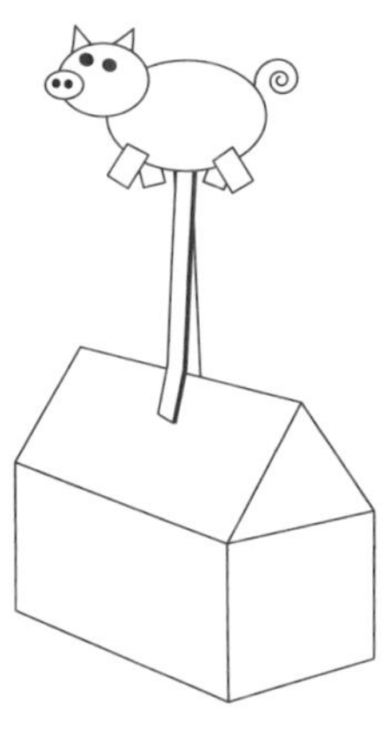

Firefighting

Art/Craft

- Cut out red construction-paper firefighter hats; decorate with your initials or your age on the front (see directions).
- Draw a dalmation outline on white paper, then use different materials to add black spots: try any crazy rubber stamp shape (or your thumbprint!) pressed onto a washable black inkpad, a purchased black Bingo stamper, chunks of sponge dipped into washable black poster paint in a foil piepan, or bits of black ribbon cut up and glued on.
- Make a "firefighter" ladder for all your bean-bag animals to climb up and down (or just hang out on!) Buy two wooden yardsticks and a bag of craft sticks. Lay the yardsticks side by side on a newspaper-covered table. Arrange the craft sticks laying across the yardsticks, overlapping to both edges. Glue them in place and let dry for an hour (see directions). Let the animals climb!

Indoors

- Bring out any toy fire trucks, and take turns driving them around the room (or house). Build a block house then crank up your "ladder" to reach. Put on raincoats (do you have any yellow slickers?) with belts around them. Stuff tube socks with newspapers to make "hoses," and make whooshing noises as you pretend to tackle the fire!
- Practice a fire drill in the house, starting with "Stop-Drop-and-Roll." From each room, how would you get out in a hurry? Try crawling around the house and checking that doors are cool to the touch.
- Where would everyone meet when you get outside?
- Go around the house and test all the smoke detectors to see if they need fresh batteries.
- Who can say their address and phone number for an emergency phone call?

Music

"House on Fire" (Busytown Radio: The Big Traffic Jam)*

Hints for Your Own Situation...

Have older children use a toy telephone to practice calling 911, or the correct emergency number for your town.

☆ ☆ ☆

On nice days, firefighters may pass the time playing a game of catch, so you may want to do it, too! They also have to move fast, so see how quickly you can run to your fire-drill meeting place.

☆ ☆ ☆

Instead of a block tower, get a big cardboard box, and draw on it to look like a tall building with lots of windows. Color orange and red flames coming out.

☆ ☆ ☆

Be sure to explain they should never try to put out a real fire—just get out of the house fast!

Snack-time

Children can make their own "ladders" from strips torn off string cheese, or by using thin pretzel sticks stuck together with peanut butter.

☆ ☆ ☆

Plain spaghetti or ramen noodles can be piles of tangled "hoses."

☆ ☆ ☆

Frost a sheet-cake with a fire-engine decoration. On white frosting, outline the truck with red icing, and draw windows, ladders, etc. with yellow (or black). Use chocolate-cream sandwich cookies for wheels.

Outdoors

- On a hot day, get out the hose; let the children spray different trees or objects. Use plastic pails to play bucket brigade, passing them along to each other (then perhaps watering a garden). They can wear plastic raincoats (and boots if you have them), or everyone can agree if they want themselves to be hosed down! If you have a plastic hydrant sprinkler, all the better.
- If you have a toy fire engine, pretend you're the firefighters taking care of it, and give it a soapy wash.
- Lay a ladder flat on the ground, and practice stepping through the spaces (hold toddlers' hands for balance).

Books

Curious George Visits the Fire Station by Margaret and H.A.Rey
(Houghton Mifflin 1985) (2/3)

ABC Fire Dogs by Ida DeLage
(Garrard Publishing Company 1977) (4/6)

I Want To Be A Firefighter by Edith Kunhardt
(Grosset & Dunlap 1989) (4/6)

Fire! Fire! Said Mrs. McGuire by Bill Martin Jr.
(Harcourt Brace & Co. 1996) (4/6)

I Want To Be A Firefighter by Linda Lee Maifair
(Sesame Stree/Golden 1991) (4/6)

Fire Engines by Anne Rockwell
(E.P.Dutton 1986) (2/3)

Smokey the Fireman by Richard Scarry
(Golden Western 1988) (4/6)

Fire Trucks by Hope Irvin Marston
(Cobble Hill/Dutton 1996) (4/6)

The Fire Station by Robert Munsch
(Annick Press Ltd. 1994) (4/6)

Big Red Fire Truck by Ken Wilson-Max
(Scholastic Cartwheel 1997) (2/3)

Videos

Robert Munsch: Angela Visits the Fire Station
Fire & Rescue (Fred Levine)*
Sesame Street Visits the Firehouse*

Art/Craft Materials

red construction paper
white paper
black markers
scissors, tape
wide (¾") craft sticks
2 wooden yardsticks
Tacky glue
poster paint or markers

Art/Craft Directions

Firefighter Hat

1) Draw this shape on a 9"x12" piece of red construction paper. Cut around the outside oval shape, and cut out the inside part that is shaded.

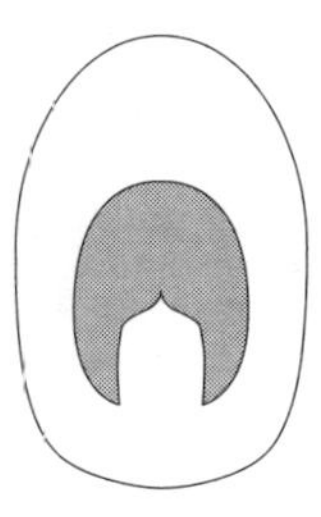

2) Cut a white piece of paper in the shape shown, about 3" across, to make the front "emblem."

Draw the child's initials and/or age on the front in black marker.

Paste the emblem to the front of the hat.

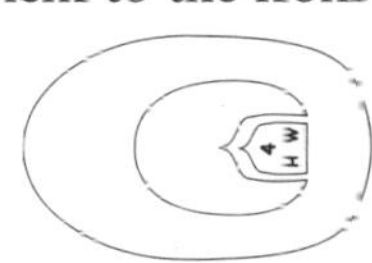

3) When you put the hat on the child, the front emblem part naturally pops up. If the head opening is not big enough, trim a little bit more off the inner edge.

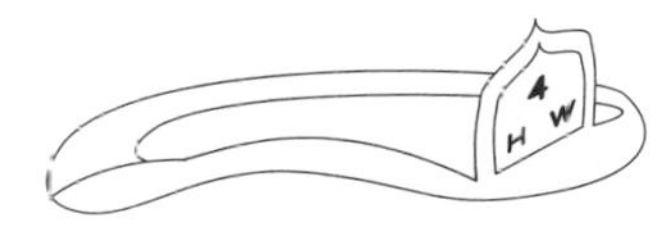

For a Little Something Extra...

Call your local firestation and ask if you and the children can be given a tour.

Ladder for Bean-Bag Animals

1) Lay 11 wide craft sticks across the two parallel yardsticks, placing them next to the 3" mark, the 6" mark, the 9" mark, etc. Glue them in place with Tacky glue, and let it sit for a good hour.

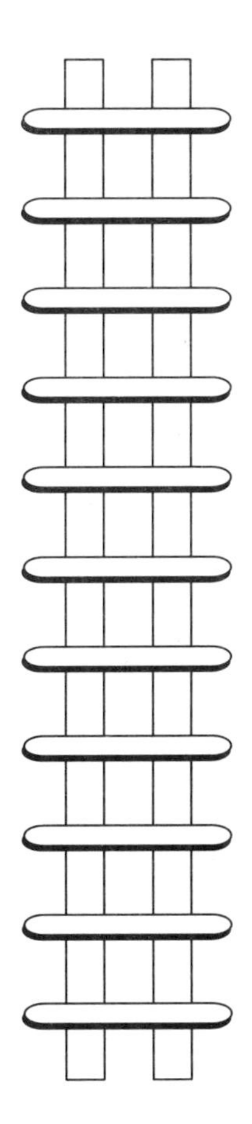

2) Use poster paints or markers to color and decorate the ladder. Have your bean-bag animals climb up it to reach the top of of a chair or table for a "rescue." Later, let them hang through the rungs to use the ladder as a storage rack.

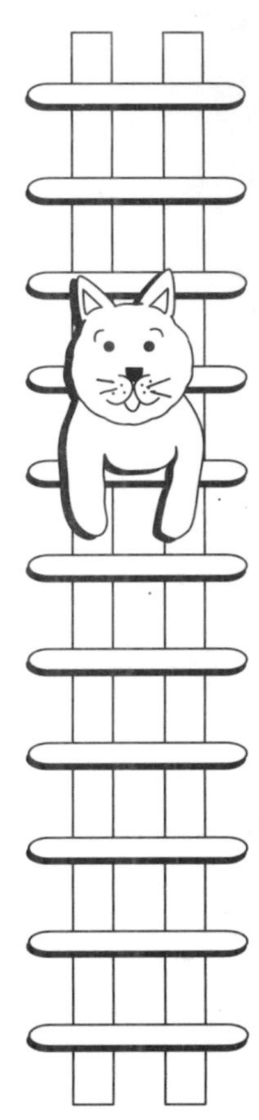

Fish/Under the Sea

Art/Craft

- Create an aquarium by lining a shoebox with blue construction paper. If you have yarn scraps in green, brown, red, or pink, glue wavy pieces around the inside to be seaweed and coral. On separate papers, color brightly striped and polka-dotted fish of different sizes. Cut them out, tape thread to the backs, and tape the free ends to hang from the inside top of the box (see directions).
- Do you have any rocks (not too small), a toy treasure box, plastic turtle, or mermaid doll you could add to the scene?
- Make fishing rods and lines by taping string or yarn to a drinking straw or a plastic ruler. On the free end, tie any kind of flat "refrigerator" magnet in which you can cut a hole. Or, get a piece of Velcro, cut a hole in the middle, and tie it on (see directions). Use for activity below.

Indoors

- Tape lengths of blue and green crepe-paper streamers hanging from the doorways of the play area, like seaweed.
- Have everyone wear bathing suits, especially in the winter! Get out beach towels, real umbrellas, sunglasses, straw hats, buckets, and plastic shovels. Set up your beach in the middle of the living room (maybe even encourage a few nap takers to lie down on the towels for a while!)
- Place a blue bath towel, old tablecloth, big scarf, etc., on the carpet to be the water. Take turns jumping onto the middle of it while everyone yells "splash!" (Amazingly simple, but they love it).
- Go "fishing" around the house with your magnet or Velcro fishing rod. What will your rod "catch?" Try to guess ahead of time what will stick and what won't.

Music

Little Mermaid (Disney); "Three Little Fishies"
Slugs at Sea (Banana Slug String Band)*
"A Sailor Went to Sea, Sea, Sea"

Hints for Your Own Situation...

For older children, complete the aquarium by securely taping clear or blue kitchen plastic wrap around the front of the aquarium for a real underwater look.

☆ ☆ ☆

Mix up a batch of sand dough for modeling castles that will keep. (Use an old pan for heating it.) Combine 1 cup of cornstarch, 2 cups of fine sand (purchased is best), and about 1½ cups of water, and stir over medium heat until thickened. Cool before using. Older children can decorate their creations with beads, tiny rocks, buttons, or shells.

Outdoors

- Makes fish faces for each other. If the weather is hot, do it with everyone in the wading pool.
- Draw fish, sharks, mermaids, seashells, etc., on the sidewalk using wet chalk for a special effect.
- If you have a sandbox, pretend it's your beach and dig with plastic shovels and pails. Sprinkle in a little water (from a spray bottle), then use plastic cups and tubs to build sandcastles. (Also, ahead of time, you can bury shells or small toys for them to uncover.)

Books

The Rainbow Fish by Marcus Pfister
(North-South Books 1992) (4/6)

Beach Party by Joanne Ryder
(Frederick Warne & C. 1982) (4/6)

A Beach Day by Douglas Florian
(Greenwillow 1990) (2/3)

An Ocean World by Peter Sis
(Greenwillow 1992) (4/6)

Blue Sea by Robert Kalan
(Trumpet/Greenwillow 1979) (2/3)

The Underwater Alphabet Book by Jerry Pallotta
(Trumpet/Charlesbridge 1993) (4/6)

How Many Fish? by Caron Lee Cohen
(Harper Collins 1998) (2/3)

The Magic School Bus on the Ocean Floor by Joanna Cole
(Scholastic 1992) (4/6)

Alistair Underwater by Marilyn Sadler
(Simon & Schuster 1990) (4/6)

Out of the Ocean by Debra Frasier
(Harcourt Brace & Co. 1998) (4/6)

Snack-time

Serve oyster crackers or Pepperidge Farm Goldfish for a snack.

☆ ☆ ☆

Especially if it's a cold day outside, hold an indoor beach picnic. With everyone in their bathing suits, spread out on the towels and eat. Cut starfish-shaped lunchmeat sandwiches (star cookie-cutters will work) or "jellyfish" peanutbutter and jelly sandwiches. Jello Jigglers cut in odd shapes make great jellyfish too. Pull string-cheese partly apart from one end to make an octopus. Shredded lettuce can be "seaweed salad" with goldfish crackers on top. Drink ocean punch by putting blue-green food coloring in water or lemonade.

☆ ☆ ☆

Half a canned pear, with mandarin orange slices stuck around it, can look like a fish with fins, or a lobster with claws.

Videos

Little Mermaid; Seabert; Free Willy
Barney—A Day at the Beach; Wee Sing Under the Sea*
Shamu & You: Exploring the World of Fish*
See How They Grow: Sea Animals (DK/Sony)*

Art/Craft Materials

shoebox
blue construction paper
yarn scraps (green, brown, red, and pink)
magnet with a hole, or a Velcro dot (hook side)
plastic straw
markers
thread, scissors, glue
white paper blue plastic wrap (optional)

Art/Craft Directions

Aquarium

1) Line a shoebox with blue construction paper.

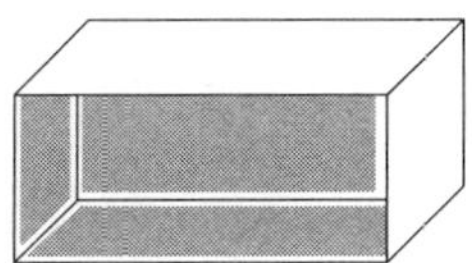

2) Glue scraps of green, brown, red, or pink yarn to sides, on bottom, and even hanging from the top, as coral and seaweed.

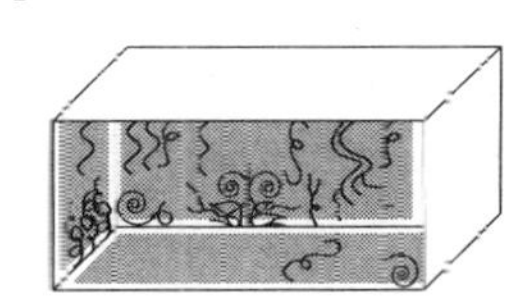

3) Draw and color bright fish on white paper, in sizes to fit inside the shoebox. Color both sides if you want. Cut them out.

For a Little Something Extra...

Even in a small yard, make your own little sandbox by pouring a bag or two of fine sand into a large tub. If you can make a corner for it outdoors, try using the big colorful round tubs that come with nylon rope handles. When play time is done, try to remember to cover it with an old trash-can lid weighted down with a rock or brick.

4) Tape varying lengths of thread, one to each fish, and tape them to the inside top of the box so that they hang down freely.

5) If you can, add real shells and rocks to bottom. Or, shape modeling dough into rocks or starfish. Can you make a treasure chest? Older children can tape blue plastic wrap stretched across the front.

Fishing Rod

1) Tape about 12" of yarn to the end of a plastic straw. Tie the free end through a hole in a magnet, or glue the end to a Velcro dot that has a hook side.

2) Go around the house and see how many kinds of things your rod will "catch."

Flags/Signs

Art/Craft

- Everyone can create a flag or pennant of his/her own, or copy one from an encyclopedia, decorating it with things that interest them. Use a construction-paper shape, then add stickers, stars cut from paper, strips of crepe-paper streamers glued on, and lots of coloring. Mount each child's flag on a separate dowel or yardstick for marching in a parade, or string them all together along one string across the side of a room, like pennants (see directions).
- Make tiny flags and tape them to unsharpened pencils. Stick them in the sides of plants in flowerpots, or all together in a little vase.
- Make a windsock out of construction paper and crepe-paper streamers (see directions).
- Explain that nowadays, we often use painted signs or lit-up signs instead of flags of old. Ask them if they can draw some well-known signs: a Stop sign, a No Parking sign, and a McDonald's sign! Draw some signs yourself, and ask children if they recognize/can read what they are: the name of the grocery store you use, their favorite toy store, the name of their preschool, a donut shop they like, etc.

Indoors

- Build castles out of wooden blocks or stacked boxes, and tape your pencil-flags to the towers.
- In a book of flags, pick ones you like, find what country they come from, and borrow library cassettes or CDs of music from those countries. Get up and dance!
- Hold lengths of crepe-paper streamers in each hand and dance with them to your favorite music.

Music

Cassettes or CDs with songs and games of different countries
"Star Spangled Banner"; "It's a Grand Old Flag"

Outdoors

- Can you see any signs from your yard or driveway? Can you guess what they are telling you?

Hints for Your Own Situation…

Older children can look up the international maritime flag symbols for the letters of the alphabet (see reference). Have each child "spell" out his/her name (maybe drawing it with markers on white paper) to make personal signs for their bedroom doors.

☆ ☆ ☆

Open up a twin-sized bed-sheet. Pretend it is a full-sized flag that has just been taken in for the night and needs to be properly folded. Teach everyone how to hold it and help with the folding (see directions).

- Have a parade around the yard, with everyone holding their flags (just watch so that no one gets poked). Sing!
- Some ancient flags used to look like windsocks; do you have a modern one? Can you use it, or one that you made, to tell which direction the wind is blowing?
- Using chalk, have a grown-up draw rectangles or triangles on the sidewalk or driveway. Toddlers can scribble colors while older children can draw a sign that shows their house, yard, favorite flower, or pet.
- Keep your eyes open for sky-writing (sky signs)!

Books

Flags by Chris Oxlade (ref.)
(Franklin Watts/Grolier 1995) (4/6)

The Sign Painter's Dream by Roger Roth
(Random House 1993) (4/6)

I Read Symbols by Tana Hoban
(Greenwillow 1993) (2/3)

Harriet Reads Signs and More Signs by Betsy & Giulio Maestro
(Crown 1981) (2/3)

The Signmaker's Assistant by Tedd Arnold
(Dial 1992) (4/6)

Signs and Symbols Around the World by Elizabeth Helfman (ref.)
(Lothrop, Lee & Shepard 1967) (6+)

I Read Signs by Tana Hoban
(Greenwillow 1993) (2/3)

Blue Bug's Safety Book by Virginia Poulet
(Children's Press 1973) (2/3)

Red Light, Green Light by Margaret Wise Brown
(Scholastic 1992) (2/3)

Flags by David Jefferis (ref.)
(Franklin Watts 1985) (4/6)

Snack-time

Cut the crusts off white and wheat bread, then cut them into even "stripes." Alternate stripes side by side on a plate. Have children use tiny star-shaped cookie cutters to cut stars from slices of cheese and meat. As desired, arrange stars on top of bread stripes, stuck on with a bit of butter or mayo, then nibble the strips as finger food.

☆ ☆ ☆

Cut pennant-shaped flags from sliced cheese, then decorate them with children's initials made from thin pretzels, slivers of apple, or rows of raisins.

☆ ☆ ☆

Cut the corners off toasted bread slices to make eight-sided signs. Squeeze a jelly STOP or anything else on the shape. Add a bacon-strip handle.

Videos
Yankee Doodle Dandy

Art/Craft Materials
wooden dowel or yardstick
construction paper
crepe paper streamers
rubber stamps, yarn
markers, paint, or crayons
scissors, string, glue stick
magazine pictures
twin-sized flat bed sheet

Art/Craft Directions

Flag/Pennant

1) Cut a basic flag shape from white or construction paper. Choose a rectangle, a triangle, or a pennant.

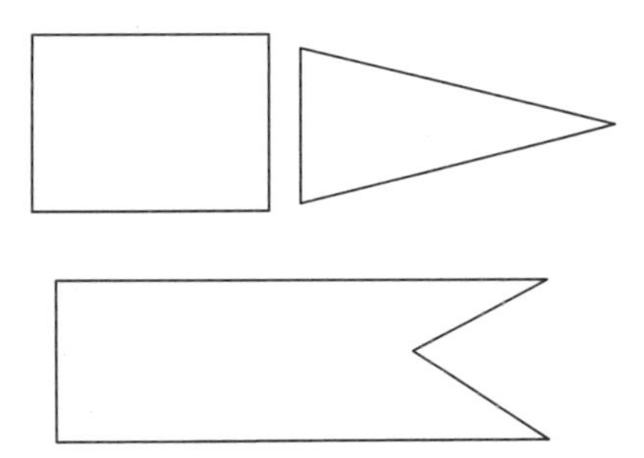

2) Draw or glue on shapes, magazine pictures, or just drawings of your favorite things. Many flags are divided into sections, so you can put one item or type of item per section.

3) Wrap a bit of the left edge of each flag around a dowel or yardstick, and tape it in place. Or, tape several flags side by side along a string, and hang them across a doorway like pennants.

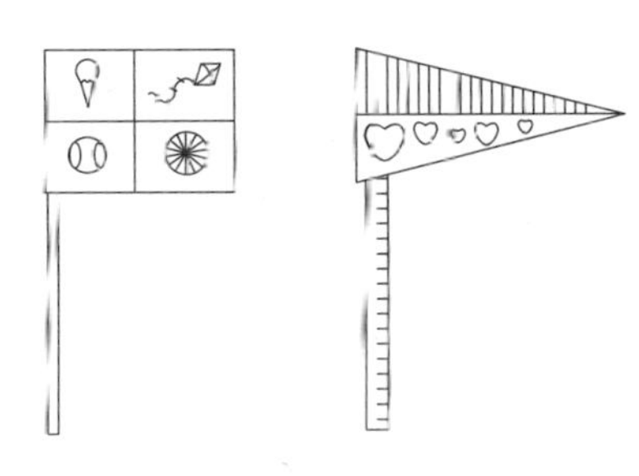

For a Little Something Extra...

For more information on flags, send a self-addressed, stamped envelope to:

Flag Research Center
3 Edgehill Road
Winchester, MA 01890
(781) 729-9410

Windsock

1) Cut a piece of construction paper in half lengthwise, to get a piece 4 ½" x 12". Decorate it to match one of your flags, or to match the season (spring flowers, summer fireworks, fall leaves, winter snowflakes). Bend the paper into a band and staple the edges together.

2) Cut crepe-paper streamers into 8 pieces, each about 24" long. Staple them around the bottom edge of the windsock. Punch 3 holes around the top edge. Tie three 12" lengths of yarn through the holes, and knot them together for hanging.

Flag Folding

1) Have each person (at least two) stand and hold onto a corner of the sheet. Fold the sheet in half length-wise.

2) Fold it in half length-wise again.

3) Fold one corner over to meet the edge, making a triangle.

4) Keep turning the triangle over to meet the next edge, until you get down to one thick triangle. Store neatly.

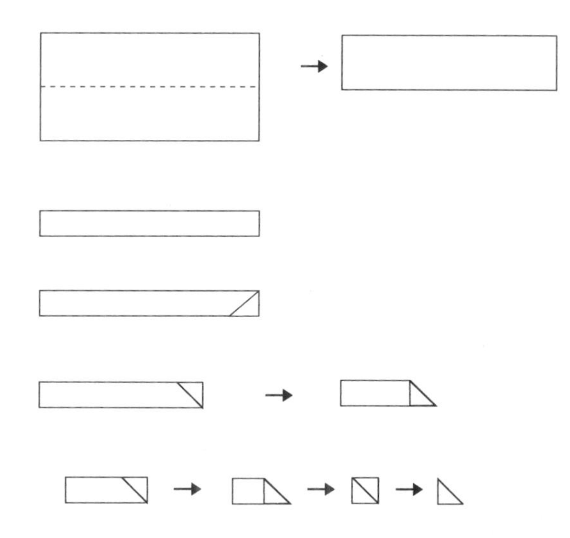

Flowers/Vegetables

Art/Craft

- Draw, paint, fold, or shape paper flowers with markers, water colors, pleated tissue paper (see directions) or modeling dough; or paste cut-out flowers (from a seed catalog) to straws or pipecleaner stems. Stick them in a vase or flowerpot, or create a 3-D picture: glue a strip of "fringed" green paper along the bottom of a full sheet of blue construction paper, then tape on the stemmed flowers to make a garden placemat (see directions).
- Glue cut-out flowers to a taped loop of green construction paper to make napkin rings.
- Make plant/seed identifier stakes for the garden by gluing flower and vegetable pictures to drinking straws or craft sticks. Seal with adhesive plastic (see directions).
- Decorate plastic tubs, frosting cups, etc., as flower pots.
- Cut potatoes in half; draw on a simple shape, then cut away the outer areas to make a potato printer. Press the potato into a shallow plate of poster paint or onto a washable ink pad, then stamp it on paper for notecards.
- In the fall, draw faces on pumpkins and squash.

Indoors

- Take flowers that you've gathered from outside, and put them in a flower press: the easy way is to layer waxed paper, a few flowers, waxed paper, several heavy books, and then repeat the process; check on them in a few weeks.
- Lead a scavenger hunt through the house, collecting names of things that have flowers on them (a picture on the wall, towels, sheets, a spoon, etc.). Try to let each child find five things.
- Add a few drops of blue food coloring to a tall glass of water. Put in a stalk of celery or a carnation flower. Check it every few hours, and see the color rise up.

Music

Everything Grows (Raffi)

Hints for Your Own Situation...

Younger children can use a vegetable scrubber to clean potatoes or carrots for an adult to cut up.

☆ ☆ ☆

If you have a garden outdoors or in, an older child can help pick tomatoes, beans, carrots, etc. (Younger children will pick anything, whether it's what you wanted or not!)

☆ ☆ ☆

Save seeds from your own purchases of apples, pears, oranges, acorn squash, pumpkins, watermelons, cantaloupe, avocados, etc. Use them to start your own seedlings, in pots or between two wet paper towels in a sealable bag. Who knows, you may have great luck with them transplanted to an outdoor garden!

Outdoors

- Cover a leaf with tracing paper and do a crayon-edge rubbing on top of it. Use several colors, cut them out, and glue them onto a piece of construction paper for a collage.
- Look at flowers under a magnifying glass. Take them apart and talk about the shapes, colors, and textures of each part. What does each part do?
- Plant seeds, collect bouquets, harvest some vegetables, or weed the garden (with supervision!). In cold weather, look to see what plants are still visible, and if they look different than they did in spring and summer.
- Draw chalk pictures on a sidewalk, then use a watering can to "erase" them.

Books

Seeds by George Shannon
(Houghton Mifflin 1994) (4/6)
Planting a Rainbow by Lois Ehlert
(Harcourt Brace Jovanovich 1988) (2/3)
The Gardener by Sarah Stewart
(Farrar Straus Giroux 1997) (4/6)
The Tiny Seed by Eric Carle
(Picture Book Studio 1987) (4/6)
Flower Garden by Eve Bunting
(Harcourt Brace & Co. 1994) (2/3)
Mouse & Mole and the Year-Round Garden by Doug Cushman
(W.H. Freeman and Co. 1994) (4/6)
An Edible Alphabet by Bonnie Christensen
(Dial/Penguin 1994) (4/6)
Grandpa's Too-Good Garden by James Stevenson
(Greenwillow Books/William Morrow & Co. Inc. 1989) (4/6)
Alphabet Garden by Laura Jane Coats
(Macmillan Publishers 1993) (4/6)
Jack's Garden by Henry Cole
(Greenwillow Books 1995) (2/3)

Snack-time

Cut bread into petal shapes, then arrange with leaves cut from sliced cheese and stems made from sliced celery, pretzel sticks, or strands of string cheese.

☆ ☆ ☆

For older children, serve raw veggies with a ranch dressing dip. Stick some slices and chunks together with toothpicks to make crazy dipping creatures.

☆ ☆ ☆

Older children may enjoy sunflower seeds to eat.

☆ ☆ ☆

Treat children to potato chips—not what we usually think of as vegetables!

Videos

Ballet of Flowers*; Hullaballoo: Everything Grows (DK)*
The Magic Schoolbus Goes to Seed

Art/Craft Materials

tissue paper or facial tissue in several colors
plastic straws, pipe cleaners
scissors, tape
blue and green construction paper
seed catalogs for pictures, or empty seed packets
wide craft sticks or short dowels

Art/Craft Directions

Pleated Tissue Flowers

1) Take 2 pieces of different colored tissue paper, 7"x10" for big flowers. Lay them on top of each other, and fan pleat them together.

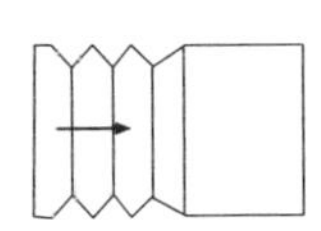

2) Twist a pipe cleaner around the center, then gently spread out the pleats in layers. For a different look, before you pleat the papers together, color on them with markers. The color really will show through both sides of the tissue.

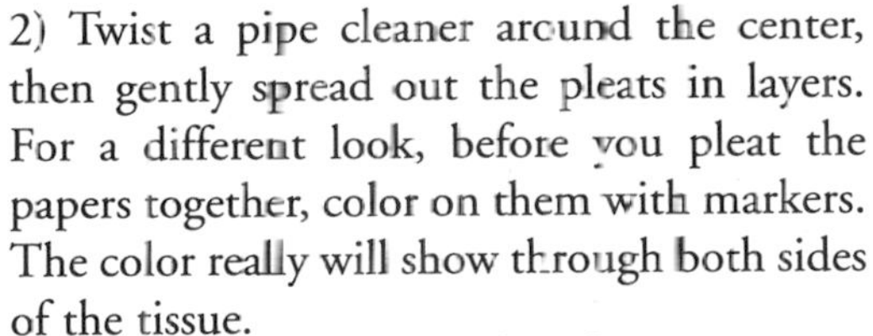

3) For smaller, fluffier flowers that look like chrysanthemums, use 2 pieces of different colored facial tissues. Cut them in half length-wise, and stack them, so that you have 4 layers, about 4"x8½". Pleat them together.

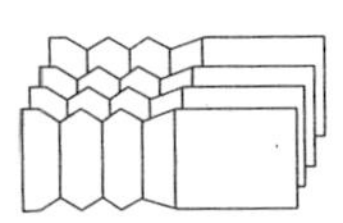

4) Cut two tiny triangles from the center, opposite each other, being careful not to cut all the way through. Twist a pipe cleaner around the middle. Cut fringe or snips on the ends. Gently spread out all the layers.

For a Little Something Extra...

Plant an indoor garden in a clear plastic rectangular box (like a shoe storage box), and put some seeds near the edges. As the plant grows, you'll be able to see the roots through the sides of the box. Try different plants, so you'll see different root colors and shapes.

Check out these Web sites: www.garden.com and www.icangarden.com/kidz.htm

☆ ☆ ☆

Call (800) LET-GRO, the National Gardening Assocition in Burlington, Vermont, for info.

Garden Placemat

1) Cut a strip of green construction paper about 2"x12". Cut fringe along one edge, and gently "ruffle" it for grass.

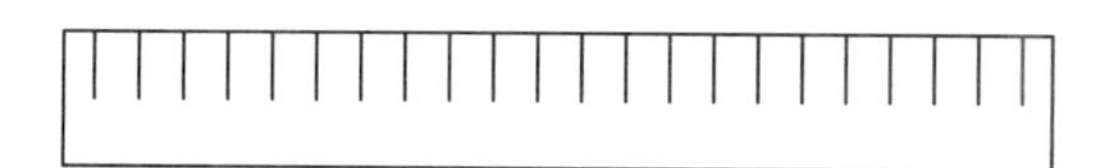

2) Glue the "grass" along the bottom edge of a piece of blue construction paper. Glue or draw a yellow sun and white clouds.

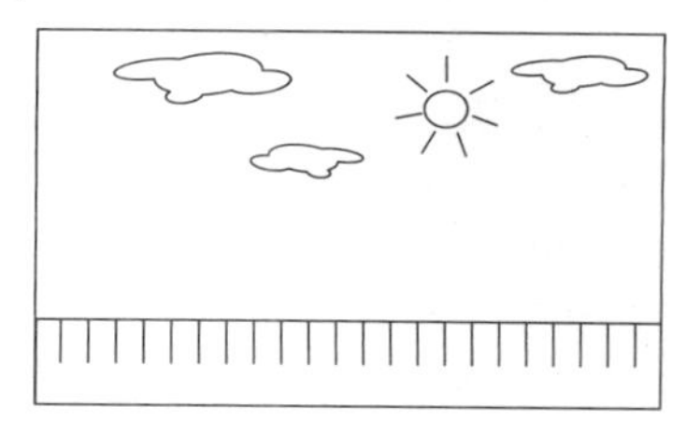

3) Slip the stems of one or two of the flowers you've made into the "grass," and tape them in place. Leave room in your flower arrangement to put a plate in the middle of the placemat.

Plant Stakes

1) Cut out pictures of flowers or vegetables from seed catalogs or from empty seed packets. Tape them to wide craft sticks, or short pieces of dowel.

2) Cut 2 pieces of clear contact paper to fit just a bit bigger than the picture. Cover the front and back sides of the picture, sealing it at the overlapping edges. This will make it weatherproof for using in an outdoor garden.

Fruit/Trees

Art/Craft

- Cut up apples into different shapes of thick slices. Dip them into washable poster paints to make apple prints on paper or thin cardboard for placemats (see directions).
- Collect leaves and have a grownup iron them between pieces of waxed paper (with a plain paper protecting the iron). Or, protect leaves between two layers of clear Contac paper. Tape tiny leaves onto strips of posterboard to make bookmarks, or large leaves onto folded paper to make greeting cards (see directions).
- Glue one rectangle of light blue felt to a piece of cardboard (from the back of an 8½ x 11 pad). Use felt scraps to cut some green hill shapes and a brown tree with branches. Let the children cut out five apple shapes you've traced on light green felt (see directions; play game below).

Indoors

- Have children "pick" the apples off your feltboard as you all sing "Farmer Brown Had Five Green Apples" (see end of this section for words). The more noisily you all "eat," the better.
- Plastic fruit that "slices" in half and goes back together with Velcro is a great addition to your toy collection. Wash them in tubs of water, cut them on real cutting boards with plastic knives (combs and craft sticks work, too), and "sell" them or "serve" them to stuffed animals.
- Pretend you are trees growing in an enchanted forest. Crouch down as low as you can, then slowly (perhaps to music), start stretching up and spreading your arms out. Go all the way up to your tippy toes, then dance in a circle, waving your branches left, right, high, low, and around.

Music

Bananaphone (Raffi)*
Dirt Made My Lunch (Banana Slug String Band)*
Family Garden (John McCutcheon)*
Trees, Trees, Trees (Rainbow)*

Hints for Your Own Situation…

Collect apple, orange, and lemon seeds. Every couple of days, take one seed and put it in a self-closing plastic bag between two damp paper towels. Use permanent marker to write the date on the outside. Repeat this five or six times. As time goes on, watch to see if they sprout in the order of planting. Transfer sprouts to pots of dirt after the second set of leaves have appeared.

☆ ☆ ☆

Get some small green plastic fruit baskets (the kind strawberries come in), and buy ribbon narrow enough to fit in the holes. Older children can weave ribbon around the sides, then tape a piece across the top for a handle. Use to keep treasures, or to hold a gift.

Snack-time

Cut up real fruit (bananas, melons, apples, peaches, strawberries). Serve on plates with a scoop of vanilla ice-cream and strips of cinnamon toast for an unusual treat. Talk about the different kinds of plants on which fruit can grow (banana plants, melon vines, blueberry bushes, apple trees, etc.)

☆ ☆ ☆

Serve raisins to older children, and talk about where raisins come from.

☆ ☆ ☆

Serve applesauce, then let older children use plastic knives to cut apples into chunks for making fresh applesauce later!

Outdoors

- Depending on the fruit of the season, sit outside and eat watermelon, cantelope, grapes, apples, strawberries, or bananas (cut up as necessary). Ask which ones have seeds they eat, and seeds they don't eat. If it's hot, rinse your hands with the hose.
- Use crayons and plain paper to do bark rubbings on different trees in the yard.
- Draw colorful fruit on the sidewalk with chalk.
- See how many kinds of different types of leaves everyone can find. Look for yellow leaves, round leaves, or weed leaves! Find maple wings, dandelion fluff, or pine cones. Collect them and look at them under a magnifying glass to see how each type carries its seeds.

Books

Fruit: A First Discovery Book by Jeunesse/Bourgoing
(Scholastic Cartwheel 1989) (4/6)

The Way of the Willow Branch by Emery & Durga Bernhard
Gulliver Books/Harcourt Brace & Co. 1996) (4/6)

Eating the Alphabet by Lois Ehlert
(Harcourt, Brace & Co. 1989) (2/3)

Alphabet Garden by Laura Jane Coats
(MacMillan Publishing 1993) (4/6)

Johnny Appleseed by Patricia Demuth
(Grosset & Dunlap 1996) (2/3)

Parsley by Ludwig Bemelmans
(Harper & Row 1955) (4/6)

A First Look at Leaves by Millicent Selsam & Joyce Hunt
(Walker and Co. 1972) (4/6)

The Tree: A First Discovery Book by Jeunesse/Bourgoing
(Scholastic Cartwheel 1989) (4/6)

The Giving Tree by Shel Silverstein
(Harper Collins 1964) (4/6)

Red Leaf, Yellow Leaf by Lois Ehlert
(Harcourt Brace Jovanovich 1991) (2/3)

Videos

Johnny Appleseed*; Eyewitness: Tree*

Art/Craft Materials

apples
washable poster paints
construction paper or posterboard
waxed paper
clear contact paper
leaves, ribbon scraps
cardboard (from an 8½"x 11" paper pad)
felt squares (light blue, dark green, light green, and brown)

Art/Craft Directions

Apple Print Placemats

1) Cut an apple into different shapes of thick slices, including the seed part. You can make some of them look like letters of the alphabet.

2) Dip the pieces into shallow tubs of washable poster paint, and "print" with them on a piece of construction paper or posterboard (cut to 9" x 12").

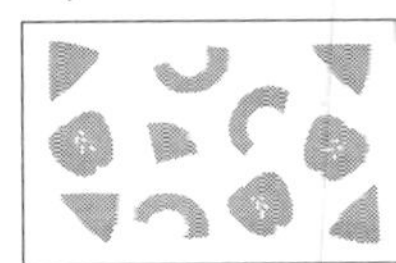

Bookmarks/Cards

1) Collect leaves and arrange them face-up in rows or patterns, on one piece of contact paper. They can be in rows to be bookmarks, or just all over to be card fronts (you'll cut apart later).

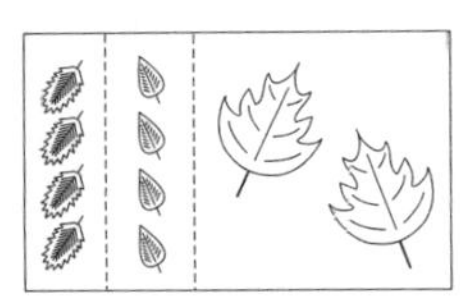

2) Place a short length of ribbon (about 4") so that it sticks to the contact paper at the top edge of the bookmarks. Lay a second sheet of contact paper on top of the first to seal in the leaves.

For a Little Something Extra...

Find out if there are any Pick-It-Yourself fruit orchards or farms in your area, and plan ahead for going during the right month.

Five Green Apples Storyboard

1) Glue light-blue felt to a piece of 8½" x 11" cardboard. Cut out grass and a hill from dark and light green felt, and glue them onto the bottom of the blue felt.

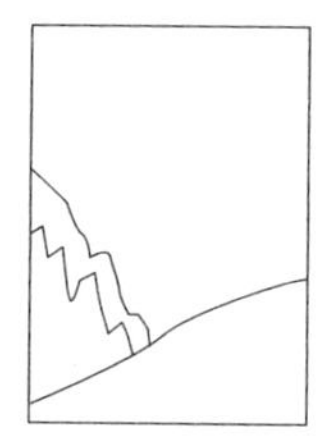

2) Cut out a brown felt tree with several branches. Cut out 5 apple shapes from light green felt. Place them on the tree branches, and take them down one by one while you sing the Five Green Apples song.

Five Green Apples Song

Farmer Brown had five green apples, hanging on a tree.
Farmer Brown had five green apples, hanging on a tree.
Then he PLUCKED one apple, *(take one off the tree)*
And he ate it hungrily...*(make lots of chomping noises),*
Leaving...four green apples, a-hanging on a tree.

Farmer Brown had four green apples, etc. (count down)

(Song ends with: Leaving ... NO more apples, a-hanging on a tree!)

Geology

Art/Craft

- Paint rocks with poster paints to make paperweights. Decorate to make faces, ladybugs, bumblebees, etc. Glue or tape on paper legs or wings if desired (see directions).
- Collect small rocks and buy bags of colored sand. Fill plastic bottles (squeeze honey or jam bottles, large plastic spice bottles, plastic peanut-butter jars) by layering some rocks and then some sand, then more rocks, and a different color of sand. Use as paperweights, or just decorations.
- Make "marble" eggs: hard-boil some eggs then let them cool. Roll them on a countertop to slightly crack the shells all over in fine lines, but not so hard as to really break the shell apart. Use food coloring to dye eggs as usual, but let them sit in the colored liquid for at least 15 minutes (the longer the better). The fine cracks will hold the color and let some inside. Both the shells and the inside will look like marble (see directions)!
- Buy a package of sugar cubes at the grocery store, and use them to build pyramids, towers, and walls.

Indoors

- Dress up in shorts and boots, strap on your backpacks, and go "mountain climbing" around the house (up and down stairs, over pillow piles).
- In the kitchen, with a dishpan of water, see how rocks change appearance when you get them wet, in and out.
- You can buy tiny geode rocks at some museums for $1; wrap one in a towel and tap gently with a hammer; inside will be a sparkly crystal lining.
- Use a magnifying glass to look at crystals of salt and sugar. Compare to any cut-glass "gems" you have in rings.

Music

Any "rock" music; Oldies for Kool Kiddies*
Rhythm of the Rocks (Marylee & Nancy);* "The Big Rock Candy Mountain"

Hints for Your Own Situation...

Start to grow crystals in a jar. This will take a week overall, but will be worth it (see directions).

☆ ☆ ☆

Make a crystal jewel T-shirt. Buy a plain T-shirt, some jewel craft glue, and package of assorted flat-back craft jewels. Arrange them as desired on the front of the T-shirt, and around the neckline, and glue them in place.

☆ ☆ ☆

Make a volcano. Place about ½ cup baking soda in a plastic bowl. Pour vinegar over it and watch the "eruption."

Snack-time

Serve Rocky Road ice cream.

☆ ☆ ☆

Build a "mountain" or pyramid by slicing squares of cheese, each a little smaller than the one before, and stacking them up.

☆ ☆ ☆

Find rock candy sticks or strings at a penny-candy store, or taste the ones you made yourself.

☆ ☆ ☆

Make Jello jigglers in bright jewel colors, and cut into diamond shapes.

Outdoors

- Go rock-hunting in your yard or garden—see how many different colors and textures of pebbles or rocks you can find. Sort them by size, type, or color.
- See which rocks make a mark on the sidewalk or driveway (a piece of brick, a lava rock, decorative marble, a bit of granite, a chunk of limestone, etc.)
- Draw with colored chalk—it's made from rocks.
- "Paint" rocks with paint brushes dipped in water; see how they change between wet and dry.
- If you have any hills, climb up them and roll down; otherwise, sing "The Bear Went over the Mountain."

Books

Winnie-the-Pooh and the Pebble Hunt (Walt Disney) (Golden/Western 1982) (2/3)

Let's Go Rock Collecting by Roma Gans (Harper Collins 1997) (4/6)

Climbing Kansas Mountains by George Shannon (Bradbury Press 1993) (4/6)

Sylvester and the Magic Pebble by Willaim Steig (Windmill Books 1969) (4/6)

High in the Mountains by Ruth Yaffe Radin (Macmillan 1989) (4/6)

Rocks in My Pockets by Marc Harshman & Bonnie Collins (Cobblehill/Dutton 1991) (4/6)

The Mountain that Loved a Bird by Alice McLerran (Scholastic 1993) (4/6)

Across Blue Mountains by Emma Chichester Clark (Harcourt Brace Jovanovich 1993) (4/6)

Planet Dexter's Crystal Factory by Irene Trimble (ref.) (Planet Dexter/Addison-Wesley 1995) (6+)

Roxaboxen by Alice McLerran (Lothrop, Lee & Shepard) (4/6)

Videos

Eyewitness: Rock & Mineral*
The Pebble and the Penguin
Wee Sing in the Big Rock Candy Mountain*

Art/Craft Materials

rocks of various shapes and sizes
  (smooth are best, but others can be interesting)
washable posterpaints
construction paper, glue
sugar, water
yarn
pencil
empty jam jar
hard-boiled eggs
food coloring, water

Art/Craft Directions

Rock Paperweights

1) Wash the rocks and decide which way should be "up." Paint on a back-ground body color, and let dry.

2) Paint eyes, dots, stripes, etc., all over the rocks. Cut out wings, a head, and legs to turn the rocks into bugs, or add a tongue to create a frog or a lizard. Glue the paper parts on.

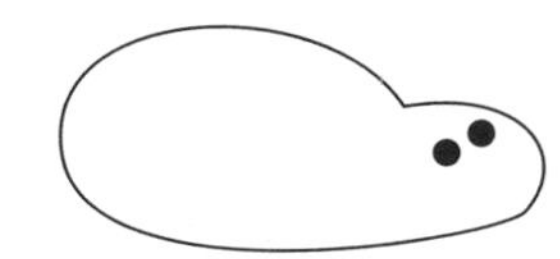
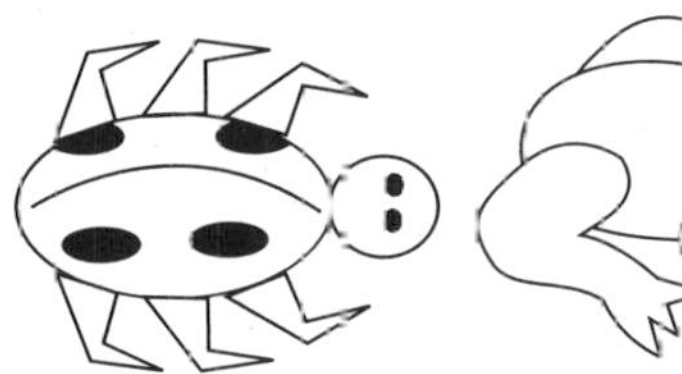

For a Little Something Extra…

Read the newspapers or call your community arts center to see if any rock collecting shows will be held in your area. Ask at your library if there is a local "rock-hound" club, and whether they allow visitors (specifically the older children) to a meeting.

☆ ☆ ☆

Look up "gems" in an encyclopedia to see pictures showing the beautiful variety of colors and shapes, or check out the Web site of the Smithsonian's National Museum of Natural History: http://galaxy.einet.net/images/gems/gems-icons.html

Grow-Them-Yourself Crystals

1) Mix ½ cup of sugar with ¼ cup of water in a bowl, and stir until all the sugar has dissolved. Tie a length of yarn to the middle of a pencil, so that it will be slightly shorter than the jar.

2) Dip the yarn until the bowl until it is soaked. Balance the pencil over the jar on the rim, with the yarn hanging down inside. (The jar helps keep away drafts.) Watch over the next hours for crystals to form, or pour the mixture into the jar so the yarn stays in the liquid. Check in one week.

Marbled Eggs

1) Hard-boil eggs. Let them cool so that you can handle them, but leave them in their shells.

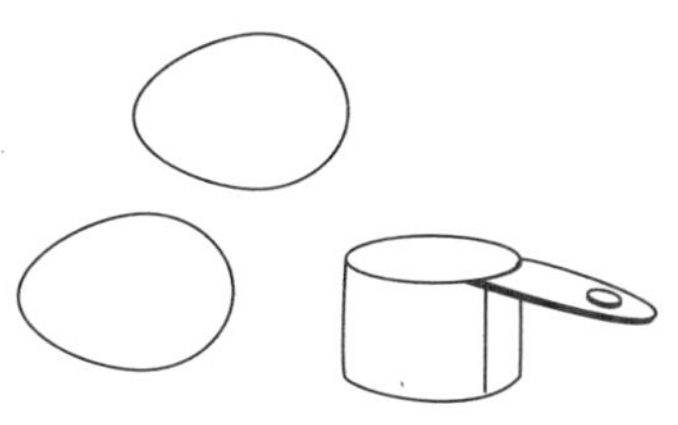

2) Roll the eggs with the palm of your hand across a countertop, or gently between your hands, so that the eggs get fine cracks all over the shell.

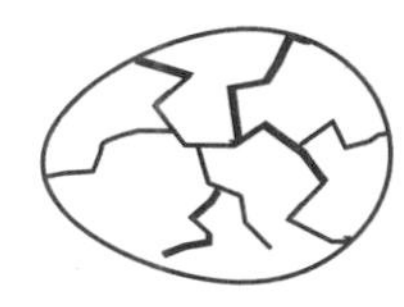

3) Set out small bowls of water, and mix a few drops of food coloring in each one. Do at least red, yellow, and blue. If you have more than 3 eggs, also mix up purple, green, and orange.

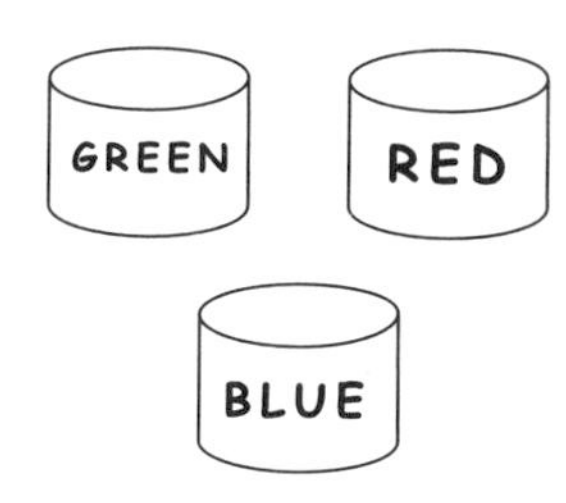

4) Gently set one egg in each bowl. Let them sit for 15 to 20 minutes, then remove them to drain on paper towels. The shells will have colored cracks. (If you're not going to eat them right away, put them in the refrigerator.) When you remove the shells, the eggs themselves will display beautiful "marbelized" coloring.

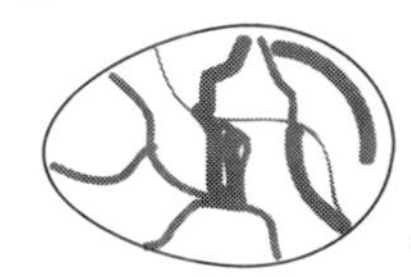

Hair

Art/Craft

- Let children cut up newspapers, catalogs, or old magazines to find pictures of lots of different styles, lengths, shapes, and colors for hair. Older children can sort them by color or length. Paste them all over a posterboard, and print in the middle "Hair Salon: Open for Business," for the shop you'll set up below.
- Cover shoeboxes, small gift boxes, baby-wipe boxes, etc., with stickers and wrapping paper to make a "hair stuff" organizer (one box for combs, one for headbands, one for elastics, one for barrettes, etc.) Tape or staple them together (see directions).
- Draw dogs, cats, tigers, giraffes, gorillas, etc., and give them crazy "hair-dos."
- Use yarn to make silly ponytails or wigs (see directions).

Indoors

- Set up a hair salon/barber shop. Get out curlers, combs, barrettes, elastics, headbands, and scrunchies (wash everything before and after sharing, and be careful of younger children using elastics). Take turns doing each other's hair in wild ponytails, braids, and swoops. Slick down hair with styling gel, then swirl it into funny curves. Have some small plastic mirrors and full-length mirrors around—and let them fix your hair!
- Use craft sticks and soapy bubbles (or real shaving cream) to pretend to give each other a shave.
- Gather dolls with long hair and practice putting in clips.
- On a floor-length mirror (could also be on a hand-held one or a medicine cabinet), tape pieces of construction paper cut to look like hair-dos, about six inches long. Have each child step up to the mirror and see their reflection "through" the hair-do; take photos!

Music

Ants (Joe Scruggs, includes "Rapunzel Got A Mohawk")*

Outdoors

- Swing on a swing and let the wind go through your hair.

Hints for Your Own Situation...

Ahead of time, take some photos of the children and have enlarged black and white or color paper copies made. Trim them so just their faces show, then glue them to plain paper. Let the children draw new hairstyles on themselves with markers or crayons.

☆ ☆ ☆

Teach older children the basics of braiding. Use three pieces of yarn, each 24" long, tied in one spot to the back of a chair.

☆ ☆ ☆

Avoid having scissors around when it's actually hair salon time, or you're bound to end up with experimental haircuts. Blunt children's scissors will cut hair!

☆ ☆ ☆

Feeling extremely ambitious? Give the dog a bath.

- Blunt children's scissors will cut grass! Go outside and give a haircut to bits of lawn (where approved), or trim some weeds.
- Use a magnifying glass to see the hairs on your arms and legs. If the season is right to buy a fresh peach, use the magnifying glass to look at its "hair."
- Buy a bubble "lawn-mower." Let everyone take turns giving the grass a "haircut" while you create bubbles.
- Bring out cookie sheets for everyone. Squirt on shaving cream, and do silly fingerpainting.

Snack-time

Buy frozen individual pizzas to decorate as faces. Help children cut up sliced cheese or meat in shapes for eyes or ears. They can use carrot curls, alfalfa sprouts, and lengths of string cheese and arrange them around the edges as hair. Offer olive slices for eyes, and any other foods that they'll actually eat to make noses and mouths.

Books

Don't Cut My Hair! by Hans Wilhelm
(Scholastic 1997) (2/3)

The Queen with Bees in Her Hair by Cheryl Harness
(Henry Holt & Co. 1993) (4/6)

Haircuts for the Woolseys by Tomie DePaola
(Putnam 1989) (4/6)

How Emily Blair Got Her Fabulous Hair by Susan Garrison Beroza
(Bridgewater Books 1995) (4/6)

Camilla's New Hairdo by Tricia Tussa
(Farrar Straus Giroux/Newfield 1991) (4/6)

An Enchanted Hair Tale by Alexis DeVeaux
(Harper & Row 1987) (4/6)

My Barber by Anne & Harlow Rockwell
(Macmillan 1981) (2/3)

Madame LaGrande and Her So High, to the Sky, Uproarious Pompadour by Candace Fleming
(Alfred A. Knopf 1996) (4/6)

The Princess Who Lost Her Hair by Tololwa M. Mollel
(Troll 1993) (4/6)

Moostache by Margie Palatini
(Scholastic/Hyperion 1998) (4/6)

Videos

Rapunzel; Arthur's Eyes plus Francine's Bad Hair Day
Ramona: The Great Hair Argument*

Art/Craft Materials

small to medium, open boxes of all sizes (from rings, checks, earrings, writing paper, paper clips, chocolate, etc.)
wrapping paper
stickers, markers
scissors, stapler, tape
yarn (about 20 yds. and about 40 yds.)
ribbon
plain barrette
construction paper

Art/Craft Directions

Hair Organizer

1) Cover sides and bottom of different sizes of open boxes, using colorful wrapping paper (or construction paper).

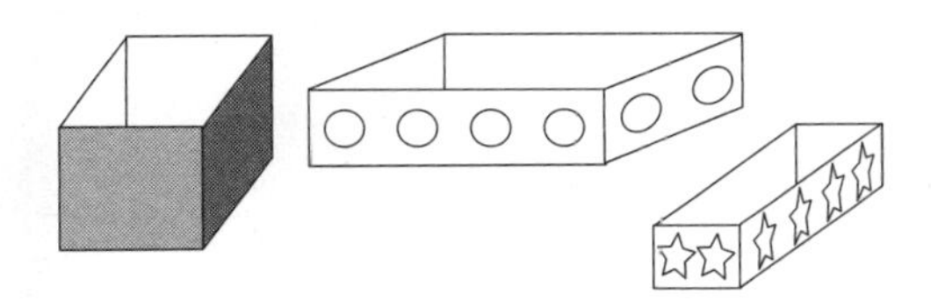

2) Lay the boxes side by side until you find an arrangement you like. Tape or staple them together to make an organizer for all your hair items. If you'd like, glue one long ribbon all around the outside.

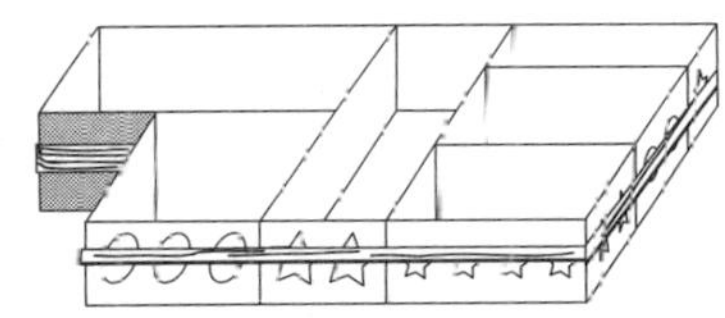

Ponytail Wig

1) For an add-on ponytail, cut lengths of yarn twice the final length that you want. Lay at least 30 lengths side by side on a table.

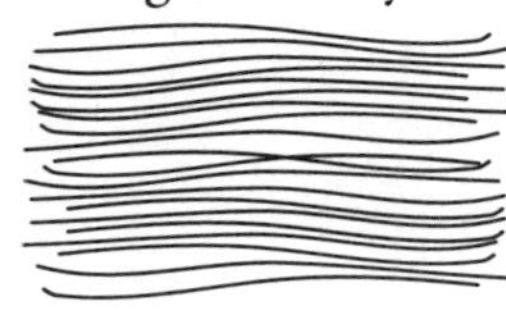

2) Gather the lengths in the middle with a short piece of yarn, and tie loosely.

For a Little Something Extra…

Grow "hair." Save egg-shells that are at least half-way unbroken, and an egg-carton. Gently draw a face on one side of each shell with a crayon or marker. Fill them part way with potting soil and sprinkle in a little grass seed. Rest the shells in the carton, in a sunny spot, and keep them watered with an eye-dropper. In a week, the face will start to grow grassy hair!

3) Bend the bundle in half, and tie again with another yarn scrap, this time tightly, about 2" down from the first knot.

4) Slip a barrette through the top knot, and clip it to someone's hair. It often helps to make a tiny, real ponytail first, to have something to anchor the pretend ponytail.

5) You can also use this for making a braid.

Wiglet

1) Cut a 9" diameter circle out of construction paper (the color of the yarn you want to use). Snip out a wedge about 3" wide, and overlap the edges to make a wide cone shape. Staple the edges together, and cover the staples with tape. This will be the base of the wiglet.

2) Cut lots (40 or more) of strands of yarn, twice the length you want the wiglet to be. Glue them all over the cap, letting them hang down as you want (you can trim the front pieces to make bangs). Punch 2 holes on either side, and thread pieces of yarn through to tie under the chin.

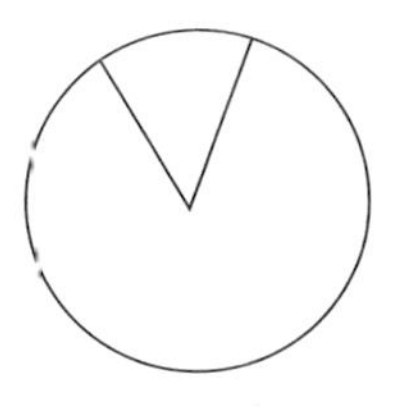

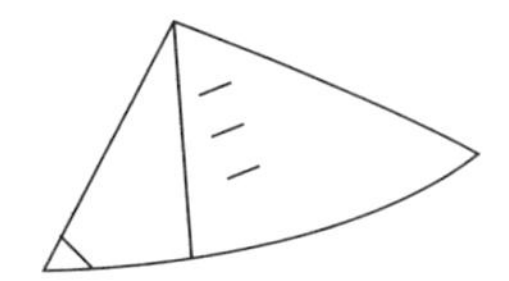

Hats/Shoes

Art/Craft

- Make paper hats like sailboats or round hats with brims. Decorate them with stickers, ribbons, streamers, and small flowers (see directions).
- Decorate plain visors, straw hats, or baseball hats (buy them at craft stores). Cut shapes of favorite things from felt and glue them on with Tacky glue. Or, use fabric paint or markers to draw your own designs.
- On posterboard, draw several child-sized heads with funny hats and hairstyles. Don't draw the faces; instead, cut out oval shapes under the hair. Hold the sheet up in front of a mirror, and have the children take turns poking their own faces through the openings (see directions).
- Decorate sneakers or the ends of shoe laces.

Indoors

- Collect all the hats, helmets, kerchiefs, crowns, and caps in the house; dress up and role play. Be police officers, firefighters, artists, queens, race-car drivers, construction workers, peasants, etc.
- Have each child close his/her eyes and pull a hat out of a big bag or pillow case; can they figure out by feeling which one it is?
- Toss soft balls or kooshis into upside down hats set in a row side by side, or grouped together like a big target.
- Save enough empty tissue boxes to have a pair for each child. Have a grown-up use scissors to enlarge the top slot enough for children to slip in their feet. Walk or "skate" around in them as crazy shoes.
- Collect everyone's shoes in a pile in the middle of the room. Have a race to find three pairs each. Or, have everyone leave the room, then take away one shoe, and see if they can figure out which shoe is missing.

Music

"Skater's Waltz," "Mexican Hat Dance," "Easter Bonnet"

Hints for Your Own Situation...

Take photos of the children's faces showing through the funny hat posters. Instant photos, though expensive, are fun once in a while.

☆ ☆ ☆

Older children can try acting out the story *Caps for Sale* by Esphyr Slobodkina. Let one child be the cap peddler, and the others be the monkeys, then take turns.

Snack-time

Cut one piece of bread into as large a circle as possible; cut a matching circle of balogna or other meat to place on it (the brim). Cut a small circle from another piece of bread and place on top in center (the crown); wrap a length of carrot shaving, string cheese, or American cheese around the small circle (the ribbon).

☆ ☆ ☆

Use the same idea to bake two sizes of round sugar cookies. Layer them small on large, and decorate with frosting to look like ribbons or flowers.

Outdoors

- Play "frisbie" with soft hats or baseball caps. Stand in a circle and toss one across or around.
- See how high in the air you can toss a hat.
- "Paint" your sidewalk with paint brushes and water. Take turns stepping into the wet part, then walking on a dry section. See how different the shoeprints look; on a hot day, do it with bare feet! Walk with your hands on the next person's waist; the marks will look like a caterpillar!
- Put a pair of shoes on your feet and another pair on your hands. Walk on all fours around the yard. What animals could you be?

Books

Ho for a Hat by William Jay Smith
(Little Brown & Co. 1989) (4/6)
Caps For Sale by Esphyr Slobodkina
(Harper & Row 1968) (4/6)
P.B. Bear Catch that Hat! by Lee Davis
(Dorling Kindersley 1997) (2/3)
Princess Abigail and the Wonderful Hat by Steven Kroll
(Holiday House 1991) (4/6)
Three Hat Day by Laura Geringer
(Harper & Row 1985) (4/6)
Martin's Hats by Joan W. Blos
(William Morrow & Co. 1984) (4/6)
Old Hat New Hat by Stan and Jan Berenstain
(Random House 1970) (2/3)
Uncle Foster's Hat Tree by Doug Cushman
(E.P.Dutton 1988) (4/6)
The 500 Hats by Dr. Seuss
(Vanguard Press 1938) (4/6)
A Hat for Minerva Louise by Janet Morgan Stoeke
(Dutton Children's Books 1994) (2/3)

Videos

Madeleine and the Bad Hat
Richard Scarry's Best Busytown Video Ever
The Cat in the Hat Comes Back

Art/Craft Materials

newspaper
stapler
stickers, ribbons, lace
scissors, tape, glue
small silk flowers
feathers (optional)
wide (about 2") craft ribbon
white posterboard
markers

Art/Craft Directions

Admiral's Hat

1) Tear ½ sheet of newspaper to make one admiral's hat.

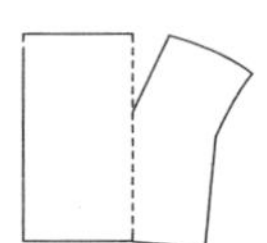

2) Fold down in half.
Fold corners down.
Fold wide bottom edges up.

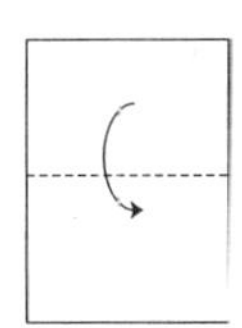

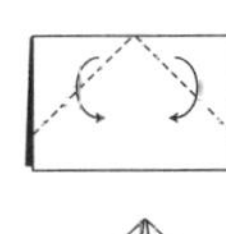

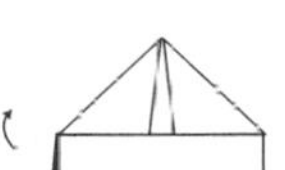

3) Fold flaps in half, back down to bottom edge. Staple corner edges.

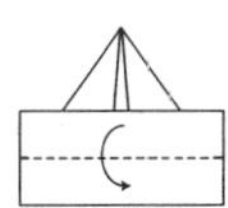

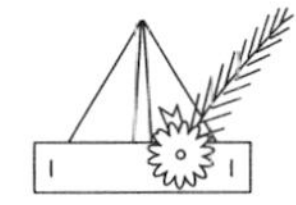

Wide-brimmed Hat

1) Cut a circle about 16" in diameter from posterboard. Cut an oval from the center, about 5" x 7".

2) Decorate the hat brim by gluing on bits of lace and ribbon, or taping on some tiny flowers. Set the brim on child's head, and drape a wide piece of ribbon across the top, hanging down on either side. Anchor it with tape, and tie the ends under the chin.

3) For princess hats, see Castles/Royalty. Other hat ideas are in the sections on Detectives, Firefighting, Kitchen Fun, and Zoo/Safari.

For a Little Something Extra...

Start collecting tiny souvenir pins by swapping with friends or finding them when you travel. Pin them on a favorite baseball cap to show off some of your favorite things!

☆ ☆ ☆

Order a Madeleine's Hat pinata from Birthday Express: (800) 424-7843

Face-Hat Cutouts

On large sheets of posterboard, draw several full-length figures with funny bodies (or just heads). Cut out the face area. Prop up the posterboards taped between two chairs and let the children poke their heads through the face openings while the others watch. Or, let each child hold one up in front of herself while standing in front of a full mirror, so she can see the effect for herself. Take photos!

Fashion Model

Cowboy

Artist

Inventions

Art/Craft

- Make toy telephones from two paper cups and a length of string. Be careful with younger children and the string (see directions).
- Ahead of time, for each child, fill a bag with age-safe nifty "stuff:" empty film cannisters, tiny boxes, craft sticks, empty spools from thread and ribbon, large buttons or lids from milk jugs, fabric scraps, tiny empty plastic bottles, plastic spoons, toilet-paper tubes, etc. Give one to each child, along with a roll of tape, a glue stick, crayons, and markers. Let their imaginations run wild as they invent "something." Let them tell you what it is and does.

Indoors

- Get out any broken cameras, computer keyboards, real or toy telephones, clocks, baby monitors, etc. that you've hung onto, and play pretend with them. Ask children how to "use" them, and what they think the different parts do.
- Buy the game Mousetrap. For younger age groups, just have fun putting it all together and making it work, over and over (don't worry about actually playing the game). Watch out for the small balls and gamepieces—toddlers may be tempted to eat them.
- Use wooden blocks, thin books, game boards, balls, plastic cups, etc., to build a device that will send a ball from the top of a chair seat to the other side of the room (see directions for ideas). A real Rube Goldberg invention!
- Go through the house and see where you can find the following inventions in use: levers (hand can-opener), springs (paper hole-puncher), gears (electric mixer, can opener), electricity (lights, radio, TV, tape player), and wheels (bed, chair). Outside, there may be a pulley (flag pole) and a gear (a sprinkler). How about others?

Music

"Why Do They Make Things Like They Do?" (Disney Children's Favorites V.3)
& "The Marvelous Toy" (V. 4)*

Hints for Your Own Situation...

If children no longer put things in their mouths, and can perhaps handle a screwdriver, let them try to take apart a broken toy, camera, or clock to see the parts inside. Clean up well afterwards.

☆ ☆ ☆

Go around the house, pointing to things that were invented. Ask children what would have been used to do the same job before those items existed (mixer vs. egg beater, computer vs. typewriter, Morse Code telegraph vs. telephone, etc.)

☆ ☆ ☆

The thermos bottle is an invention with no moving parts. Who knows how it keeps hot things hot and cold things cold?

Snack-time

Invent a new snack. Put out various plastic measuring cups, spoons, bowls, and tall clear cups plus different kinds of ingredients, and let the children come up with their own combinations. Try milk, water, instant chocolate or strawberry powder, juices, sliced grapes or bananas, yogurt, oat cereal, graham crackers, sugar, grated cheese, and perhaps food coloring. What do they call their creations?

Outdoors

- Get a horseshoe magnet or bar magnet for each child to use as a "metal detector." Go hunting around the yard, touching everything you can think of to see if the magnet sticks to it. Talk about them; are there certain types of things it will stick to and won't (plants versus toy cars in the sandbox; the side of the house versus the tricycle)?
- Invent some new game using a ball or a bean-bag or a pile of smooth rocks. (Stand backwards and throw the ball over your head to each other.) Invent a way to walk (two steps, one hop, and a clap).

Books

Archibald Frisby by Michael Chesworth
(Farrar/Straus and Giroux 1994) (4/6)

Alistair's Time Machine by Marilyn Sadler
(Simon & Schuster 1986) (4/6)

What Does It Do? by Daniel Jacobs
(Raintree Publishers 1990) (2/3)

Click! A Book About Cameras by Gail Gibbons
(Little, Brown and Co. 1997 (4/6)

The Camera—A First Discovery Book by Claude Delafosse
(Scholastic Cartwheel 1993) (4/6)

Odds 'n' Ends Alvy by John Frank
(Four Winds Press/Macmillan 1993) (4/6)

Marta's Magnets by Wendy Pfeffer
(Silver Press 1995) (4/6)

The Wonderful Towers of Watts by Patricia Zelver
(Tambourine/William Morrow 1994) (4/6)

The Berenstain Bears Fly-It! by Stan & Jan Berenstain
(Random House 1996) (4/6)

What's Inside? Toys by Angela Royston
(Dorling Kindersley 1991) (6+)

Videos

Cro series*; How It's Done 1 & 2*
Harriet's Magic Hats: Photographer and Computer Specialist* (5/6)
The Great Inventors*
The Magic School Bus Getting Energized

Art/Craft Materials

2 paper cups
sturdy string (not kite string, 5 to 10 feet)
scissors
ideas for ball launchers: tennis balls, wooden blocks, empty oatmeal can, wastebasket, game boards, dominoes

Art/Craft Directions

Paper-cup Telephone

1) With scissors, poke a small hole in the bottom of each paper cup.

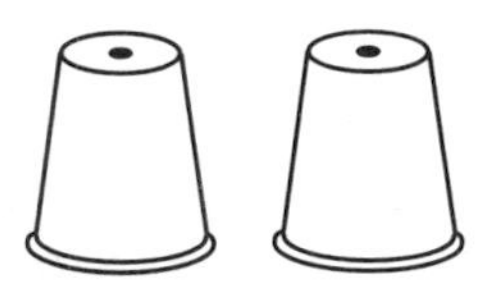

2) Thread the string through the holes, and tie several knots inside the cups, so the strings won't pull through.

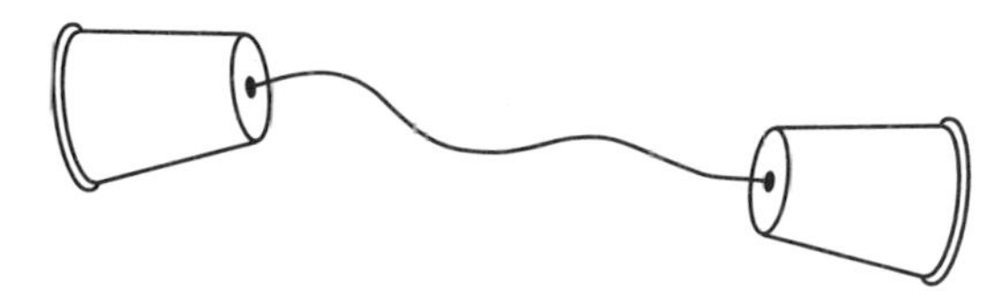

3) Pull the string tight. Have one child hold a cup to his ear, while a second child speaks into the other cup.

For a Little Something Extra...

Visit a museum that might have a telescope, a telegraph, and a Victrola record player, or old cars, light-bulbs, and washing machines.

☆ ☆ ☆

See if you live near a "Scrap Box" type of store, where you can pay (usually) $1 to fill a paper bag with your choice of neat leftovers from local manufacturers.

Ball Launcher #1

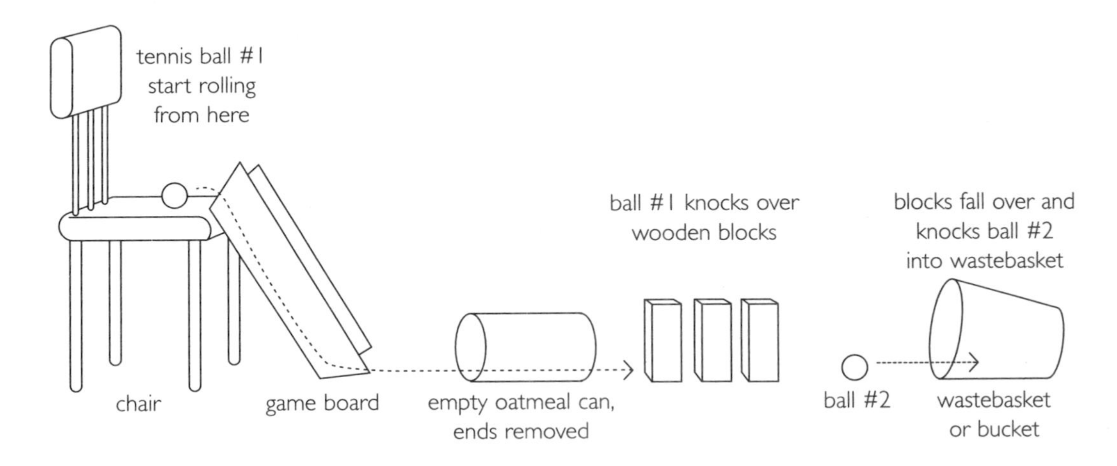

Ball Launcher #2

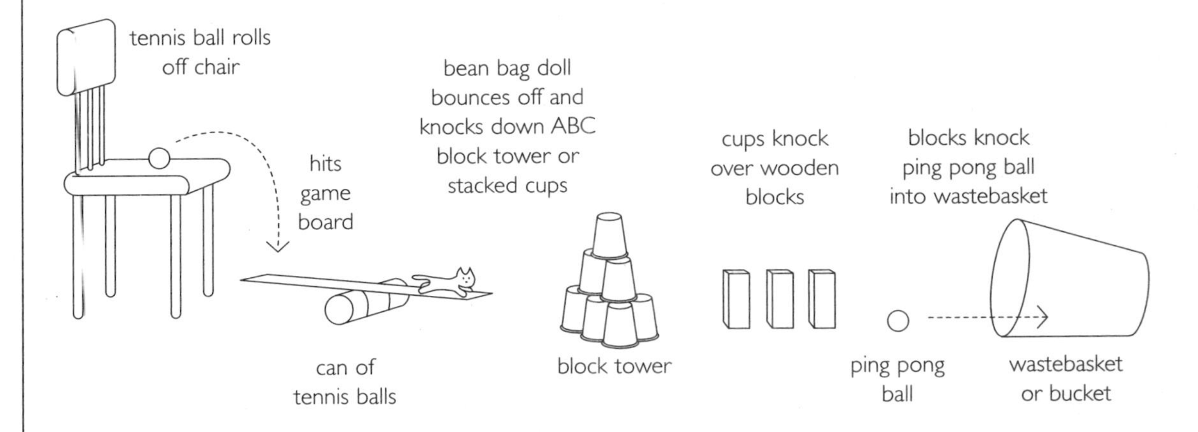

Kitchen Fun

Art/Craft

- Add food coloring to water, then mix with vegetable oil in a sealed bottle (small flavored-water bottle is good); tip back and forth—they don't mix!
- Make chef hats by pleating white paper and adding a band around the bottom (see directions).
- Turn plastic or wooden spoons into puppets by drawing a face (you may need permanent markers) on the bowl of the spoon, then tie a ribbon around its "neck" for a scarf.
- Trace around cookie cutters with black markers on white paper. Staple the pages together to make your own coloring books.
- Use cookie cutters to cut pretend cookies out of modeling dough. Let children use real spatulas and cookie sheets to practice "baking."

Indoors

- Make modeling playdough or real pretzel dough and shape dough into their initials (see directions).
- Toddlers are the right height for a "copy-paper box" stove and oven. Color black circles on the lid (or glue circles of black construction paper). On the front, cut 3 sides of a rectangle to pull down as an "oven door."
- Gather together several dozen different plastic tubs and their lids (soft margarine, frosting, storage bowls, plastic spice bottles, etc.) Put all the lids in one pile and the bowls in another. Have children match bowls with lids.
- Build towers from nesting bowls or cups.
- Collect lots of measuring cups. Set out a dishpan of water, and try pouring from one size cup to another. Will two of one size all fit into one of another size?
- Buy candy molds and use with microwavable candy.

Music

Happiness Cake (Linda Arnold)*
"Baking a Cake" (Shining Time Station: Birthday Party)*

Hints for Your Own Situation...

With older children, let them see the "magic" of whipping cream. Pour 1 pint of heavy cream into a bowl. Let the children help, first trying a fork, then an old-fashioned egg-beater (if you have one). Then, have an adult use the electric mixer and show how really stiff and white the cream becomes.

☆ ☆ ☆

If you'd like, add a few tablespoons of sugar, and serve on their pudding snack (or something else they'd like to try).

☆ ☆ ☆

Do the same experiment with egg whites (save yolk for scrambled eggs). See how the liquid changes from clear to pure white. (Toss out, or use in a baked meringue recipe.)

Outdoors

- Carefully mix a little baking soda and vinegar (outdoors is a good place, since the children will always complain about the smell). What happens with different amounts?
- Create mudpies or wet-sandy cookies.
- Gather all the measuring cups. Fill several dishtubs or buckets partway with water, and experiment with filling one whole cup with three of the ⅓ cups, etc. Or, do the same activity in a sandbox.
- On a warm day, build a small ramp. Put an icecube in the middle, and a small ball behind it. See how long it takes for the cube to melt and the ball to roll down.

Books

Babar Learns To Cook by Laurent de Brunhoff
(Random House 1978) (4/6)
The Magic School Bus Gets Baked in a Cake by Linda Beech/Joanna Cole
(Scholastic 1995) (4/6)
Alexander's Midnight Snack by Catherine Stock (ABCs)
(Clarion/Houghton Mifflin 1988) (4/6)
Pretend Soup by Mollie Katzen & Ann Henderson (ref.)
(Tricycle Press 1994) (3/6)
Jake Baked the Cake by B.G. Hennessy
(Viking Penguin 1990) (4/6)
Florence and Eric Take the Cake by Jocelyn Wild
(Dial Books for Young Readers 1987) (4/6)
Mr. Putty and Tabby Bake the Cake by Cynthia Rylant
(Harcourt Brace & Co. 1994) (4/6)
Dudley Bakes a Cake by Peter Cross
(G.P.Putnam 1988) (4/6)
Bunny Cakes by Rosemary Wells
(Dial/Penguin 1997) (2/3)
Walter the Baker by Eric Carle
(Simon & Schuster 1972) (4/6)

Snack-time

Make pizza dough from a mix. Shape into several mini pizza crusts and spread with prepared sauce. Let children sprinkle on shredded cheese and any other toppings that they like.

☆ ☆ ☆

Mix instant chocolate pudding. Top with the whipped cream you made!

☆ ☆ ☆

Ask children how they would cook/bake: pie, chicken, cake, bread, rice (the answers may be unusual!)

Videos

The Magic Schoolbus Ready, Set, Dough
Milk & Cookies*

Art/Craft Materials

white paper (8½" x 11")
scissors, tape, ruler

Art/Craft Directions

Chef Hat

1) Tape 2 sheets of white paper end to end (use 3 sheets for a grown-up hat).

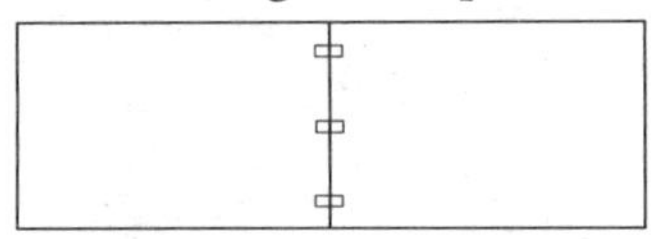

3) Cut another sheet of paper into 3" strips, and tape them end to end.

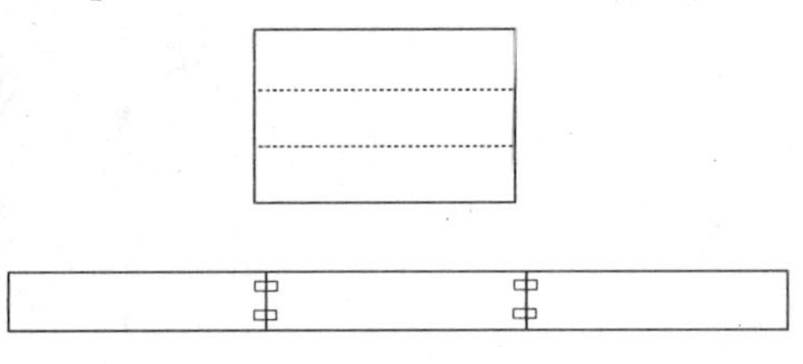

5) Loosely fold the strip up and over the pleated edge. Again, don't completely flatten the pleats. Tape the band in place on the front side, in about 4 places. The band will be lumpy, but it will stay in place.

2) Pleat the length of the paper, making tiny overlaps.

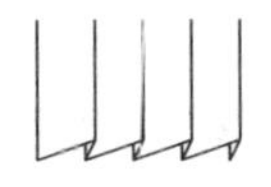

4) Slip half the width of the long strip under one edge of the pleated paper. Tape the band to the pleats only at about 4 places, without pressing the pleats flat.

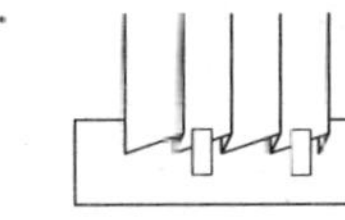

6) Wrap the hat around child's head, and overlap the edges to fit. Tape in place.

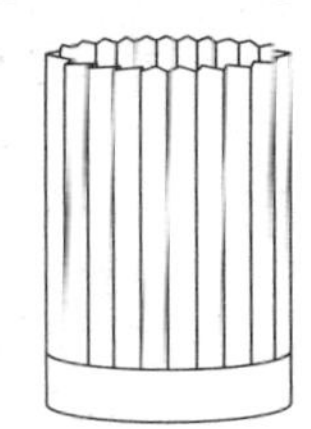

For a Little Something Extra...

Gold Medal Flour offers a children's cookbook for $2. The order form is always on their bags of flour; however no proof of purchase is required.

Gold Medal
Alpha-Bakery Cookbook
P.O. Box 5119
Minneapolis, MN 55460-5119

Modeling Dough

1 cup flour
¼ cup salt
2 teaspoons cream of tartar

Stir together, then add:

1 cup water
2 teaspoons food coloring
2 teaspoons vegetable oil

Stir and cook over medium heat (it looks sticky). Turn it onto a floured board and knead it with a little more flour. Store in a tightly covered container.

Pretzel Dough

¾ cup warm water
½ envelope yeast
1 teaspoon sugar
2 cups flour
½ teaspoon salt
1 egg

Mix warm water, yeast and sugar. Separately mix salt and flour. After 5 minutes, add yeast mix to flour mix. Shape dough into initials, animals or fun shapes. Brush them with the beaten egg, and bake at 425 degrees for 12 minutes.

Christine Playdough
2 cup fl
2 tbl oil
2 cup water
1 cup salt
4 tsp cr of tartar
color

Library

Art/Craft

- Make bookmarks from construction paper and wide fabric ribbon (or strips of wrapping paper or wallpaper scraps). Use tiny cookie cutters or stencils to trace shapes that you'll glue to the ends of the strips (see directions).
- Make a special bookcover by cutting up one large brown grocery bag per book. Fold and tape the cover onto the book, then decorate it with markers (better than crayons here), rubber stampings, and stickers (see directions).
- Make your own coloring book. Gather any almost used-up coloring books, and carefully tear out any remaining sheets (the more old books the better). Stack the pages alternately with new plain paper. Decorate construction paper to make front and back covers. Staple them all together, and perhaps bring out new crayon boxes.

Indoors

- Set up a lending library. Take books and set them up in a row on a bench, table, or desk. Take turns being the librarian and checking out the books by stamping slips of paper. Use any kind of rubber stamp, although date stamps are fun; use washable ink pads (they're worth it!)
- Put a big, random pile of story books in the middle of the floor, and take turns sorting them. Have one child pick out three Little Golden Books, another child find two Little Critter books, and another child look for a book about a bunny, etc. Have everyone help shelve them in any order they choose (e.g., shortest to tallest).
- Set up a "reading nook" in one corner of the room for story time, and put a big box in another corner for "puppet play;" stock it with any puppets you have, or use this chance to get out old socks and make some more!

Music

"Marian, the Librarian" (The Music Man)

Hints for Your Own Situation...

Libraries offer so much by way of cassettes, CDs, and software-to-go! Use this chance to organize your own tapes and CDs, etc. Let older children help print names on white address labels, and put one on each plastic box—now the children will be able to read their own choices. If you wish, add a dot of color to mark different types (lullaby music, dance music, showtunes, etc.)

Snack-time

Take six or eight slices of bread, cut off the crusts, and make one multi-layer sandwich. Peanut butter is good, but anything else that will be fairly "sticky" will work. Or, make a number of different sandwiches and toothpick them together. Set the stacked sandwich on its side on a large plate. This is your row of "books." Have each child come up and ask to "take out" the sandwich of their choice.

Outdoors

- On a nice day, put some of your favorite books in a wagon and make your own "BookWagon" or "Bookmobile" as these have been called (read *Clara and the Bookwagon*). Bring it around the yard and make pretend delivery stops at various "houses" (the robin's house, the caterpillar's house, the puppy's house). Would they like to read *Round Robin, The Hungry Caterpillar,* and *Poky Little Puppy*? Who else might like one?
- Set up an outdoor reading spot, under an umbrella or a favorite tree, on a big rock, a beach towel, or some little chairs.

Books

How My Library Grew by Dinah, by Martha Alexander (H. W. Wilson Co. 1983) (4/6)

Walter's Magic Wand by Eric Houghton (Orchard Books 1989) (4/6)

The Library by Sarah Stewart (Farrar Straus Giroux 1995) (4/6)

Clara and the Bookwagon by Nancy Smiler Levinson (Harper & Row 1988) (4/6)

Aunt Lulu by Daniel Pinkwater (Macmillan 1988) (4/6)

I Like the Library by Anne Rockwell (E.P.Dutton 1977) (2/3)

ABC for the Library by Mary E. Little (Atheneum 1975) (4/6)

Nicholas at the Library by Hazel Hutchins (Annick Press 1990) (4/6)

Just Open a Book by P.K. Hallinan (Ideals Children's Books 1995) (2/3)

Alistair in Outer Space by Marilyn Sadler (Simon & Schuster 1984) (4/6)

Videos

The PageMaster; Arthur's Lost Library Book
Encyclopedia Brown and the Flaming Beauty Queen

Art/Craft Materials

construction paper
wallpaper scraps (optional)
stencils, catalog pictures, cookie cutters
scissors, tape, glue
ribbon (thin, about 4" to 8")
shaped paper punchers
brown grocery bags (or heavy wrapping paper)

Art/Craft Directions

Bookmarks

1) Cut construction paper or wallpaper into strips about 6" long and 1¼" wide. The ends can be straight, angled, or rounded.

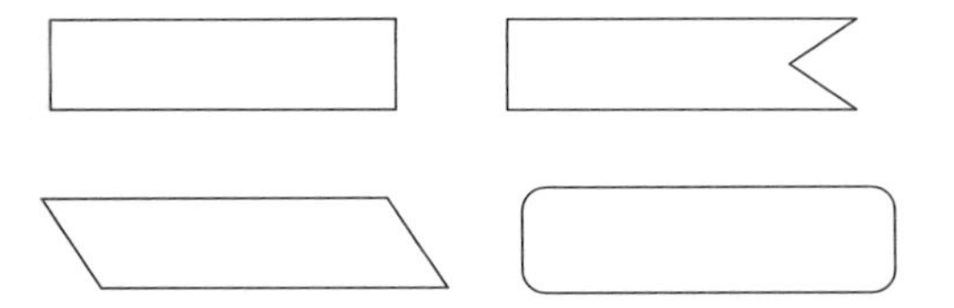

2) Use stencils or cookie cutters to cut shapes from contrasting colors, or from catalog ads for colorful flowers or favorite foods. Special paper punch shapes are extra fun.

3) Lay out an arrangement of the shapes that you like, layering them on each other, or just putting one at the top of the bookmark.

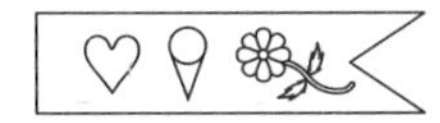

4) Glue the layers in place, then either glue a 6" thin ribbon to the back of the top edge, or punch a hole in the top edge, and loop the ribbon through and into itself.

For a Little Something Extra...

When possible, spend some time at the library, perhaps for an organized story hour. Often, children who can print their name are allowed their own cards. Ask for free bookmarks. Also, local elementary schools (perhaps within walking distance) will often let adults come in with younger children and borrow books.

Bookcover

1) Brown grocery bags make the sturdiest bookcovers, but you can work with heavy wrapping paper. With a bag, cut it up one side, and cut off the bottom rectangle.

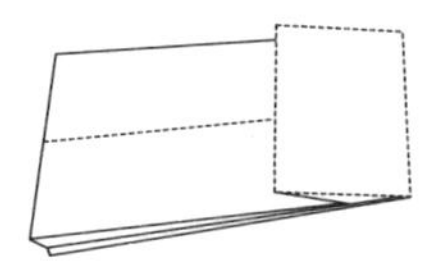

2) Spread the paper bag out flat. Lay the book that you want to cover (hard or soft cover book, but hardcover is a little easier) open on top of the paper, centered on the paper, with the pages facing up.

3) Bend the top edge up over the book to make a crease, move the book away, and bend the paper down. Repeat this for the bottom edge. Bend up at least one inch, if possible; more is okay.

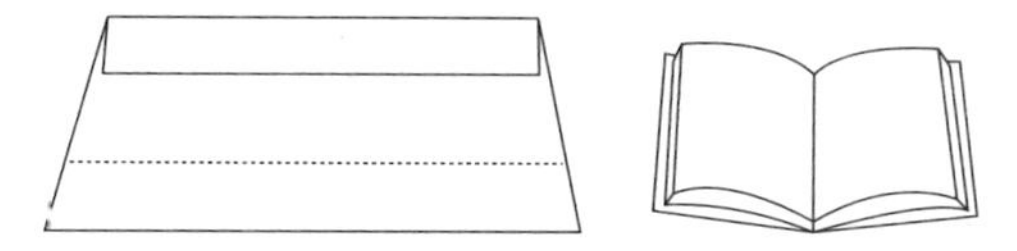

4) Lay the book closed on the paper, and fold the cover over it, roughly in half. Let the extra paper hang out on the right, then crease it against the edges, and bend both flaps to the inside of the book.

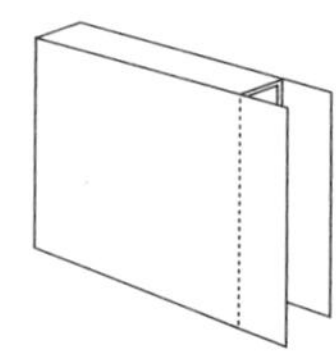

5) Lift the front cover, and slide the book front into the "pocket" formed by the folded paper. Repeat for the back cover.

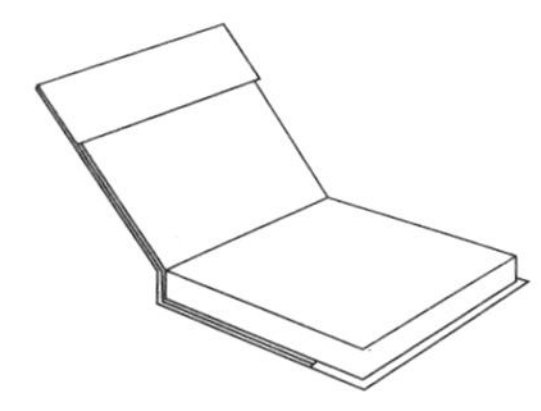

6) Tape the cover edges at the top and bottom, to make the inside and outside flaps stay together. Decorate the cover front and back; write the title and author, or just draw some of the characters or things that are special in the book. You can add your name, too.

Maps/Traveling

Art/Craft

- Collect old maps (from AAA, a gas station, hotels, etc.). Especially if you have one of your own state, cut out a section (the right size for a placemat or a sign for your bedroom door) that includes your town, but make the overall shape that of your state. Use a marker to circle your town; write "Sue lives here" and add an arrow. Mount it onto cardboard with gluestick; if desired, cover with clear Contac paper (see directions).
- Draw a "treasure map" that shows pictures of items in rooms in the house, to follow later (below).
- Use a cardboard box to make a traveling "lap desk" (see directions).

Indoors

- Put together a map puzzle (regular or magnetic). Have the younger ones pick out all the pieces of the same color, or count the states whose names begin with a certain letter. Have them learn which state is theirs, or where they've lived before.
- Spread out a map of the world on the floor. Play a guessing game: "I see a continent/country/state. Its name begins with 'N' and it's next to...." What is it?"
- Use the map you made earlier to go on an indoor treasure hunt with small prizes. Plan ahead to hide new crayons, new books, etc., along the way, and something bigger at the end (maybe under a sofa pillow), after leading them on a good trek.
- On a local map, point out towns you know, and talk about what is there (the movie theater, a favorite restaurant, a toy shop, a state park, etc.) On a town or city map, find and mark friends' houses, the library, their own house, a school, a church, the firestation, etc.

Music

A Car Full of Songs (Tom Paxton)*

Outdoors

- Draw outlines of a country or state on the sidewalk in chalk; use them for hop scotch, Giant Step, or tricycle-riding.

Hints for Your Own Situation...

Older children can each draw their own treasure map, and have the other children try to follow it. As they take turns, the mapmaker gets to hide a "treasure" at the end.

☆ ☆ ☆

Set up a box as a "vending machine" filled with special treats (M&M bags, small packages of peanut butter and crackers, gum, and different treats). Label them with prices (four cents, ten cents) and let older children practice their money skills, picking coins from a coin jar to "buy" items they want as they stop on their "trips."

☆ ☆ ☆

Play travel agent, especially if you've picked up lots of color brochures over the years. Plan a trip.

Snack-time

Offer children their favorite traveling foods: juice boxes, snack-packs of cheese and crackers, individual bags of chips, small bags of Cheerios, and sandwiches packed in plastic boxes.

☆ ☆ ☆

Make "license plates:" use tubes of ready-made icing to decorate graham crackers with numbers and letters. Or, do it with squeeze cheese on double saltine crackers.

- Get a compass and mark north, south, east, and west on the wall of the house, the fences, a tree, or bush (with paper signs or chalk). Tell the children "walk three steps north, then go five steps east, etc." to get to some goal (a hidden treat, a prize, their lunches!). For younger ones, say, "Take three steps to the fence, then stop; now go one step to the house." The really little ones will just run around and think they're doing great; be sure to reward them, too.

Books

As the Roadrunner Runs by Gail Hartman
(Bradbury/Macmillan 1994) (4/6)
The Way to Captain Yankee's by Anne Rockwell
(MacMillan Publishing Co. 1994) (2/3)
The Secret Birthday Message by Eric Carle
(Thomas Y. Crowell Co. 1972) (2/3)
Me on the Map by Joan Sweeney
(Trumpet/Scholastic 1996) (4/6)
Amelia's Fantastic Flight by Rose Bursik
(Henry Holt and Co. 1992) (2/3)
Toot & Puddle by Holly Hobbie
(Little, Brown & Co. 1997) (4/6)
Lucky's 24 Hour Garage by Daniel Kirk
(Hyperion 1996) (4/6)
The Whole World in Your Hands by Melvin & Gilda Berger
(Ideals Children's Books 1993) (4/6)
Gifts by JoEllen Bogart
(Scholastic 1995) (4/6)
Going Places by Frances Lawton
(Discovery Toys/Walker 1988) (2/3)

Videos

Winnie the Pooh's Grand Adventure
Harriet's Magic Hats: Weather Forecaster (5/6)*

Sunken Treasure (Reading Rainbow)
The Tots Find a Treasure Map*

Art/Craft Materials

old maps
scissors, gluestick
posterboard
contact paper
white paper
markers, rubber stamps
corrugated cardboard box (the size that reams of copy-paper come in)
small boxes (like bank-check size, with lids)

Art/Craft Directions

Map Placemat or Sign

1) Get a map of your state, and find your town on it. Trace or draw the outline of your state (or any shape you want). Keep the whole piece about 12" x 18".

2) Use a dark marker to circle where your town is on your new map. Cut an arrow from white paper, about 1" x 6". Write "(your name) lives here" on it, and tape it near your town so that it points to it.

3) Using a gluestick, glue your map shape to a piece of posterboard, then cut the posterboard to the same map shape. Cover the map side with clear contact paper. Use as a placemat, or as a sign for your bedroom door.

For a Little Something Extra...

Write to Tourist Boards or Chambers of Commerce in towns you'd like to visit, to get free color brochures from around the country. Use them when you play Travel Agent, and cut them up to use as part of your placemat map collages.

Traveling Lap Desk

1) Draw an arch on each side of the copy-paper box (bottom only). Have a grown-up cut out these arches with strong scissors.

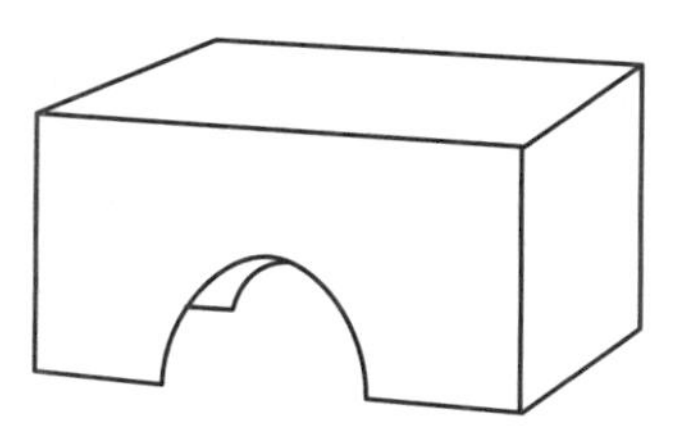

2) Glue small box bottoms on top of desk. Put on the lids.

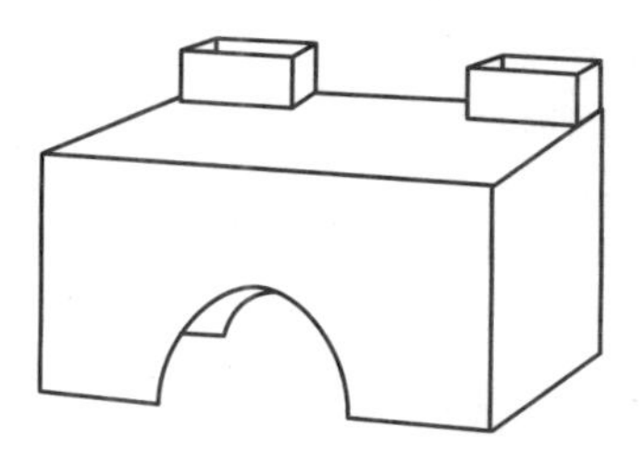

3) If the box is plain, decorate it directly with child's name, markers, rubber stamps, etc. If it has printing on it, cover the outside surfaces with white paper taped around the edges, then decorate.

4) Store crayons and markers in the small boxes. Set desk over legs of seated child. Adjust cut-out openings if you need them wider.

Musical Instruments

Art/Craft

- Make drums out of oatmeal containers with fabric or paper stretched over them. For little children, after you use a rubber band to fasten it, go over the band with a wide strip of packing tape to secure it (see directions).
- Cool Whip containers with lids also make good little drums; decorate them with markers and stickers.
- Fold waxed paper over a comb and blow on it like a harmonica for a traditional kazoo sound.
- Fill a baby-wipe box with three or more metal juice-can lids and close it. Shake for a nice, loud sound!
- Have children draw to the beat of some music. What does it make them think of? Talk about the sounds.

Indoors

- Collect any rattles, shakers, bells, horns, or toys that make music or noise. Add any "instruments" you've made. Gather them in one place and have each child choose an "instrument" to set up a band. Take turns having one child be the conductor (with a wooden spoon) or the leader of a parade around the room. How do different pieces sound with different kinds of songs?
- Are there any music boxes, or animals that have a music box inside? Take turns playing them (then see what it sounds like when they're all going at once!)
- Voices are wonderful musical instruments. Share some songs you know, or buy a book of children's songs and have everyone learn some new ones.
- Put on some rock 'n roll music. Play the "air" guitar, "air" trumpet, and "air" drums while you dance along.

Music

Rythms on Parade (Hap Palmer)*; I Love a Parade (Boston Pops)*
Peter and the Wolf

Hints for Your Own Situation...

Make a "guitar" by stretching rubber bands of different thicknesses around an empty facial tissue box. Tape them at the sides, and strum them across the rectangular opening (see directions).

☆ ☆ ☆

Collect different sizes of empty plastic bottles, from salad dressings, sodas, water drinks, maple syrup, etc. Try blowing across the tops of them, or filling them with different amounts of water and tapping on them. Can you put them in order of lowest notes to highest?

Snack-time

Frost a rectangular sheet cake with white or chocolate frosting, then use darker icing to make five thin lines across the middle (to look like a musical staff), a G-clef symbol, and some half and quarter notes (see directions).

☆ ☆ ☆

Cut grapes in half, lay a tiny pretzel stick alongside, and put "flags" made from cheese at the top, to look like musical notes.

☆ ☆ ☆

A half of a pear, or some slices, with pretzels laid down the middle and two more coming out the top, can be a guitar or mandolin.

☆ ☆ ☆

Pretzel rods can be flutes, Oreos and tiny pretzel sticks can be snare drums, a Ding Dong can be a bass drum, and Bugle snacks are...bugles!

Outdoors

- On a nice day, dress up for a parade, and bring all your instruments outdoors. March around the yard, and take turns who is the leader.
- Collect any metal wrenches you have. Tie strings around them, and hang them from a branch or railing. Tap them with a rubber mallet or a wooden spoon. Listen for the different tones that come from different lengths.
- Bring out a tape player and put out chairs (or use stepping stones) to play musical chairs. Change the pace with different types of music, or play hopping on one foot.

Books

I Like the Music by Leah Komaiko
(Harper & Row 1987) (4/6)
A Little Night Music by Charles Micucci
(William Morrow & Co. Inc. 1989) (4/6)
The Musical Life of Gustav Mole by Kathryn Meyrick
(Child's Play Intl. 1989) (4/6)
Zin! Zin! Zin! a Violin by Lloyd Moss
(Simon & Schuster 1995) (4/6)
The Animals' Song by David L. Harrison
(Boyds Mills Press 1997) (2/3)
Hurricane Music by Barbara Bottner
(G.P.Putnam's Sons 1995) (4/6)
The Little Band by James Sage
(Margaret K. McElderry Books 1991) (4/6)
The Birthday Trombone by Margaret A. Hartelius
(Doubleday 1977) (2/3)
One Dancing Drum by Gail Kredenser and Stanley Mack
(S.G.Phillips 1971) (2/3)
Meet the Orchestra by Ann Hayes
(Gulliver/Harcourt Brace Jovanovich 1991) (4/6)

Videos

Fantasia; The Orchestra (Peter Ustinov)*
Disney Fun with Music Sing-Along; The Music Man
Mister Roger's Neighborhood - Making Music*
Wee Sing Marvelous Musical Mansion*

Art/Craft Materials

oatmeal or cornmeal container
fabric (cotton type) to cover one end (about 6" square)
packing tape
large rubber bands, different widths
empty facial tissue box

Art/Craft Directions

Oatmeal Drum

1) Cut fabric into a circle 6" in diameter. Lay it over the open top of the oatmeal can.

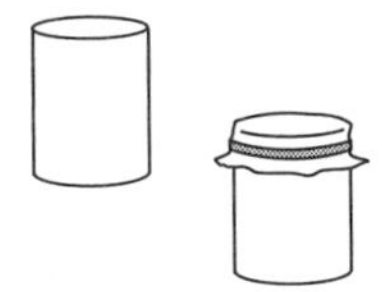

2) Secure the fabric with a rubber band; pull fabric tight. Tape the rubber band and the edges of the fabric to the can.

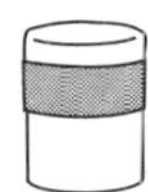

Box Guitar

1) Gather 6 rubber bands of different widths, large enough to stretch around the facial tissue box. Remove the plastic strip from inside the box.

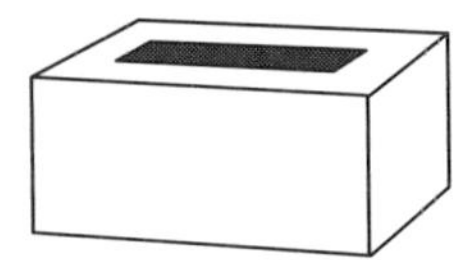

2) Spread the bands around the narrower width of the facial tissue box, over the open slot. Tape the bands to the sides.

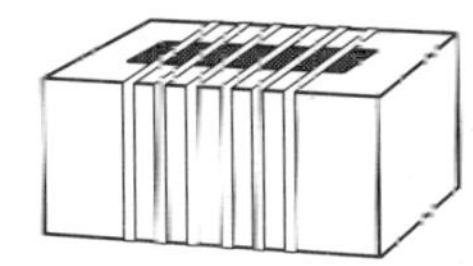

Musical Cake

1) Frost a rectangular cake with white or light-colored frosting. Fill a cake decorator tube with dark chocolate or dark-colored frosting (or buy a few tubes of different colored icing gels). Draw five straight lines across the middle of the cake.

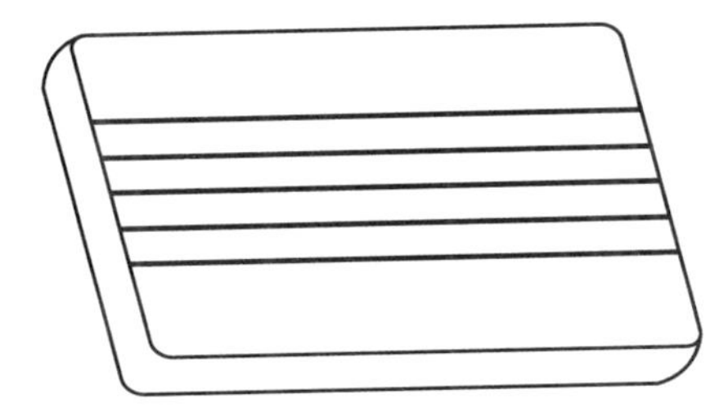

2) With a different color than the lines, add a G-clef symbol and as many musical notes as you wish. Make some of them different from each other. Use quarter notes, eighth notes, whole notes, and half notes. For a birthday, do the first six notes of the Happy Birthday song:

For a Little Something Extra...

If your community offers them, go to an outdoor noontime concert.

Nursery Rhymes

Art/Craft

- Make name placecards for each child's place at the lunch or dinner table. Each child can choose from objects named in nursery rhymes (suggest: egg, spider, pumpkin, dish/spoon, pail, dog bone, shoe, sheep, star, horn), getting ideas from a Mother Goose book. Draw one on each card for little ones to color; older ones can do it all themselves (see directions).
- Make sheep to help in acting out different rhymes. Cut a shape from posterboard. Glue cotton balls on one side, and scraps of black yarn to the other, and mount on an unsharpened pencil or paint mixing paddle (see directions).
- Make Humpty Dumpty sit on a wall (or window sill). Cut a large oval from white paper. Draw or glue on eyes, nose, mouth. Cut long strips of construction paper and accordian pleat them to make arms and legs. Cut out and glue on hands and feet (see directions).

Indoors

- Read a nursery rhyme, then take turns acting it out. Make up motions to go with the poems, and sing any of the songs you know (Old King Cole, Little Bo Peep, Eensy Weensy Spider, the King is in his Counting House, Baa Baa Black Sheep–use your sheep "puppets.")
- Dress up as nursery rhyme characters: the Queen of Hearts, the Knave of Hearts, Little Bo Peep, Little Boy Blue, etc.
- As you read one of the nursery rhyme books, notice how many different kinds of animals they mention. Give your best imitation of the sounds those animals can make.

Music

Mainly Mother Goose (Sharon, Lois & Bram)*
Classic Nursery Rhymes (Hap Palmer)*
"With Apologies to Mother Goose" (W. Ryan/Disney's Children's Favorites V. 3)*

Outdoors

- Hide mittens, let the "little kittens" find them; have pie!

Hints for Your Own Situation...

Invent silly parts for rhymes everyone knows. Say "Mary had a little..." and let them call out something like "peanut!" Then "Its fleece was white as..." and they might add "pajamas!"

☆ ☆ ☆

Make up stories about what happens after the end of your favorite rhyme or story. "Jack and Jill opened up a business that built elevators, or gave people helicopter rides to tall hills!" or "Miss Muffet and the Eensy Weensy Spider decided to open an outdoor cafe, with lots of umbrellas in case it rains!"

- Get in some exercise and try jumping over the moon (a small ball), running a race to carry a pail of water, climbing in a big chair (Humpty Dumpty's wall), and running around to look for Bo-Peep's sheep. Swing on swings and sing Rock a Bye Baby. If it's nice out, go barefoot and count off the rhyme "This Little Piggy Went to Market."
- Teach the finger game "Here is the church, here is the steeple, open the doors, here's all the people."

Snack-time

Mix up sugar cookie dough. Let children "roll it, pat it, and mark it" with the letter of their first name, and anyone else they want. Bake and enjoy!

☆ ☆ ☆

Make hard-boiled eggs and let the children crack them open.

☆ ☆ ☆

Serve milk from the Cow that jumped over the Moon, honey from the Owl and the Pussycat, bread from the Bakerman, mini-pies from the Pieman, pickles from Peter Piper, or water from Jack and Jill, and plums from Jack Horner.

Books

Animal Crackers by Jane Dyer
(Little Brown & Co. 1996) (2/3)

Moon Jump—A Cowntdown by Paula Brown
(Viking/Penquin 1993) (4/6)

Two Cool Cows by Toby Speed
(G.P. Putnam's Sons 1995) (4/6)

Tomie de Paola's Mother Goose by Tomie de Paola
(Putnam 1985) (4/6)

Mary Had a Little Lamb by Sarah Josepha Hale/Bruce McMillan
(Scholastic 1990) (2/3)

The Missing Tarts by B.G. Hennessy
(Viking Kestrel 1989) (2/3)

To Market! To Market! by Peter Spier
(Doubleday 1967) (4/6)

Mother Goose: Seventy-Seven Verses with Pictures by Tasha Tudor
(Random House 1989) (4/6)

Nursery Rhymes by Maud Humphrey
(Derrydale/Random House 1992) (2/3)

A Stitch in Rhyme by Delinda Downes
(Borzoi/Knopf 1996) (4/6)

Videos

Richard Scarry's Best Sing-Along Mother Goose Video Ever!;
Barney's Magical Musical Adventure
The Mother Goose Video Treasury (1-4)*
Mary Had a Little Lamb (Jim Henson)*
Wee Sing King Cole's Party*

Art/Craft Materials

construction paper
white paper
markers, scissors, crayons
gluestick
rubber stamps (optional)
white and black posterboard
white cotton balls
black yarn scraps (optional)
paint stirrer or pencil

Art/Craft Directions

Nursery Rhyme Placecards

1) Cut white paper into rectangles about 1½" x 4½". Cut a piece of colored construction paper 4" x 5".

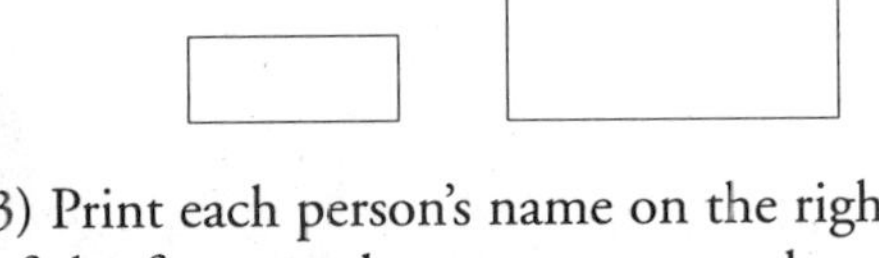

2) Fold the construction paper in half. Glue the white paper so that it is centered on one side of the construction paper.

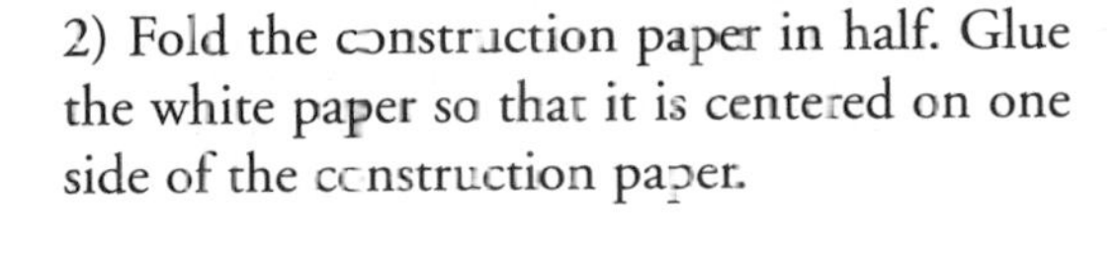

3) Print each person's name on the right side of the front, and use crayons, markers, rubber stamps, etc. to decorate the left side with some nursery rhyme person, animal, or thing.

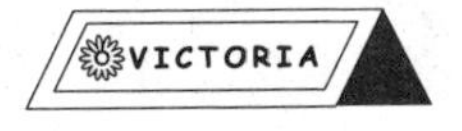

4) On the backs, you can write the name of the nursery rhyme that your chosen picture came from. Use these at dinner and get the grown-ups to guess the rhyme's name.

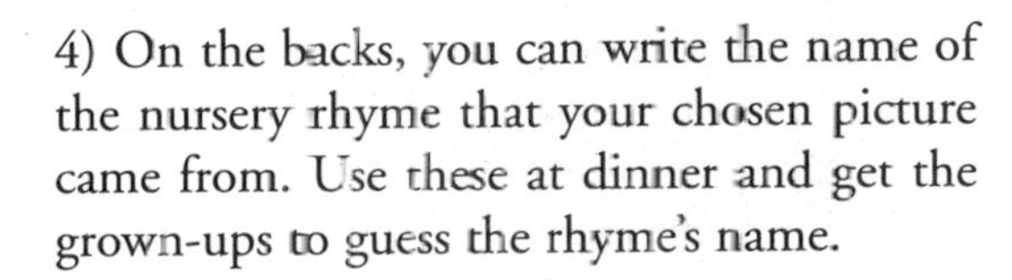

For a Little Something Extra...

Buy the software "Mixed-up Mother Goose" from Sierra. It comes with a music CD with more than thirty unusual versions of nursery rhyme songs.

Sheep Puppet

1) Cut one sheep out of white poster-board, and one out of black posterboard. Glue them together, with a paint stick or pencil in between the two layers.

2) Glue the cotton balls all over the white side. If you have black yarn scraps, glue them on the black side. Hold the paint stick as a handle, and turn the puppet as needed to tell stories (Baa Baa Black Sheep, Mary Had a Little Lamb, etc.)

Humpty Dumpty Decoration

1) Cut an egg shape and 4 strips from a piece of white paper. Pleat the 4 strips into about 1" folds.

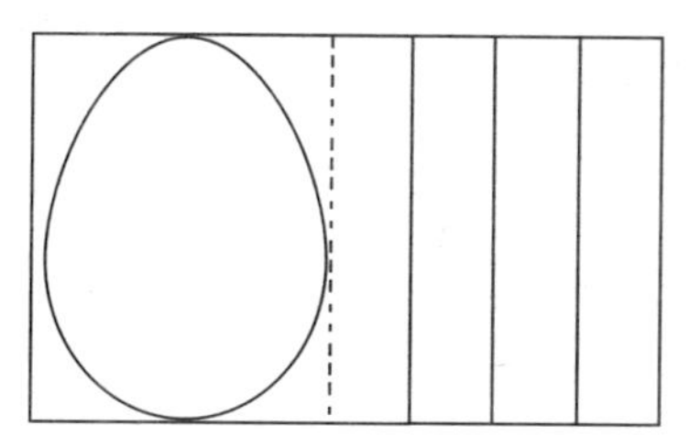

2) Glue or tape the pleated strips to the back of the egg shape, as arms and legs. Draw an egg face, then color or glue on cut-out clothes, hands, and feet.

Old-Fashioned Days

Art/Craft

- Make paper pleated fans to keep cool. You can decorate white paper with markers, then fold it, or fold construction paper and then decorate it with stickers. Wrap the handle with a bit of ribbon and let some hang down for fancy style (see directions).
- Make sunbonnets in two styles (just a brim in front, or a brim all around) from posterboard. Decorate them with colored markers and ribbons (see directions).
- Make a boy or girl doll by wrapping yarn around a length of cardboard, then cutting and tying off different sections. You can glue on felt eyes, nose, etc., and make clothes from pieces of felt (see directions).

Indoors

- This is definitely a good time for dress-up—get out long skirts, roll pants up to the knees for britches, put on suspenders, and use grown-up shirts and long-sleeve blouses rolled up at the sleeves. Knee-socks, caps, aprons, and floppy hats would all work.
- Pretend you're back in the mid-1800s. Notice there's no TV, CDs, computers, radio, or phones. Go around the house and see what you do have. (Books, spoons, wooden and china bowls, chalk, candlesticks, rugs, knitting needles, flower vases, balls, tops, dolls, dollhouses, whistles, etc.)
- Make gingerbread cookies and decorate them with raisins and white icing.
- Play at cooking using only bowls, spoons, whisks, and rolling pins. Play at cleaning using only brooms to sweep and "beat" rugs clean. Collect wooden blocks to bring in "firewood."

Music

"Bicycle Built for Two"; "Yankee Doodle Dandy"
"And the Band Played On"

Hints for Your Own Situation...

Older children can make butter by putting about 2 tablespoons of heavy whipping cream into a clean, empty baby-food jar. Have each child shake it a lot—even jump up and down with it! Slowly, a lump of real butter will form. The leftover liquid is buttermilk!

☆ ☆ ☆

Feeling really ambitious? Make applesauce or a loaf of homemade bread from scratch.

Snack-time

Fill a plastic pail with apple slices, a bread roll, a chunk of cheese (cut in slices), and a purchased miniature pie-type pastry, covered with a cloth napkin. Ladle water with a soup ladle into paper cups.

☆ ☆ ☆

Make old-fashioned lemonade by cutting 2 or 3 real lemons in half, squeezing out the juice, pouring the juice into a medium pitcher of water (3 or 4 cups), and mixing in lots of sugar (½ cup or more) to taste.

Outdoors

- Do you have jump-ropes, bouncing balls, a top to spin, and chalk for drawing? These are all toys that children might have played with a hundred or more years ago.
- If it's cold and snowy, pull each other around on sleds.
- Try to keep a hula hoop rolling along the ground by tapping it with a stick (a paint stirrer is good, since it's not pointed).
- In warm weather, set up a clothes line for drying, perhaps between two patio chairs. Get out doll clothes or bandanas or a few real clothes, and wash them (with supervision) in two dish tubs (for soapy water and clean water). Use clothes pins to hang them up to dry.

Books

An Old-Fashioned ABC Book by Elizabeth Allen Ashton
(Viking/Penguin 1990) (2/3)

When I Was Young in the Mountains by Cynthia Rylant
(E.P. Dutton 1982) (4/6)

Ox-Cart Man by Donald Hall
(Viking Press 1979) (4/6)

Winter Days in the Big Woods by Laura Ingalls Wilder
(Harper Collins 1932/1994) (4/6)

Harvest Song by Ron Hirschi
(Cobblehill/Dutton 1991) (4/6)

Mountain Wedding by Faye Gibbons
(William Morrow 1996) (4/6)

McGraw's Emporium by Jim Aylesworth
(Henry Holt and Co. 1995) (4/6)

The Great Pumpkin Switch by Megan McDonald
(Orchard Books 1992) (4/6)

Theres' Nothing to Do! by James Stevenson
(Greenwillow 1986) (4/6)

The Long Way Westward by Joan Sandin
(Harper & Row 1989) (4/6)

Videos

The Olden Days Coat*; The Secret Garden, Wee Sing: Grandpa's Magical Toys*

Art/Craft Materials

white paper, posterboard (colored is nice)
markers, stickers
thin ribbon (about 2 ft.)
tape, stapler, scissors
ribbon (½" wide, 1 yd.)
16" lace (optional)
yarn (about 30 ft., plus scraps)
felt scraps

Art/Craft Directions

Paper Fan

1) Pleat a sheet of white paper; for a fuller look, tape 2 sheets together end to end before pleating.

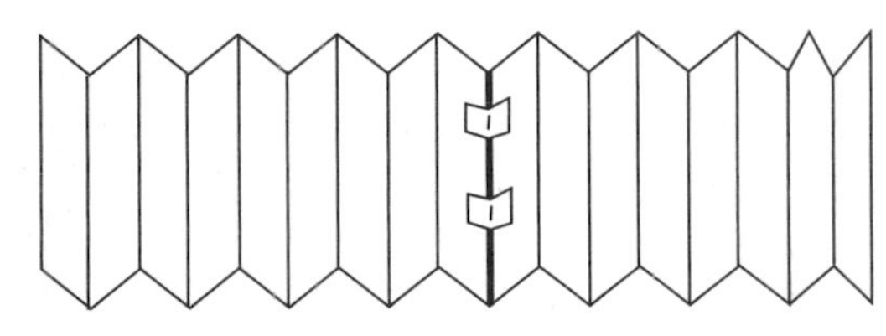

2) Flatten out the pleats gently, and use markers, stickers, etc., to draw designs on the fan. Refold, and gather it on one end. Staple and tape that end.

3) Cut 2 pieces of thin ribbon about 12" each. Fold them in half and tape them to the handle of the fan.

For a Little Something Extra...

Go fly a kite in a safe, wide open area.

Sunbonnet

1) For the type of bonnet that has a wide brim all around, and a scarf to tie it down, see the section Hats/Shoes.

2) For a Prairie-Girl Bonnet, cut the shapes shown out of posterboard. The curves can be approximate.

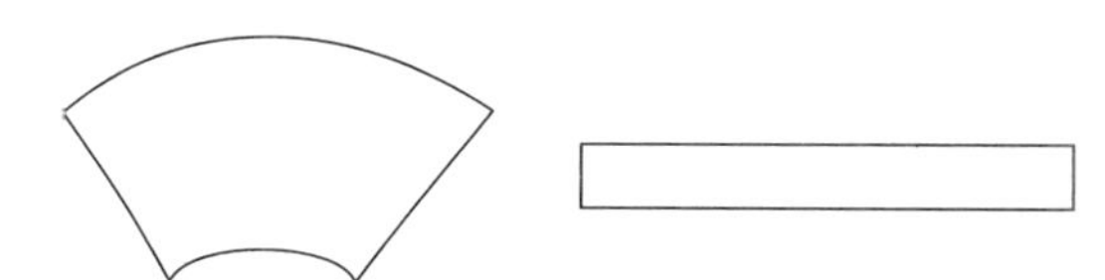

3) Bend the bonnet into a bowed shape, and staple the band across the back, checking to see that it fits the child. Staple 18" ribbon ties to the front corners. Staple lace around the front edge.

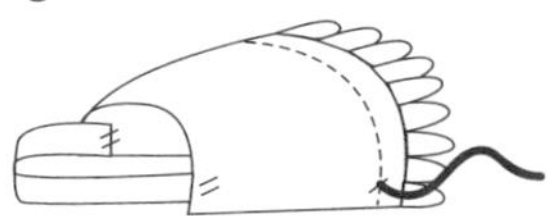

Yarn Doll

1) Wind all the yarn around a scrap of 6" x 3" cardboard. Slip another piece of yarn through the top, and tie off tightly. Cut open the bottom edges of yarn.

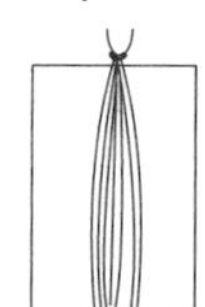

2) Use scrap yarn to tie the bundle at about 1½" down from the top. Separate ¼ of the yarn to the left, leave ½ in the middle, and leave ¼ of it to the right. Tie off the left and right sections at the half-way points, then trim the ends almost to the ties.

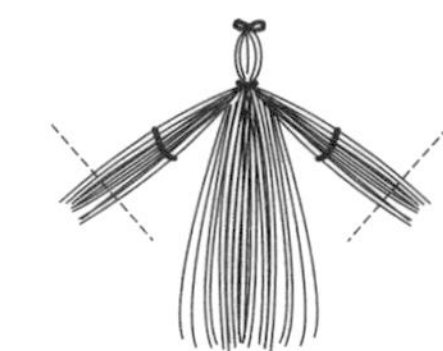

3) Tie off the center bundle down another 1½". If you spread out the remaining yarn at this point, you have a girl doll in a dress. For a boy doll, divide the remaining length in half, and tie both sections off just above the ends. Decorate both types with felt scrap eyes, nose, and mouth.

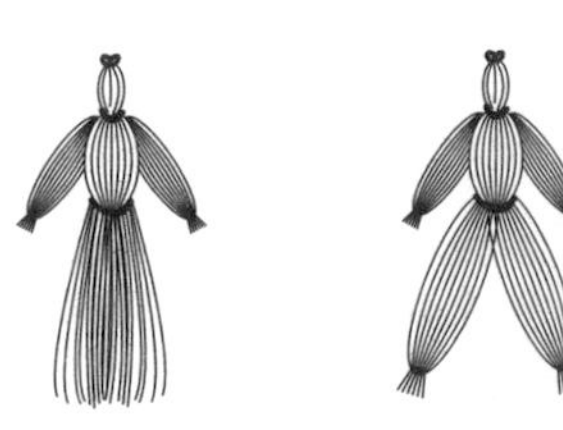

Pirates

Art/Craft

- Make a spyglass by decorating and "nesting" paper towel tubes and toilet paper rolls (see directions).
- Make black pirate hats and eye patches from black construction paper and yarn (see directions).
- Make cardboard swords from paper towel tubes, wrapping paper tubes, or flat cardboard, covered with foil and decorated (see directions).
- Decorate and tape together pieces of construction paper, cardboard, and ribbon to make a parrot, then safety-pin it to your shoulder (see directions).
- Make a treasure map: draw a map with crayons (not washable markers). Put in lots of trees, rivers, mountains, and lakes as guideposts. Tear the paper's edges to make them jagged, wrinkle it, and then smooth it out. Soak a tea bag in water, squeeze it lightly, then rub the wet bag over your map to make it look brown and very old.

Indoors

- Push several sofas/chairs together facing each other, then pile in for a pirate ship. Take turns deciding who has "permission to come aboard," who walks the plank, and where you're sailing. See any land or sharks?
- If you can get a large box, draw on the outside to make it a ship (cut round openings in the sides for portholes; cut a small hole in the top to stick a broom down through as a mast). Let everyone decorate it.
- Dress up in pants rolled to the knees, t-shirts or long-sleeved shirts tied at the waist (do you have any striped ones?), and scarves knotted around necks and heads. Shower-curtain loops can work as earrings (just loop them around ears). Try dancing a jig (hornpipe dance) and swabbing the deck.

Music

Disney's Peter Pan
I'm a Happy Pirate (Doug & Gary)*

Hints for Your Own Situation…

Older children can practice tying knots with sturdy white cord (thicker than kite string, but not as rough as twine). Show them a square knot and a half hitch. Get a library book to show you fancier knots.

☆ ☆ ☆

If the children can handle a plastic knife, they can make "scrimshaw" by carving their initials into a bar of dry white soap. Brush over it with dirt or dry cocoa powder, so that the lines really show. Wipe off the surface.

Snack-time

Serve crackers for your parrots (and you!) Serve fresh fruit because that was very important to sailors. However, they usually lived on hardtack (biscuits). Try infant biscuits or tea biscuits. Older children may try beef jerky.

☆ ☆ ☆

If you have a big thermos or cooler with a dispenser, fill it with water and pretend it's a barrel of precious fresh water in the midst of a salty sea. Set it outside on a table or upside down box and serve drinks in mugs.

Outdoors

- Have each child take turns hiding a "treasure" in the yard (under leaves, under a wheelbarrow, in a window-box, or actually buried in dirt or a sandbox, if that's okay), and let the others search for it.
- Make a treasure map ahead of time, that leads to a point in the yard. Decorate a plastic box (such as a baby-wipe box) as a treasure chest: cover it with brown grocery-bag paper and taped strips of gold gift ribbon. Have everyone put a "treasure" in it (or fill it ahead of time with new treats). Have an adult hide (bury?) it, then all the children can follow the map to hunt for it together.
- In a sandbox or all on a rock, sing "Row Row Row Your Boat."

Books

Do Pirates Take Baths? by Kathy Tucker
(Albert Whitman & Co. 1994) (4/6)

Richard Scarry's Pie Rats Ahoy! by Richard Scarry
(Random House 1994) (4/6)

The Pirate Queen by Marianne MacDonald
(Barron's 1992) (4/6)

It Was a Dark and Stormy Night by Janet & Allan Ahlberg
(Viking/Penguin 1993) (4/6)

Pirate School by Cathy East Dubowski
(Grosset & Dunlap 1996) (4/6)

The Pigrates Clean Up by Steven Kroll
(Bill Martin/Henry Holt 1993) (4/6)

Mrs. Pirate by Nick Sharratt
(Candlewick Press 1994) (2/3)

Sheep on a Ship by Nancy Shaw
(Houghton Mifflin 1989) (2/3)

Once Upon a Pirate Ship by Mircea Vasiliu
(Golden Western 1974) (4/6)

I Wish I Had a Pirate Suit by Pamela Allen
(Viking Penguin 1990) (2/3)

Videos

Muppet Treasure Island
Peter Pan

Art/Craft Materials

paper towel tube
toilet paper tube
construction paper (red or black)
felt (yellow or gold)
scissors, stapler, tape
yarn (black)
paper towel or wrapping paper tube
stiff cardboard
foil
colored Post-It notes (optional)

Art/Craft Directions

Spyglass

1) Cover both the paper towel tube and the toilet paper tube with red or black construction paper. The small tube will fit in the big tube, with room to spare.

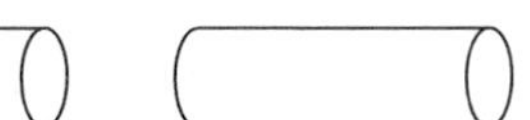

2) Cut 4 strips of yellow or gold felt about ½" wide, and long enough to go around the ends of both tubes exactly. Glue them on, and if needed, trim to have no overlap.

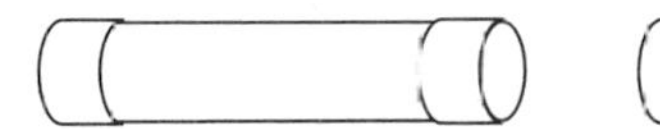

3) Slide the smaller tube into the larger one. It will be a very snug fit (you may have to slightly bend in the end of the small tube to actually get it in), but this will keep the tubes together.

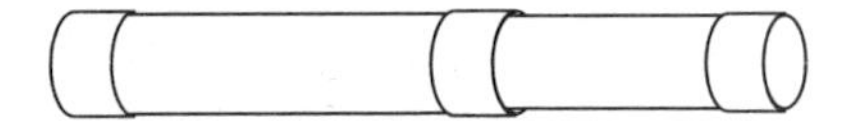

4) "Operate" the spyglass by twisting the smaller tube and sliding it in and out of the larger tube. Try not to pull it all the way out.

Pirate Hat and Eyepatch

Tape two 9"x 12" pieces of black construction paper end to end for the front; repeat for the back. Draw and cut out this shape, then staple the top and sides together. Add a white skull and crossbones. Use a scrap of black, with yarn ties, for the eyepatch.

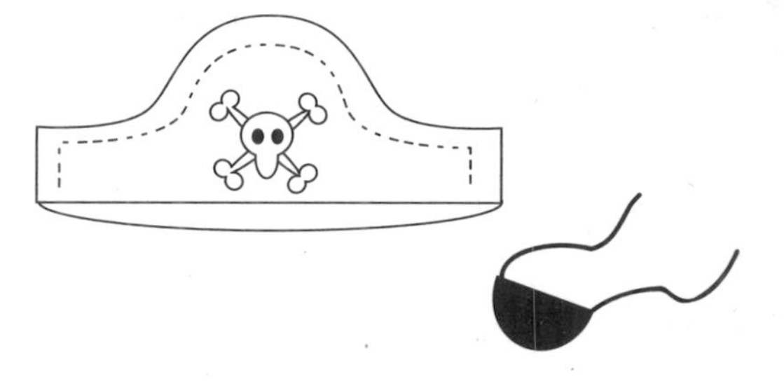

Swords

Round: See Castles/Royalty

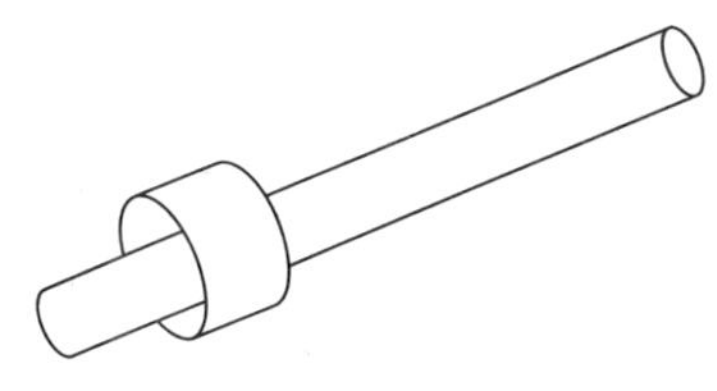

Flat:
Cut this shape from stiff cardboard and cover it with foil.

Parrot

1) Cut 2 pieces of green construction paper into parrot shapes.

2) Decorate one side of each with bits of colored paper (Post-It notes, the long thin paper-marker types, work very well) for the beak, wings, and tail feathers.

3) Tape the two sides together all around the edges, except for the legs. Tape or safety pin the parrot's legs, spread apart, to the shoulder of your shirt. Polly want a cracker?

For a Little Something Extra...

Write to the New England Pirate Museum for information about pirate life. The address is: 274 Derby Street, Salem, MA 01970.

Post Office

Art/Craft

- Make and decorate cards (birthday cards, holiday cards, I Love You cards, post cards); write letters and send pictures to friends and relatives (or each other).
- Cover empty tissue boxes, or one large cardboard box to look like a house or sidewalk mailbox (see directions).
- Decorate plain paper and envelopes to create your own set of stationery. Use rubber stamps, repeating a pattern all around the edges, or just in a corner. Use markers and rulers or stencils to make an edging. Show children how to draw their initials, and make a pattern out of them.
- Collect used postage stamps and let the children glue them together on paper to make a collage or design.
- An envelope with the flap up looks like a house. Glue one to a piece of paper, and decorate it to be your house (see directions).

Indoors

- Set up a post office: collect paper, rubber stampers, ink pads, pencils, a scale, stickers to use as stamps, and anything that helps it all look "official." Arrange a table or desk as the post office, and take turns as the Post Master and customer. What do you do at a post office? Buy stamps, envelopes, empty boxes, and postcards.
- Use a bathroom scale (or postal scale) to weigh different toys. Guess which ones weigh the closest to each other.
- Use a set of magnetic letters to practice spelling your name, names in your family, friends' names, your street name, and the name of your town. Copy them to help you address your cards and letters.

Music

"Please, Mr. Postman, Look and See"
"Return to Sender" (Elvis)
Mail Myself to You (John McCutcheon)*

Hints for Your Own Situation...

Older children can design their own stamps. Get a sheet of white self-adhesive address labels (the kind that run through a printer). Use them as oblongs, or cut them in halves or thirds. Use fine-line markers to create a stamp that shows something they like to do, a place they have been, or a favorite book character.

☆ ☆ ☆

Ahead of time, save several weeks' worth of mail to get envelopes with many different stamps and postmarks. Have children sort them by numbers (postage value), size (square or rectangle), and type (people, places, or things).

Outdoors

- Use an unsharpened pencil or plastic knife to practice writing and drawing in wet sand, snow, dirt, mud, or a patch of clay. If you don't have those, use some modeling dough flattened onto a cutting board and shaped into a rectangle (the way ancient Romans made marks on sheets of wax); or, just write with chalk.
- If you can go for a walk, see how many house numbers or building numbers you can read. Pretend to be the postal person: did you think that the numbers were easy to find?
- Set up an outdoor mailbox, and take turns sending each other "leaf" notes. Or, how about a note in a bottle?

Books

What the Mailman Brought by Carolyn Craven
(G.P. Putnam's Sons 1987) (4/6)
The Jolly Postman or, Other People's Letters by Janet/Allan Ahlberg
(Little Brown & Co. 1986) (4/6)
The Jolly Christmas Postman by Janet & Allan Ahlberg
(Little Brown & Co. 1991) (4/6)
No Mail for Mitchell by Catherine Siracusa
(Random House 1990) (2/3)
The Dove's Letter by Keith Baker
(Harcourt Brace Jovanovich 1988) (4/6)
Katie Morag Delivers the Mail by Mairi Hedderwick
(Little Brown & Co. 1984) (4/6)
Mystery of the Lost Letter by Olive Blake
(Troll 1979) (4/6)
Don't Forget to Write by Martina Selway
(Ideals Children's Books 1992) (4/6)
Never Mail an Elephant by Mike Thaler
(Troll/Whistlestop 1994) (2/3)
Hail to the Mail by Samuel Marshak
(Hentry Holt & Co. 1990) (4/6)

Snack-time

Use frosting to decorate graham crackers to look like envelopes with addresses. Use squares of chocolate bars as stamps and return address labels (or, for older children, the address label could be a stick of gum broken in half).

☆ ☆ ☆

Decorate one large sheet cake with white frosting as an envelope, then use colored icing to write in the names and the address where you are.

Videos

The Video Guide to Stamp Collecting (5/6)*
Postman Pat (Fisher-Price)*; There Goes the Mail*

Art/Craft Materials

facial tissue box (250 count size)
construction paper (black, red, blue, and green)
scissors, tape
sheet of cardboard
Velcro strip (2" self-stick)
markers
brass fastener
paper towel tube
cereal box
shoe box
white envelope (small)

Art/Craft Directions

House Mailbox

1) For a mailbox on a post, take a tissue box and cover it with black construction paper, even over the slot. Remove one end, and cut a new one out of cardboard. Cover that with the black paper, and tape it to the bottom only of the new end. Stick the Velcro on the edges of the box and door so that you can close the door. Draw numbers on the sides.

2) Cut a red paper flag to tape to the side of the box. Tape it on, or use a brass fastener so that you can spin it up or down. If you want, tape a paper towel tube to the bottom of the box, and prop it up in a bucket or with books stacked around the bottom.

3) For a wall-type box, tape shut the top of a cereal box. Cut away an angled lid. Cover the box top and bottom with black paper, and put numbers on the front.

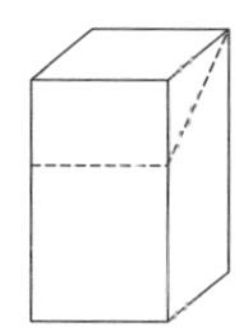

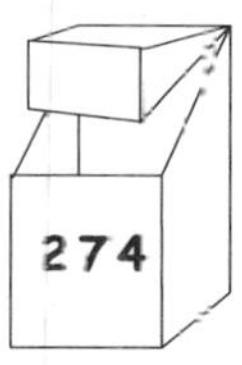

City Street Mailbox

1) Tape the lid onto a shoebox, and set the box on its end. Cover it with blue construction paper, and add some red and white paper, ribbon, or marker stripes. If you're really ambitious, draw the eagle symbol on white paper, and glue it on. Cut a slot in the upper front. Draw on legs.

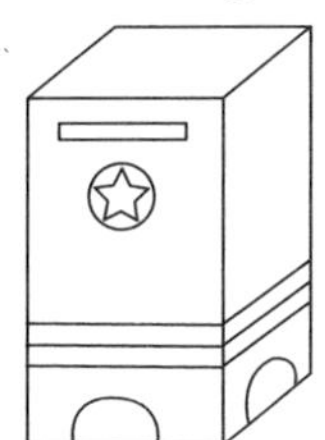

2) Cut a piece of blue construction paper the width of the shoebox, and 8" x 10" x 10" long. Tape this piece over the top of the upright end, making a loop that goes up from the front and down to the back.

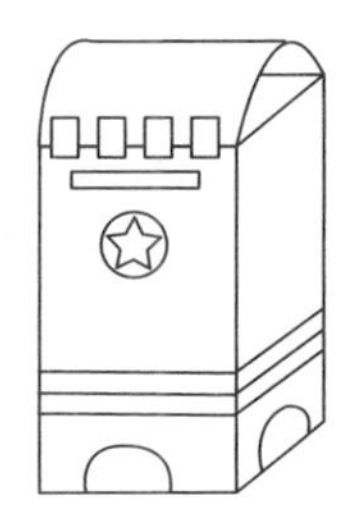

Envelope House Art

1) Glue a strip of green paper fringe along the bottom of a piece of blue construction paper, to make grass and the sky.

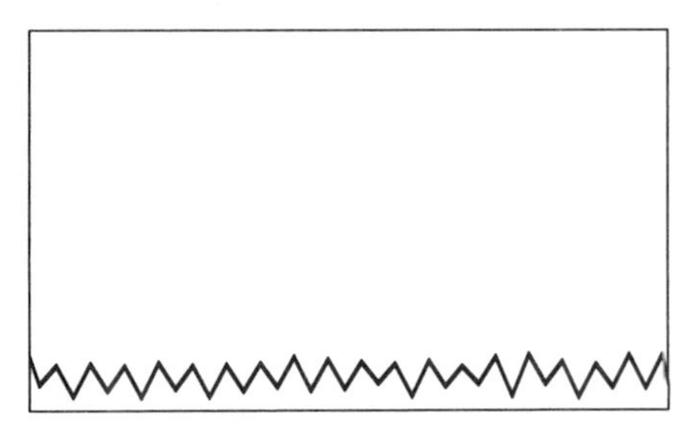

2) Open up the flap on an envelope. Glue the envelope, address side facing up, on the blue paper, just above the grass. Draw on doors, windows, and other house decorations.

For a Little Something Extra...

Call the U.S. Postal Service for a free start-up stamp-collecting kit (stamps, magazines, and posters): (888) 782-6738

Rain

Art/Craft

- Make a rainbow mobile from lengths of colored ribbons (gift ribbon or craft ribbon) or yarn, construction paper, and cotton balls. Put a sun on one end and clouds on the other (see directions).
- Get out the water color paints. Try painting a picture on paper, letting it partly dry, then spraying it with a mister—it will look like rain drops fell on it.
- Tell children every cloud has a silver lining, then make one. Take plastic Easter eggs, tape a length of yarn to one side. Cover with Tacky glue, and stick on cotton balls. Fill them with silver foil-covered chocolate candies, and hang them from the ceiling or doorway (or deliver them to someone who needs cheering up) (see directions).

Indoors

- Set up umbrellas and toss small balls (raindrops or hail) into them from across the room.
- Buy inexpensive prisms (sometimes at antique stores, from old chandeliers) and, ahead of time, hang them from threads where light will shine on them. Let the children "discover" the rainbows on sunny days, and create your own rainbows on rainy days using flashlights.
- Gather a number of fabric and material scraps: felt, cotton, vinyl, or latex (a picnic tablecloth or shower cap), plastic (small bag), wool, satin, a towel, etc. Use a spray mister bottle or eyedropper to spray water droplets on each. Predict, then talk about, which fabric will "bounce" the water off, and which ones will get really wet.
- Spray water on the leaves of a plant and on the dirt, and see which parts soak up the water first.
- Sing and act out "Eensy Weensy Spider."

Music

"April Showers" (Bambi); "It's Raining, It's Pouring;"
Swinging on a Rainbow (Cheryl Kirking);*
"Somewhere Over the Rainbow"; "Rainbow Connection" (The Muppet Movie)

Hints for Your Own Situation...

Use crayons to color rainbow colors all over a piece of white paper. Color all over, very hard with black crayon on top of the rainbow crayoned paper. Use a toothpick to scratch a drawing into the black, and let the rainbow colors come through.

☆ ☆ ☆

Buy each child a small, inexpensive watering can. Children can take charge of a certain plant or part of a garden to provide its very own "rain."

☆ ☆ ☆

Try finding an object for every color of the rainbow in each room of the house. Take turns being first.

Snack-time

Fill ice-cube trays with water, adding a drop of different food coloring to each one, then freeze. Use in clear cups of water for a cooling rainbow drink.

☆ ☆ ☆

Make "lightning" cheese sandwiches or toast: take the crust off slices of oval bread (e.g., Italian) and cut the edges in and out to look like puffy clouds. Cut slices of American cheese (or other types) into zig-zag strips for lightning. Lay the strips on the bread, and if desired, lightly toast them under a broiler.

☆ ☆ ☆

Make a batch of sugar cookie dough, divide it into six parts, and mix in six rainbow food colors. Roll bits of dough into lengths, and press them side by side to make rainbow cookies.

Outdoors

- If the rain won't stop, gather at a window, or out on a porch (if it's not lightning out) and see and hear how different the world seems during the rain.
- When the rain stops, find a puddle, get everyone into boots, and go splashing. Get out the chalk and draw on the wet sidewalk. Look for rainbows and draw your own.
- Use big brushes to paint water pictures on sidewalks.
- If you want it to rain, go outside and jump, dance, and holler your very own rain dance!
- On a hot day, have everyone put on raincoats and boots, or just bathing suits. Get out the sprinkler or a hose with a sprayer nozzle, and make your own rain for fun.

Books

The Rain Puddle by Adelaide Holl
(Lothrop, Lee & Shepard Co. 1965) (4/6)
Johnny Lion's Rubber Boots by Edith Thacher Hurd
(Harper & Row 1972) (2/3)
Stormy Day by Claire Henley
(Hyperion Books for Children 1993) (4/6)
In the Rain with Baby Duck by Amy Hest
(Candlewick Press 1995) (2/3)
It Chanced to Rain by Kathleen Bullock
(Simon & Schuster 1989) (4/6)
Rain Talk by Mary Serfozo
(Margaret K. McElderry Books 1990) (4/6)
We Hate Rain! by James Stevenson
(Greenwillow Books 1988) (4/6)
Mud Puddle by Robert Munsch
(Annick Press Ltd. 1995) (4/6)
The Enchanted Umbrella by Odette Meyers
(Gulliver/Harcourt Brace Jovanovich 1988) (4/6)
Cloudy with a Chance of Meatballs by Judi Barrett
(Atheneum 1984) (4/6)

Videos

Singing in the Rain; Winnie the Pooh and the Blustery Day
Rainy Day Adventure (Joanie Bartels)*

Art/Craft Materials

construction paper
white cotton balls (or yellow, optional)
red, orange, yellow, blue, green, and
purple ribbons or yarn (1 ft.)
scissors, Tacky glue, tape
crayons
hanger (optional)
silver-foiled candies

Art/Craft Directions

Rainbow Mobile

1) For a simple mobile, tie lengths of colored yarn or ribbon to a hanger, in rainbow color order. Cut out a cloud from white paper to hang at one end, and a sun from yellow paper to hang at the other ends.

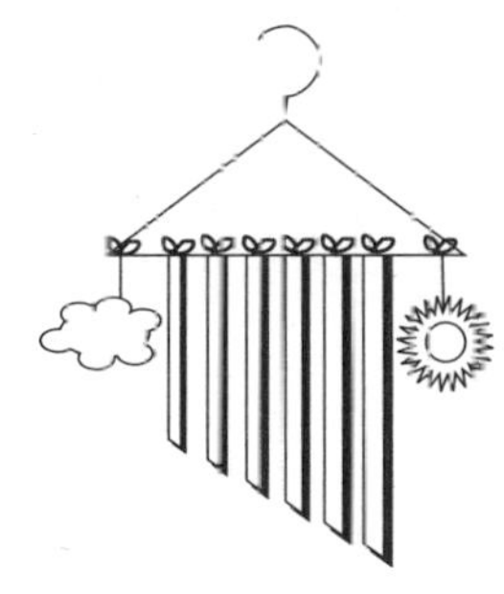

1) For a mobile that takes a little longer, cut 2 sun shapes out of yellow paper, and 2 cloud shapes out of white paper.

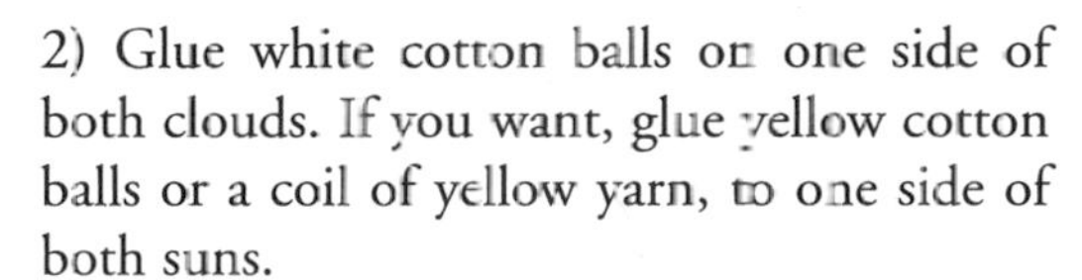

2) Glue white cotton balls on one side of both clouds. If you want, glue yellow cotton balls or a coil of yellow yarn, to one side of both suns.

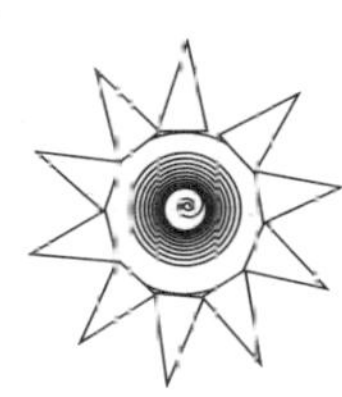

For a Little Something Extra...

Make a rain gauge by cutting the top off a milk jug and using a permanent marker to mark inches down one side. Put it outside and check it after a rainstorm, to see how much rain fell in an hour.

☆ ☆ ☆

Watch The Weather Channel on television.

3) Cut a rainbow arch out of white paper. Draw five arcs so that you divide the arch into six spaces. Color them in with rainbow colors, starting with red on the outside (the longest stripe), then orange, yellow, green, blue, and purple.

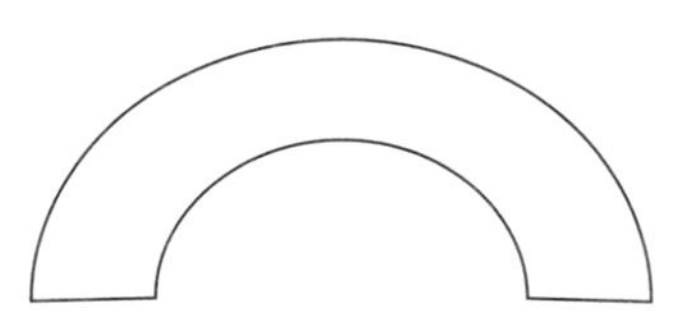

4) Glue the clouds on either side of one end of the rainbow. Glue the suns on either side of the other end. Hang it from a piece of yarn taped to the top center.

Silver-Lining Cloud

1) Cover a plastic Easter egg with Tacky glue. Stick white cotton balls all over both halves.

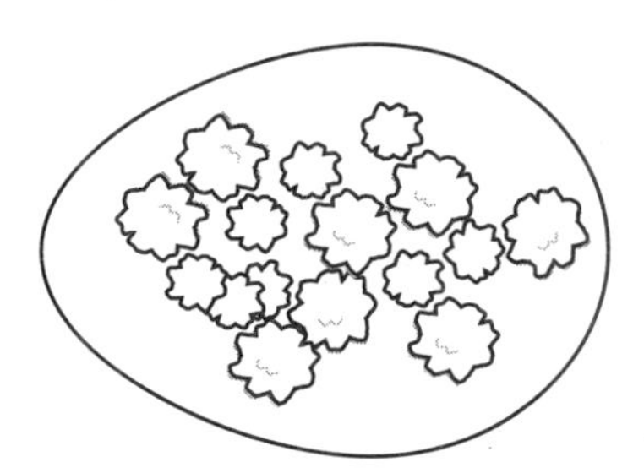

2) Fill the "cloud" with silver candies. Add a note that says, "Every cloud has a silver lining."

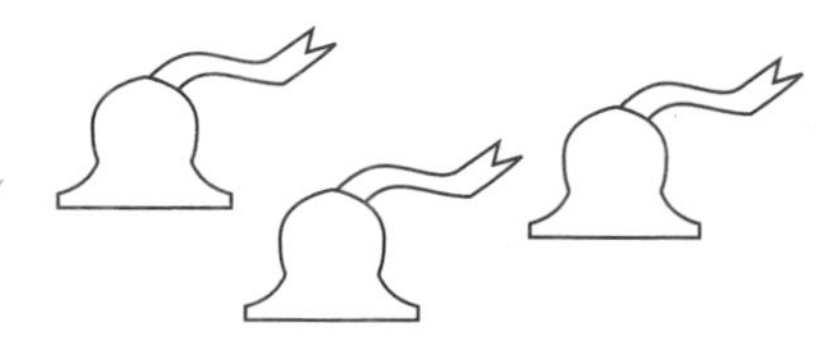

Restaurant

Art/Craft

- Make napkin rings from slices of toilet paper tubes, covered with strips of construction paper. Cut out shapes, or pictures from magazines, to decorate one part or all around the tube (see directions).
- Put together menus by cutting out pictures of food from magazines and pasting them in a column on a piece of white paper. Older children can write numbers for prices. Glue menu to construction paper (see directions).
- Make a sign for your restaurant—children will probably have some favorites and know enough to draw the logos or tell you what to draw (see directions).
- Make paper placemats that go with the theme of your favorite restaurant or food. Decorate then cut out: a big circle as a pizza, a hamburger in a bun, an ice-cream cone. If possible, cover them with clear contact paper.

Indoors

- Set up a restaurant, pizza parlor, or dessert shop. Set out a table with plastic dishes, cups and spoons. Try different ways to fold napkins. If you have plastic food, put it on a tray, ready to serve. (If not, pretend that blocks or checkers are food, or serve your real snack or lunch at your "real" restaurant.) If you have a chalkboard or whiteboard, write the day's specials.
- Take turns being the waiter, with a towel folded over your arm. Give everyone a small pad of paper and a crayon for writing down "orders." Another child can be the chef and work at a toy stove with pots, pans, spoons, and measuring cups, while others will be the diners.
- Practice carrying stacks of plastic dishes while you walk in a straight line!

Music

"Noodles, Noodles in Your Hair" (Hello Sun, Good Night Moon)*
"I Am a Pizza" (Peppermint Wings)*

Hints for Your Own Situation...

Older children may want to take your order and assemble it from the kitchen to deliver to your table. If possible, set up kitchen items so that they can get plastic plates, cups, napkins, and silverware, plus a simple snack (bread, crackers, butter, cookies, a juice box) and be real servers.

☆ ☆ ☆

Tape white paper to a table and have the children draw in the shapes of where plates, cups, forks, knives, and spoons should be placed.

Outdoors

- Set up an outdoor cafe. Get out plastic chairs or a picnic set, and lay it with a plastic tablecloth, paper plates, and plastic silverware (maybe your tea-sets or camping sets would have them). If you want to really picnic on the ground, be sure to weight down the cloth with stones.
- Have an egg-in-a-spoon walking contest. Fill plastic eggs with treats, and give children big cooking spoons for carrying one egg at a time. When they get across the finish line, open the eggs and have dessert.
- Make mud-pies, sand-cakes, or snow-muffins. Use real cake-pans and cupcake tins if allowed.
- Decorate your outdoor cafe with a string of hanging construction paper lanterns.

Books

In the Diner by Christine Loomis
(Scholastic 1993) (2/3)

Animal Cafe by John Stadler
(Aladdin/Macmillan 1986) (4/6)

Curious George Goes to an Ice Cream Shop by H.A. Rey
(Houghton Mifflin 1989) (4/6)

Marge's Diner by Gail Gibbons
(Thomas Y. Crowell 1989) (4/6)

Gregory, the Terrible Eater by Mitchell Sharmat
(Scholastic 1980) (4/6)

Alphabet Soup by Scott Gustafson
(Calico/Contemporary 1990) (4/6)

Eating Out by Helen Oxenbury
(Puffin Penguin 1983) (2/3)

Bat in the Dining Room by Crescent Dragonwagon
(Marshall Cavendish 1997) (4/6)

Dinner at the Panda Palace by Stephanie Calmenson
(Harper Collins/Newfield 1991) (4/6)

Frank and Ernest by Alexandra Day
(Scholastic 1988) (4/6)

Snack-time

Pick a theme for the type of restaurant you're making, and match your snack to that. At the pizza place, serve mini-pizzas (make your own by spreading pizza sauce on English muffins and adding shredded cheese). At the salad bar, put out bowls of cut-up lettuce, croutons, raisins, sliced tomatoes, etc. For a sub shop, give everyone a sliced roll, and set out slices of meats, cheese, and favorite toppings. For a dessert shop, set out plastic tea-cups, small plates, and a platter of cookies or snack-cakes.

Videos

Lady and the Tramp (Disney)

Art/Craft Materials

toilet paper tubes
scissors, tape, glue
construction paper
ribbon (2 ft., optional)
magazines, catalogs, ads from grocery stores
thin ribbon (2 ft. each)
posterboard
markers

Art/Craft Directions

Napkin Rings

1) Cut toilet paper tubes in half. Glue construction paper strips around outsides; tape edges down.

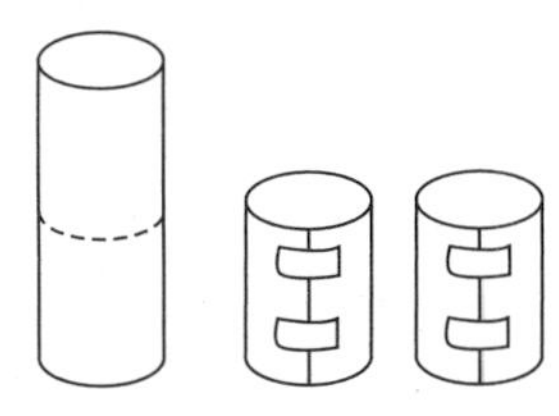

2) Cut out pictures from magazines or catalogs, and glue them around the covered tubes. If you'd like, tie a ribbon all around it with a bow. Roll up a napkin and slide it inside.

Menus

1) Look through magazines and grocery ads for pictures of prepared food dishes (a basket of rolls, a plate of dinner, a salad, a slice of cake, a pie, a vegetable dish, a glass of milk, a cup of soup, etc.)

2) Cut the pictures to sizes that will fit on a sheet of construction paper. If you have quite a few of them to choose from, sort them into groups by type.

For a Little Something Extra...

Next time you go to a favorite restaurant, take home extra napkins with printed logos to use in your pretend restaurant.

☆ ☆ ☆

On a nice day, older children can set up a classic lemonade stand. Don't go in the house and leave the children alone; instead, be sure to have everything you need together ahead of time.

3) Fold the menu in half, to make a crease down the middle. Glue the pictures on both sides of the inside, in the order of a meal (soup, bread, salad, main dishes, dessert). For older children who can print, leave spaces for writing in food names and prices.

4) Label the items, add prices, and tie a thin ribbon around and down the center fold. Write the name of your restaurant on the front, and decorate it.

Restaurant Sign

1) Write the name of your restaurant in the middle of a piece of posterboard. Decorate around it with more cut-out food pictures, marker drawings, or symbols from your own favorite restaurant.

McDruken's

2) Mount the sign on a door leading to your snack area for the day.

School

Art/Craft

- Decorate brown paper lunch bags, using markers to write each child's name, then coloring or adding stickers.
- Make a graduation cap for each child out of black construction paper and embroidery thread or yarn for a tassel (see directions).
- Make nametags for each child on red paper apples. First, write their names in large capital letters. Then, pour a box of alphabet cereal onto a plate, and help children find the letters of their names. Glue them onto the name tags under the printed letters (see directions).
- Ahead of time, get a photo of each child. Draw a schoolbus at least one foot long on yellow construction paper. Outline and cut out windows, one for each child. To the backside, tape one photo in each window so that it shows from the front. Hang for display in your "school" (see directions).

Indoors

- Set up desks (if you have them), chairs, and boxes to make a schoolroom. Do you have a chalkboard or whiteboard? Take turns so each child can be the teacher for a while. You might agree that one will teach how to draw a dog, another will teach singing the ABCs, while another will teach how to write, etc.
- On the chalkboard or whiteboard, let each child take turns drawing a picture. Everyone can contribute one sentence to making up a story about the picture.
- Get a bell (hand bell or jingle bell). Plan your day to do different things each hour or half-hour, and let children take turns ringing the bell at the right time; toddlers will of course want to ring it a lot more than that.

Music

"Mary Had a Little Lamb"
Back to School Again (Mr. Al & Stephen Fite)*

Hints for Your Own Situation...

Older children may want to spend time helping set up a whole classroom. Make one corner a story center for read-aloud circle time; set out pillows or carpet sample to sit on. Another corner can be the dress-up area, with lots of clothes, shoes, hats, etc. A third section can be the creative play kitchen or puppet theater; use large boxes upside down for tables or the stage to kneel behind. You can even make a space for quiet reading or naptimes!

☆ ☆ ☆

Decorate empty frosting canisters with stickers to make pencil/pen holders.

Snack-time

For snack time, use thermos bottles or juice boxes for drinks, and set out paper plates for each child, with an apple slice, some Cheerios, and a cookie.

☆ ☆ ☆

For lunch, have everyone pack their own food in their personalized lunch bags. Ring a bell for lunchtime, leave the "classroom," and, if it's nice, go outside for lunch and recess. If it's not nice out, go to a different room and call it the cafeteria!

Outdoors

- Get out big soft balls for throwing or kicking, chalk for sidewalk drawing, and tricycles or riding toys.
- Older children may want to try jump-ropes and bubble-blowing (you may need to blow the bubbles for younger children, but they can chase and pop them).
- Make full use of any swings or climbing structures.
- Bring some small, favorite items along outdoors for "show and tell." Sit in a circle. Each child can take a turn explaining what they're holding, and why it's so special.
- Sing "Mary Had a Little Lamb" and other favorites.

Books

School Days by B.G. Hennessy
(Viking/Penguin 1990) (2/3)

Arthur Goes to School by Marc Brown
(Random House 1995) (4/6)

My Great-Aunt Arizona by Gloria Houston
(Harper Collins Publishers 1992) 4/6)

Prairie Primer A to Z by Caroline Stutson
(Dutton Children's Books 1996) (4/6)

Miss Nelson is Missing by Harry Allard
(Houghton Mifflin 1977) (4/6)

Who Goes to School? by Margaret Hillert
(Follet Publishing 1981) (2/3)

Minerva Louise at School by Janet Morgan Stoeke
(Dutton/Penguin 1996) (4/6)

The Giraffe Who Went to School by Irma Wilde
(Treasure/Price Stern Sloan 1979) (4/6)

A Very Special Critter by Gina and Mercer Mayer
(Golden/Western Books 1992) (4/6)

The Berenstain Bears Go to School by Stan and Jan Berenstain
(Random House 1978) (4/6)

Videos

Richard Scarry's Best Busy People Video Ever!
Richard Scarry's Best ABC Video Ever!
Barney Goes to School; Learning the ABCs* (2/3)
The Huggabug Club: School Days*

Art/Craft Materials

black posterboard or construction paper
gold or yellow embroidery thread or yarn
scissors, tape, glue
red and yellow construction paper
markers, safety pins
Post Alphabet cereal
face photos of each child

Art/Craft Directions

Graduation Cap

1) Cut a square and a strip from the black paper or posterboard, as shown.

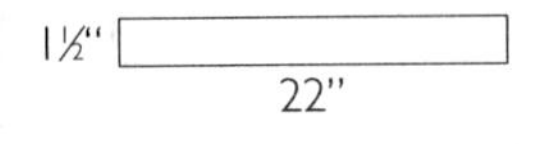

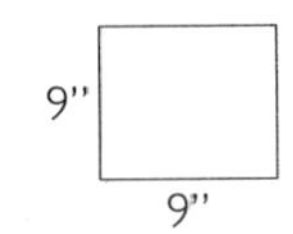

2) Bend the strip into a circle to fit the child's head. Staple the strip ends together, and tape over the staples. Tape the band to the middle of the square.

3) Cut the embroidery thread or yarn into 20" lengths (about 10 of them). Bundle them together, and, with a scrap piece, tie them in the center. Fold the bundle in half, and tie it again, about 1"down from the first knot.

4) Tape the tassel to the top center of the the cap. Cut a 1" circle of black paper, and glue this over the tassel knot.

For a Little Something Extra...

Take a "field trip" to a local elementary school. Play on the playground, and see if you can visit their library. If an older sibling is at that school, bring along lunches and have everyone eat together if the school allows.

Apple Nametag

1) Cut apple shapes out of the red paper.

2) Write each child's name in large letters with the black marker, on the upper part of each apple.

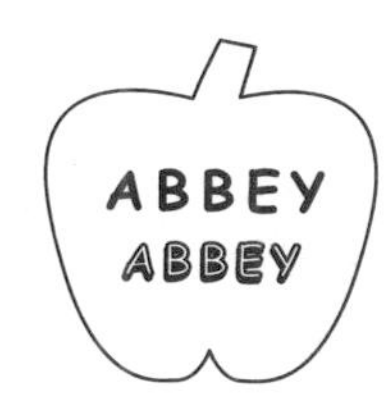

3) Find the letters to each child's name in the box of Alphabet cereal. Glue the letters to the apple, one below each written letter. Tape a safety pin to the back side.

School Bus Photo Frame

Draw and cut out a school bus shape from yellow paper. Cut out a window for each child. Tape a school face photo of each child in the windows, from the back. (Who should be the driver—a family pet?) Hang the bus up for display.

Sewing/Knitting/Weaving

Art/Craft

- Draw each child a simple picture on posterboard and cut them out. Let children use hole punchers (the different shaped ones are extra fun) around the edges. Lace them up with shoelaces or yarn (taped around the ends).
- Collect fabric scraps (you can buy inexpensive bundles in the remnant bins at fabric stores). Let children practice cutting them into crazy shapes. (Later, perhaps you can iron them with a fusible bonding layer to a sheet for a storytime "flying carpet.")
- Make a paper quilt from decorated squares glued on a long roll of white paper, or on pieces of construction paper taped together. Hang up for display (see directions).
- Make "woven" placemats from two or more colors of construction paper (you may want to cut the strips ahead of time) (see directions).

Indoors

- Find big plastic buttons, shoelaces, yarn, plastic canvas, and purchased lace-up cards; practice going in and out.
- Measuring is an important part of sewing. Let children use a tape measure to get the idea of measuring each other's height, arm length, chest size, etc., as if they were tailors getting ready to sew. Measure stuffed animals, too.
- Gather spools of thread of different colors and put them all in a box or bowl. Ask each to child to find and pick out "a red spool," "a black spool," "a light green spool," etc. If you have a lot, sort them by "all blues" or "all greens." Fabric stores often sell discontinued colors at a discount.
- Use a magnifying glass to look at many types of fabric: denim jeans, silk scarf, cotton bandana, wool sweater, nylon jacket, twill baseball cap. Show how the colors fit together differently in plaids, stripes, tweeds, and checks.

Music

Try "weaving" a favorite song: have each child sing a line.

Hints for Your Own Situation...

Older children can try doing lace-up cards in different ways: an up-and-down running stitch, or an over and over whip-stitch (see directions).

☆ ☆ ☆

Give older children the big blunt plastic needles that come with kits of plastic canvas. Let them stitch in and out of pre-cut plastic shapes, and try stitching some of them together.

☆ ☆ ☆

Older children, (who know how to hide something in their hands!) can play Button, Button, Who's Got the Button?

Snack-time

Serve Ritz crackers or RitzBits (the holes make them look like big buttons), long pretzel rods (for knitting needles) and string cheese or cherry licorice strings (like lengths of yarn). If you can't find pretzel rods, ramen noodles will look the part!

☆ ☆ ☆

Spread a patchwork of meat, cheese, bread, and vegetable slices. Cut them all into roughly the same size squares and lay them side-by-side on a large platter.

Outdoors

- Older children can find long-stemmed grasses and flowers, and try tying them in knots or strings for bracelets.
- Look around on plants, railings or porch columns during the day for delicate webs that spiders have woven.
- In the spring, set out scraps of yarn and ribbon for birds to use in their weaving. Later, look for nests and see if you can find where they've used your colorful bits.
- Use your big plastic buttons (or plastic lids from coffee cans) to play a safe form of marbles or shuffleboard by sliding one into another along a sidewalk. Mark a goal with chalk.
- If you have a chain-link fence, weave wide craft-ribbon or strips of paper in and out.

Books

The Bedspread by Sylvia Fair
(MacMillan Children's Books 1982) (4/6)

Peter's Pockets by Eve Rice
(Greenwillow Books 1989) (2/3)

The Patchwork Quilt by Valerie Flournoy
(Dial 1985) (4/6)

The Keeping Quilt by Patricia Polacco
(Simon & Schuster Books for Young Readers 1988) (4/6)

The Goat in the Rug by Charles L. Blood & Martin Link
(Four Winds Press/MacMillan 1976) (4/6)

Mr. Nick's Knitting by Margaret Wild
(Gulliver Books/Harcourt Brace Jovanovich 1988) (4/6)

Something from Nothing by Phoebe Gilman
(Scholastic 1992) (4/6)

Luka's Quilt by Georgia Guback
(Greenwillow 1994) (4/6)

Charlie Needs a Cloak by Tomie de Paola
(Aladdin/Simon & Schuster 1973) (4/6)

Eight Hands Round (Patchwork Alphabet) by Ann Whitford Paul
(Harper Collins1991) (4/6)

Videos
The Tailor of Gloucester (Beatrix Potter)

Art/Craft Materials
white or colored construction paper
colored paper scraps or wall-paper scraps
stickers
scissors, glue
long roll of paper (optional)
construction paper
tape, stapler

Art/Craft Directions

Paper Quilt

1) Cut several 9" squares of white or colored paper for each child. Decorate squares any way you want, or choose a common theme (all cars and trucks, or spaceships, or types of flowers, or all animals). Glue on bits of paper or wallpaper to add some texture. Have each child "sign" their squares.

2) Glue the finished squares side by side on on long roll of paper, or just tape them to construction paper, and tape all those pieces together to form a rectangle. Hang it up for display.

For a Little Something Extra...

Buy rubber stampers that come on wheels. Print lines running across and down a piece of paper, so that it looks like stripes woven together.

Draw a picture using just "Xs" to look like a cross-stitch pattern.

☆ ☆ ☆

Buy a classic pot-holder weaving loom (the kind with the stretchy loops).

Lace-Up Stitching

1) Doing a running stitch means you put a shoelace (or yarn) down into the first hole of your lacing card, pull it out from the backside, and push it up from the back to the front through the second hole. Go down through the third hole, and back up from underneath, through the fourth hole, etc.

2) Doing a whip stitch means you always put the tip of the shoelace into the hole from the backside, coming up to the front. The lace ends up looping over the edge of the card with every stitch.

Woven Placemats

1) Cut twelve 1" x 12" strips of multi-colored construction paper. You may want to cut up the strips ahead of time.

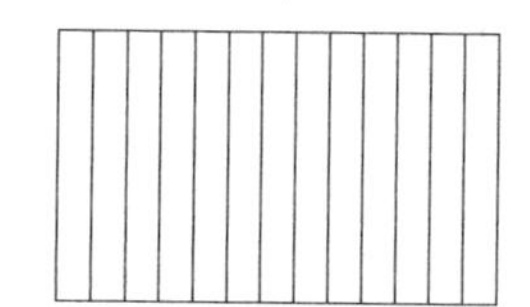

2) Fold a 9" x 12" sheet of another color of paper in half, to 9" x 6". Starting at the folded edge, cut in straight lines, 1" apart, but not all the way to the edge (leave about 1" uncut).

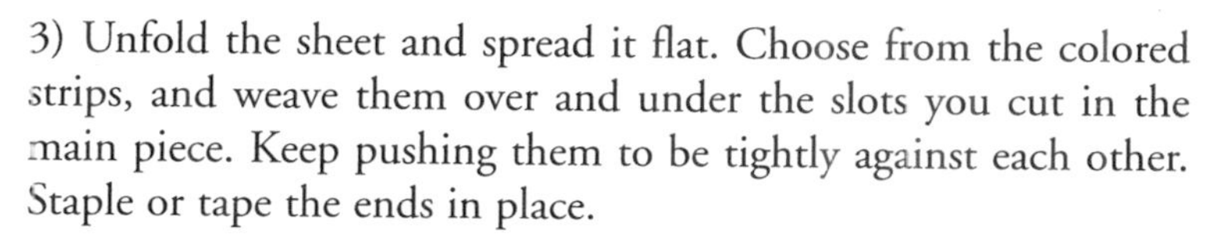

3) Unfold the sheet and spread it flat. Choose from the colored strips, and weave them over and under the slots you cut in the main piece. Keep pushing them to be tightly against each other. Staple or tape the ends in place.

Work with the children on the concept of "over" and "under" for weaving.

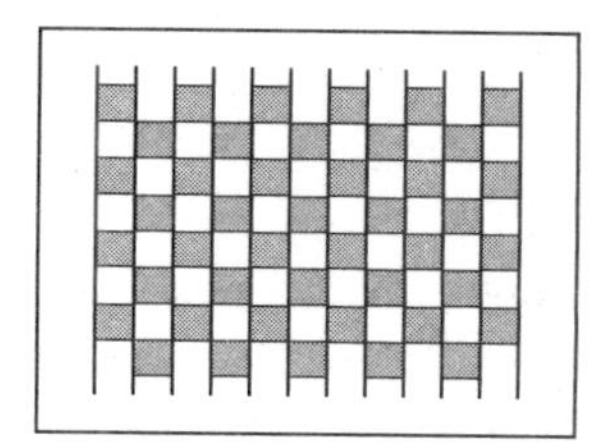

Shapes

Art/Craft

- Fold a piece of paper four or five times, then draw a person, swan, car, etc., and cut it out, so that it comes out like connected paper dolls when you unfold it (see directions).
- Fold a paper in half, unfold it, have children dab some poster paint on (randomly, or as a picture), then fold the paper over itself and gently press the two sides together. Unfold carefully—what new pictures do you see?
- Draw a picture on cardboard (white posterboard works well). Then cut up the board in randomly shaped pieces. (Or, cut up an extra photo of yourself.) Trade your pieces with another child and put together their new puzzle.
- Cover a stiff piece of cardboard with a layer of felt. Cut out geometric or random shapes from other colors of felt to create a free-form shape design board (see directions).

Indoors

- Take wooden blocks, Legos, Tinker Toys, etc., and lay them out in a pattern (symmetric, a repeating pattern, same color, same size, same shape, etc.) Have the children do their own, or try to repeat what someone else has done.
- Get out all the puzzles in the house, ones you haven't done in a long time, or new ones. Can you do them looking upside down, or without looking at a picture?
- Go on a scavenger hunt, or just a walking tour of the house, to find items of a certain shape (round, rectangular, square, crescent, oval, etc.)
- Cut different colors of construction paper into big circles, triangles, squares, etc. Tape them on the floor (looped tape on backs) and make your own "Twister" game. Call out "right hand on the green circles" or "put any foot on a yellow triangle."

Music

- Sing any kind of riddle ("puzzle") song.
- Sing "Brown Bear, Brown Bear, What Do You See?" calling out shapes (e.g., "I see a green circle looking at me," "I see a pink heart looking at me.")

Hints for Your Own Situation...

Introduce older children to the art of origami (see the reference book in the "Books" section). Regular paper or colored tissue paper will work.

☆ ☆ ☆

Give pairs of older children two identical sets of five blocks or Legos. Sit them back to back. Have one build something, then describe it to the other (without any peeks). For example, "I'm putting a long blue Lego on top of a red one, with four dots showing on the left." The other tries to reproduce the same pattern by listening, then compares. See how close you can get!

☆ ☆ ☆

Design and assemble a "Squarecrow" for a garden, using round foil piepans, rectangular boxes, long cylindrical broomsticks, etc.

Snack-time

Make sandwiches, then cut them up in squares (or with cookie cutters), and cut the edges in a few sections, too. Rearrange them in new patterns, or try to get them back together again.

☆ ☆ ☆

Buy a roll of refrigerated sugar cookie dough. Roll out and use different shapes of cookie cutters, or just cut circles, rectangles, and triangles. Make bigger cookies by laying several different shapes touching side by side.

Outdoors

- Go on a backyard shape hunt: see who can spot a square (door or window), a rectangle (wagon), a triangle (roofline), a circle (tire), a zigzag (stairway), etc.
- Blow bubbles and see what shapes they make when they stick together.
- On a nice day, bring a number of regular puzzles outside for a change of pace. For puzzles they've done several times, mix pieces from two (or more) together, and sort!
- On a snowy day, or in the sand, bring plastic cups, tubs, and containers outside to make shape prints. "Draw" circles for the Olympic rings, and squares and circles together to make a train. Use fingers or hand brooms to make big wavy curves.

Books

Alphabet Puzzle by Jill Downies
(Lothrop, Lee & Shepard Books 1988) (2/3)
Look Around! A Book about Shapes by Leonard E. Fisher
(Viking Kestrel 1987) (2/3)
Puzzles by Brian Wildsmith
(Franklin Watts Inc. 1971) (4/6)
Shapes, Shapes, Shapes by Tana Hoban
(Greenwillow 1986) (2/3)
Easy Origami by Dokuohtei Nakano (ref.)
(Puffin Penguin 1994)
The Village of Round and Square Houses by Ann Grifalconi
(Litton, Brown & Co. 1986) (4/6)
Circles, Triangles, and Squares by Tana Hoban
(Macmillan 1974) (2/3)
Color Zoo by Lois Ehlert
(Trumpet/Harper & Row 1990) (2/3)
Grandfather Tang's Story by Ann Tompert
(Crown 1990) (4/6) (includes tangram pattern)
It Looked Like Spilt Milk by Charles G. Shaw
(Harper & Row 1947) (4/6)

Videos

Clifford's Fun with Shapes; Puzzle Place series
Hullaballoo: All About Shapes*

Art/Craft Materials

piece of corrugated cardboard, at least 9" x 12"
one piece of felt, at least 9"x12"
many different colors of felt scraps
white or construction paper
scissors, tape
markers

Art/Craft Directions

Paper Doll/Car String

1) Tape two or more pieces of paper end to end. Cut along the middle and tape the ends together again, to make a long, narrow strip. Fold the whole length into pleats, 3 to 4" wide.

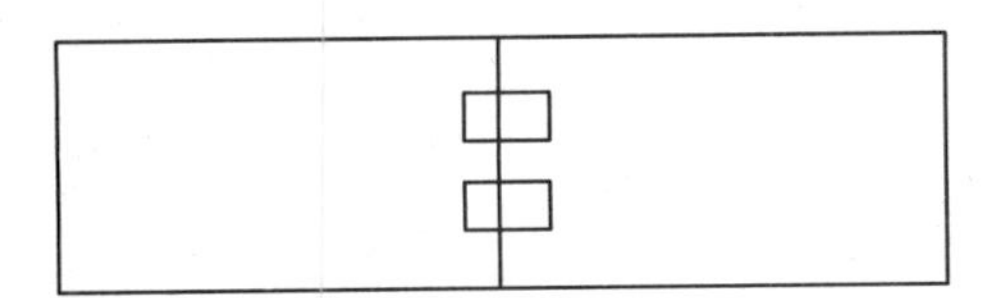

2) Draw a doll, animal, car, etc., so that it reaches to both edges of the folded stack of paper. Cut through all layers, being careful not to cut through the side folds.

3) Unfold and color each figure, either making them all match, or making each one different in some way. What looks the same and what looks different about the way your pattern repeats?

For a Little Something Extra...

Buy or cut out a set of Tangrams so children can free-form design their own patterned pictures. (ref.: *Grandfather Tang's Story* by Ann Tompert, a book with Tangrams.)

☆ ☆ ☆

Buy blank, pre-cut puzzles you can draw on yourself (Bits & Pieces: (800) 544-7297)

Shape Board

1) Cut as large a piece of corrugated cardboard as you can (at least 9" x 12"). Cut the same size of one color of felt.

2) Glue the felt to the cardboard (real glue is best for this).

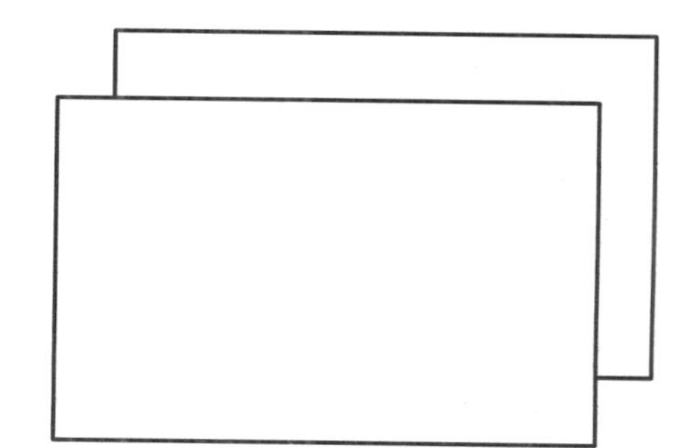

3) Cut 8 different colors of felt into at least 8 different shapes, all about 2" across. Use the following ideas, or use cookies cutters or stencils. You could also do more than one color of each shape. Use all the shapes together to make felt-board pictures from your imagination (a train, a house, a garden, an underwater scene, etc.)

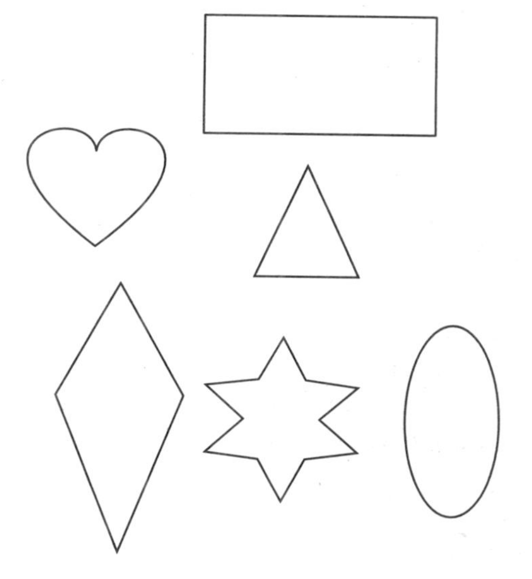

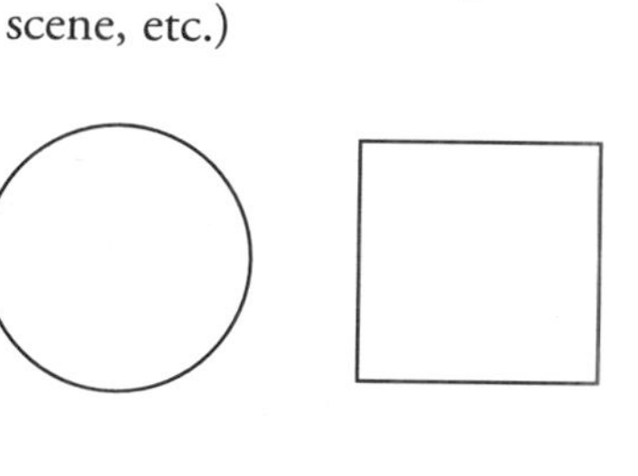

Shopping

Art/Craft

- Make signs and price tags for your own store. Gather paper bags and decorate them with pictures and the name of your store done in fancy letters (see directions).
- Make something to sell in your store: macaroni jewelry, greeting cards, sock puppets, paper airplanes, paper fans, placemats, pencil holders.
- Make a piggy bank from an oatmeal or cornmeal container (keep the lid, too), for storing the money you earn in your shop (see directions).
- Cut up advertisements from grocery stores, picking out pictures of foods from different groups, and boxes or cans with favorite brand names. Glue them by type to a roll of paper, to make a long grocery list. Maybe you can use it!

Indoors

- Gather real or pretend food, especially unopened boxes. Set up a desk or table or bench (a piano bench works well) as a store. Put groceries behind on a shelf, or on the bench as a counter. Have someone be the checkout person, and use a toy cash register, calculator, or money box. Have strips of white paper to "write" on for receipts. Use a basket for shopping, paper money (from Monopoly?), and paper bags for purchases (do you have a toy grocery cart?)
- Practice counting out change (use the paper money, and big buttons or checkers for child-safe coins).
- Try other types of stores. Set up a jewelry store with dress-up jewelry, a stuffed animal/pet store, a puzzle and game store, a sporting goods store, a musical instruments store, a model car/truck/train store, or an art supply store.
- Gather a bunch of action figures (the more different kinds, the funnier). Have them go shopping through an imaginary (or block) town; what would they need to buy?

Music

Corner Grocery Store (Raffi)*

Hints for Your Own Situation...

Older children can sort coupons by size, product type (cereal, cookies, etc.), or prices (25 cents, 50 cents, etc.)

☆ ☆ ☆

Make your own catalog. Cut up catalogs, department store ads, or magazines to get pictures of your favorite toys and games. Glue them onto sheets of construction paper and staple them together like a book. Maybe give it to someone as a "shopping guide" for the next birthday!

☆ ☆ ☆

For children who don't put small things in their mouths, dump a pile of assorted coins on the floor. Sort them by type, and practice counting them up.

Outdoors

- If possible, set up a traditional lemonade stand and sell paper fans you've folded, too. Or, on a chilly Spring or Fall day, how about offering hot chocolate and cookies? (Plan ahead for all you'll need; don't leave children alone.)
- Pretend to be different animals (squirrels, robins, snakes, dogs, bumblebees). What would you go "shopping" for? Visit different parts of the yard and choose/collect nuts, worms, grass, sticks, flowers, etc., in bags with handles.
- Can you walk while balancing an empty (or slightly filled) wicker basket on your head? In some countries, that's how people carry their shopping home.

Books

Ten Items or Less by Stephanie Calmenson
(Golden/Western 1985) (2/3)
A Fruit & Vegetable Man by Roni Schotter
(Little Brown & Co. 1993) (4/6)
Carl Goes Shopping by Alexandra Day
(Farrar Straus Giroux 1989) (2/3)
The Berenstain Bears at the Super-Duper Market by Stan and Jan Berenstain
(Random House 1991) (4/6)
Teddy Bears Go Shopping by Susanna Gretz
(Four Winds Press 1987) (4/6)
Welcome to Dinsmore, the World's Greatest Store by William Boniface
(Andrews and McMeel/Universal Press1995) (4/6)
Sheep in a Shop by Nancy Shaw
(Houghton Mifflin 1991) (2/3)
Tom and Annie Go Shopping by Barry Smith
(Houghton Mifflin 1989) (4/6)
The Supermarket by Anne & Harlow Rockwell
(Macmillan 1979) (2/3)
Market Day by Eve Bunting
(Joanna Cotler/Harper Collins 1996) (4/6)

Snack-time

Cut bread into the shape of hanging price tags; use a straw to make a hole in the triangular area. "Write" price numbers with squeezable jelly or cheese spread, or cut cheese slices, balogna, etc. into number shapes.

☆ ☆ ☆

Set up snack as if you were going to a little restaurant as part of a long day of shopping. Treat yourself to ice-cream cones or frozen yogurt and put your feet up!

Videos

Winnie the Pooh—Wind Some, Lose Some ("How Much is that Rabbit in the Window?")

Art/Craft Materials

white paper
markers
magazines & catalogs
posterboard
paper hole punch
paper bags of different sizes,
  with one side plain for coloring
yarn or embroidery thread
oatmeal or cornmeal cannister
2 toilet paper tubes
margarine tub
construction paper
pipe cleaner

Art/Craft Directions

Signs, Price Tags, and Bags

1) Cut paper or posterboard into fancy shapes (or the shape of whatever you're "selling.") Decorate with the shop's name. Hang signs up on doors in the house.

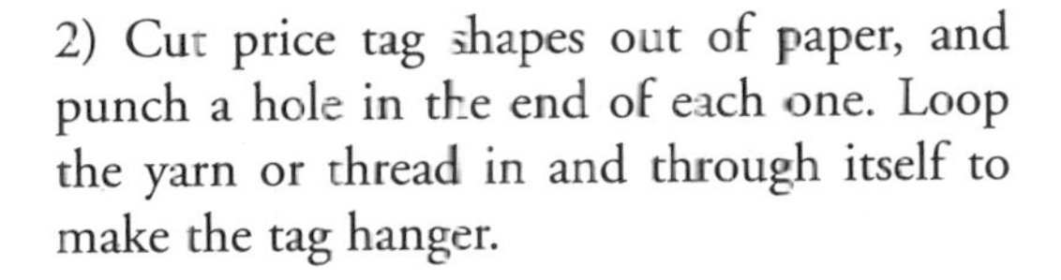

2) Cut price tag shapes out of paper, and punch a hole in the end of each one. Loop the yarn or thread in and through itself to make the tag hanger.

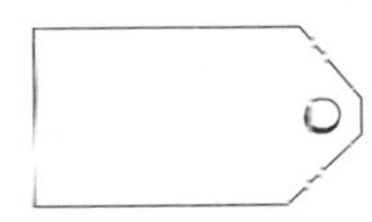

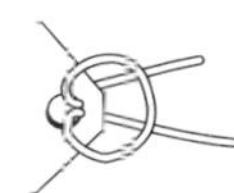

3) For shopping bags, use markers, stickers, and cut-out pictures from catalogs to decorate the blank side. Add yarn handles if you'd like.

For a Little Something Extra...

Sort out old toys and games, and set up a "swapping" store instead of a garage sale.

☆ ☆ ☆

Plan a trip to a thrift shop, giving a little spending money to each child.

Piggy Bank

1) With the lid taped on, cover an oatmeal or cornmeal container with pink construction paper. Cut out ear shapes and glue them to one end. Draw on a face.

2) Curl a pipe cleaner to make a tail, and tape this to the back end. Cut a wide slot in the back. (This is very hard to do with just scissors; you may want to leave this for later, and have an adult use a craft knife safely away from the children).

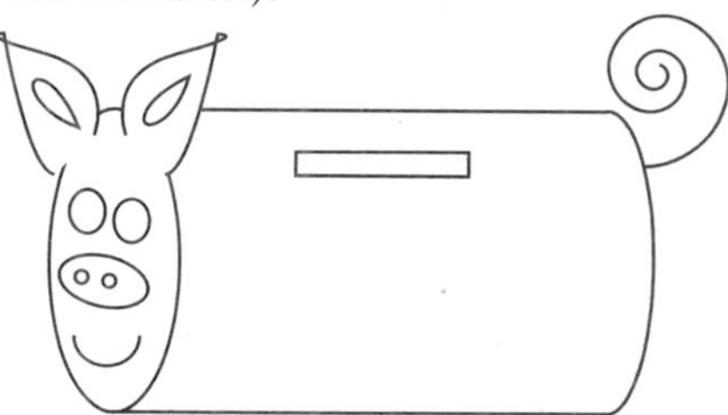

3) Cut 2 toilet paper tubes in half on a slant. They will not fit perfectly at first, but you can trim them a bit to fit better. A few snips into the tube will help, too.

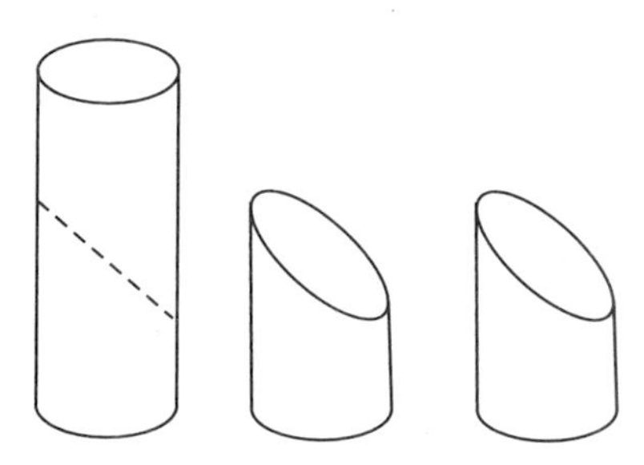

4) Flatten the legs slightly to help them fit against the curve of the can, then tape them in place against the sides and bottom.

Snow

Art/Craft

- For an easy snowman, draw three sizes of circles, one above the other, on a sheet of blue construction paper. Glue on white cotton balls to fill the circles. Add a black paper hat, eyes, mouth, and orange nose. A bit of yarn or ribbon will make a good scarf (see directions).
- Cut out classic white or colored snowflakes. It's not any harder to make a true six-pointed snowflake than it is to make a four-sided one. Tissue wrapping paper can be easier to use than plain paper, for cutting through all the folded thicknesses (see directions).
- White chalk on blue paper makes easy snowy pictures.
- Make simple stand-up snowmen by taping together white plastic laundry scoops with snipped-off handles. Stack three sets, then decorate with markers, paper, or stickers. An empty black plastic film cannister, with a circle of black paper underneath, makes a good top hat (see directions).

Indoors

- Gather in the kitchen to make snowmen: mix Ivory powdered soap with a little water, and shape it into balls and snowpeople. Arrange them on a plate (perhaps sitting on a ring of paper mittens) for a table decoration.
- If you have a plastic "saucer" sled, take turns pulling the children around the house on it.
- Dress up stuffed animals in hats, mittens, and scarves.
- Let younger children play a matching game with six or more pairs of mittens and gloves. Spread them out on the floor and have them take turns picking out the pairs.
- If you have lots of empty white baby-wipe boxes, stack them up to make an indoor "snow" fort.

Music

"Let it Snow, Let it Snow, Let it Snow"
"Frosty the Snowman"

Hints for Your Own Situation...

Let younger children draw a "squiggly" design on the folded snowflake paper for you to cut out. Older children can cut their own.

☆ ☆ ☆

For older children, build an igloo by using canned frosting to "glue" tiny marshmallows together; shape it easily by using an upside-down plastic bowl underneath for support until it all hardens. See if you can make a tunnel entrance over part of a toilet-paper roll (see directions).

☆ ☆ ☆

On a hot day, try guessing which of a number of things will melt first and last: ice cubes, a spoonful of ice cream, a crayon, a piece of chocolate, the frosting on a cookie, etc.

Snack-time

Make crispy rice cereal/melted marshmallow "snowballs."

☆ ☆ ☆

Serve Hostess Sno-Ball snack cakes.

☆ ☆ ☆

Mix up instant mashed potatos. Scoop a ball with an ice-cream scoop. Push in two peas for eyes and a row of peas for a smile (or use bits of a preferred vegetable). Use a sliver of carrot for a nose, and stick on a broccoli floweret for a top hat.

Outdoors

- If you actually have snow, pack some pans or plastic plates, and smooth the top with the back of a big spoon. Take felt-tip markers and draw pictures on the smooth surfaces; if you want, put the pans in the freezer for later.
- No snow? With a little effort, you can still pull children over the ground on plastic saucer sleds!
- Spread a thin layer of snow or leaves on the ground; lie down and move your arms and legs to make an "angel" appear.
- Move as if you were skating.
- In hot weather (not cold—your fingers could stick), use ice cubes like wooden blocks to make buildings.

Books

How to Make a Paper Snowflake by Angelina Winters (ref.)
(Patterson Printing, Benton Harbor MI 1990) (6+)
F-Freezing ABC by Posy Simmonds
(Alfred A. Knopf 1995) (4/6)
Snowballs by Lois Ehlert
(Harcourt Brace & Co. 1995) (2/3)
White Snow, Bright Snow by Alvin Tresselt
(Mulberry Books 1947/1988) (2/3)
Henry and Mudge and the Sparkle Days by Cynthia Rylant
(Bradbury/Macmillan 1988) (4/6)
A Winter Day by Douglas Florian
(Scholastic/William Morrow 1987) (2/3)
The Mitten by Jan Brett
(Scholastic/G.P.Putnam's Sons 1989) (4/6)
Snow by Roy McKie and P.D. Eastman
(Random House 1962) (2/3)
Jolly Snow by Jane Hissey
(Philomel Books 1991) (4/6)
Footprints in the Snow by Cynthia Benjamin
(Cartwheel/Scholastic 1994) (2/3)

Videos

The Snowman; Frosty the Snowman
Richard Scarry's The Snowstorm
Winter Tales (Little Bear/Maurice Sendak)*

Art/Craft Materials

blue construction paper
white cotton balls
Tacky glue, scissors
black, orange paper
yarn scraps
white paper
6 white plastic laundry detergent scoops
empty black film canister
black permanent marker (optional)
white frosting
tiny marshmallows
small bowl, toilet paper tube

Art/Craft Directions

Snowman Picture

1) Draw 3 circles, in 3 sizes one on top of each other, on a piece of blue paper. Leave enough space at the top to draw a hat. Glue on white cotton balls to fill in the circles.

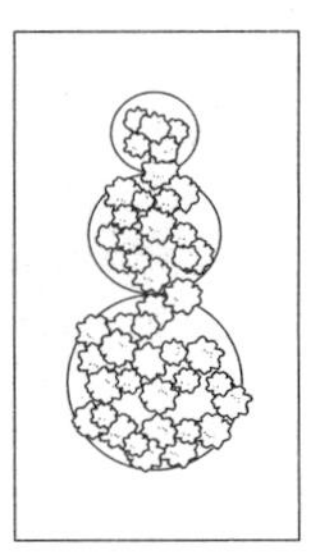

2) Cut and glue bits of black paper for a hat, eyes, and buttons, and a piece of orange paper for a scarf. Use any other scraps for arms, trees, and other parts of your picture.

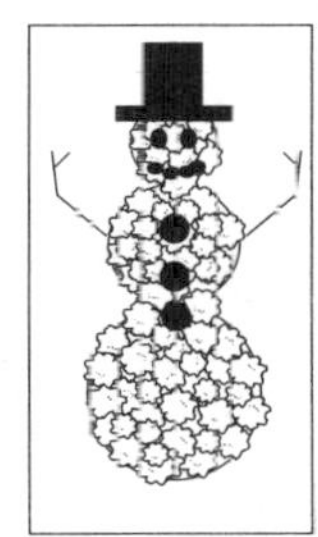

For a Little Something Extra...

Guess where in the world it might be snowing right now. Tell children that summer in your country may be winter somewhere else. Check your answers on a weather map, then eat some ice cream to get in the mood.

☆ ☆ ☆

Cut scrap paper into random pieces about 2" square. Let everyone throw it up in the air to make your own snow. Tape spoons to pieces of cardboard to "shovel" it up later.

Six-Pointed Snowflake

1) Cut a piece of white paper or tissue into a square (9" is fine). Fold it on the diagonal into a triangle, then fold the triangle into wedge-shaped thirds.

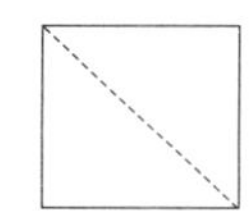

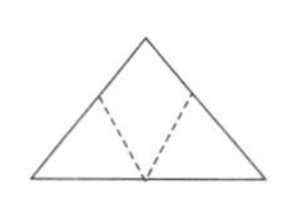

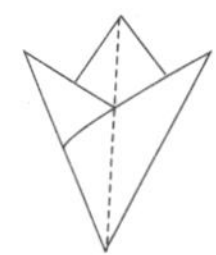

2) Fold this shape in half, and trim off the top edge as shown. Cut a snowflake pattern on all edges. Unfold and enjoy!

Stand-Up Snowman

1) Cut the handle off of 6 white laundry scoops, including the bump at the base of the handle (use sturdy scissors). Glue them edge to edge, in pairs.

2) Glue the 3 sets in a stack. Cut a 3" diameter paper circle out of black paper and glue it on the top scoop. Glue the empty film canister upside down on top of the circle. Decorate the front of the snowman with paper nose, and scarf. You can draw on the eyes, mouth, and buttons with a permanent marker.

Marshmallow Igloo

1) Turn a small bowl (with no rim) upside down on a plate. Use white frosting to stick tiny marshmallows all over the bowl and to each other.

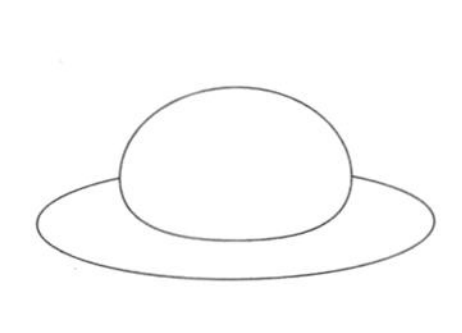

2) Cut a toilet paper tube in half, then in half again lengthwise. Push one of these pieces against one side of the igloo, and cover it with more frosting and marshmallows.

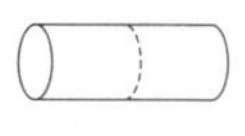

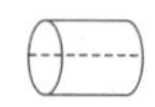

Sound

Art/Craft

- Make a "noisy" collage picture. Go through old catalogs, newspaper advertisements, and magazines, looking for things that make noise (car, truck, airplane, train, baby crying, computer keyboard, kitten lapping milk, knitting-kneedles clicking, sewing machine whirring, telephone ringing, etc.) Cut them out and glue on paper.
- Roll a piece of posterboard into a megaphone. Make several of different lengths, and vary how tightly they are rolled. Listen to which ones make louder sounds (see directions).
- Make a necklace that makes good "clacky" sounds when you dance. Ahead of time, color long pasta shapes in bowls of colored water. String them together with yarn to make necklaces and bracelets (see directions).

Indoors

- Ahead of time, gather different items that can make noises (a rattle, keys to jingle, paper to crumple or rip, small bells, a wind-up clock that ticks, a bottle with a lid that snaps open and shut, two wooden blocks you can clap together, a zipper you can pull up and down, etc.) Stand behind a big chair, have one child come behind, and hand her the item. Have her make the noise. The other children can guess what it is, then take their turn.
- Collect six or more of the same bottles (soda or water bottles). Fill them with varying amounts of water. Take turns blowing across the tops to make different notes.
- Take turns clapping wooden blocks together in some pattern (e.g., slow slow fast fast fast) and have others copy it.
- Teach some silly songs, especially ones with sound effects like "She'll Be Coming Round the Mountain."

Music

What's That Sound? (Discovery Toys)*
Rythms on Parade (Hap Palmer)*

Hints for Your Own Situation…

If you're sure children are old enough not to put rice, popcorn kernels, or dry beans in their mouths, make noise shakers with paper plates. Fold plate in half, staple closely around the edges, filling it with beans just before stapling shut. Decorate it with markers, crayons, bits of ribbon or crepe paper taped or stapled to hang from edges (like a tambourine) (see directions).

Snack-time

For older children, pop popcorn in the microwave. Guess when the first kernel will pop, and listen until it's all done.

☆ ☆ ☆

Serve "noisy" food: crunchy carrots or apples, snappy crackers or gingersnaps, a "crackling" bowl of crispy rice cereal with milk, and slurpy slices of watermelon.

☆ ☆ ☆

What can you eat perfectly quietly? Try a banana, some yogurt, an ice-cream cone, or a slice of cheese.

Outdoors

- Look for ways you can make different kinds of sounds outside: tapping a stick on a log or rock, blowing on a blade of grass for a buzzing sound, clicking a stick along a picket fence, brushing against a wind chime, drumming your hands on a trashcan lid, etc.
- Sit very quietly outside and listen to the sounds around you. Can you hear a bird? What direction is the sound coming from? Can you hear a lawn-mower, leaf-blower, dump-truck, fire-engine siren, other children, a dog barking, a jet airplane, a helicopter, a fly, or a bumblebee?

Books

Mrs. Merriwether's Musical Cat by Carol Purdy
(G.P.Putnam's Sons 1994) (4/6)
Indoor Noisy Book by Margaret Wise Brown
(Harper & Row 1942; entire series) (2/3)
Richard Scarry's Splish-Splash Sounds by Richard Scarry
(Western/Golden Books 1986) (4/6)
The Magic Schoolbus in the Haunted Museum by Joanna Cole
(Scholastic 1995) (4/6)
Chicka Chicka Boom Boom by Bill Martin and John Archambault
(Simon & Schuster 1989) (2/3)
The Listening Walk by Paul Showers
(Harper Collins 1991) (2/3)
City Sounds by Rebecca Emberley
(Little Brown & Co. 1989) (2/3)
I Hear by Rachel Isadora
(Greenwillow 1985) (2/3)
Jungle Sounds by Rebecca Emberley
(Little Brown & Co.1989) (2/3)
Night Noises by Mem Fox
(Trumpet/Harcourt Brace Jovanovich 1992) (4/6)

Videos

Household Marching Band;* Basil Hears a Noise (Jim Henson)*

The Magic Schoolbus in the Haunted Museum
Wee Sing Marvelous Musical Mansion*

Art/Craft Materials

sheets of paper or posterboard
tape, stapler, scissors
pasta and macaroni tubes
bowls for water
food coloring
newspapers
yarn or string
paper plates
popcorn kernels or dry beans
crepe-paper streamers

Art/Craft Directions

Megaphone

1) Cut paper or posterboard into an arc shape. Make three or four different ones, using different lengths and widths of the arcs. Use pot lids or records to help you make the circles.

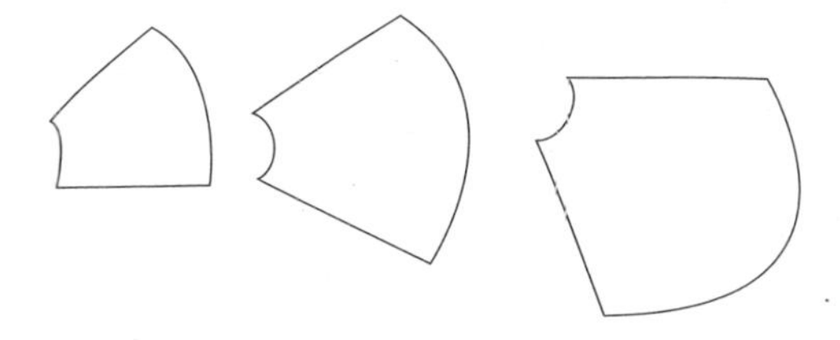

2) Curl up the megaphones and tape the straight edges together. Try them out to see if one sounds louder than the other; does a posterboard megaphone sound different than one of the same size made just out of paper?

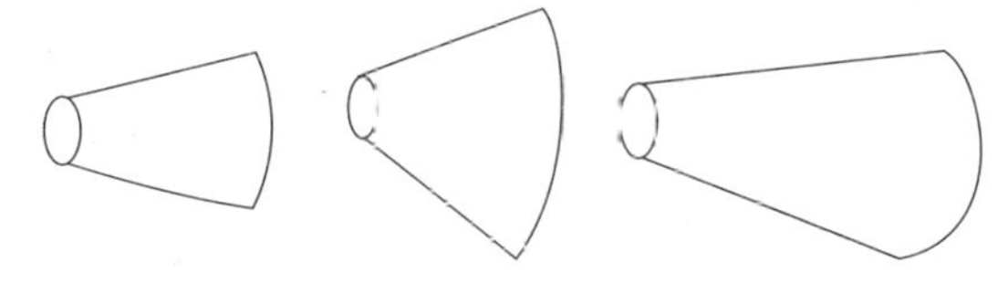

"Loud" Macaroni Necklace

1) Put 3 tablespoons of water and a few drops of food coloring in each bowl. Fill bowl with about ½ cup of pasta. Stir the pasta until it is all the desired color (about 3 minutes).

2) Use slotted spoon to scoop pasta onto newspapers. Let dry, then string into necklaces and bracelets with yarn or string.

Noise Shakers

1) Decorate the undersides of 2 paper plates.

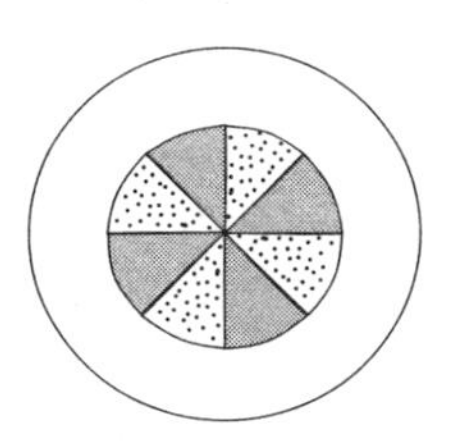

2) Staple the plates together, edge to edge, almost all the way around. Leave about a 2" opening. Fill the shaker with ½ cup of popcorn kernels or dry beans.

3) Staple the opening shut. Cut 6" lengths of crepe-paper streamers and staple them around the edges of the shaker.

4) Hold the shaker by the middle with the thumb and fingers. Shake, shake shake!

For a Little Something Extra...

Look in your newspaper to find out when there will be a community children's concert, perhaps at a park, school auditorium, or at the library. Outdoor events are extra fun, as you can usually get up to jump, dance, clap, and sing along!

Surprises!

Art/Craft

- Make top hats out of black construction paper (see directions).
- Make a "presto!" wand out of craft ribbon or crepe paper wrapped and glued around a dowel, unsharpened pencil, or rolled up newspaper (see directions).
- Use Crayola ColorOvers to draw "surprise" pictures—the colors will change as you first use the "under" markers then draw on top using the "over" markers.
- Buy classic "magic slates" (usually found with coloring books): even the youngest are amazed when pictures appear and disappear!

Indoors

- Gather together any stuffed or plastic rabbits, decks of cards, silk flowers (watch out for stems), and large handkerchiefs. Set up a table with a tablecloth and spread out the items, including an upside-down hat. Have children take turns being a "master of surprise" by covering an item with a handkerchief, pulling the item away from the back and dropping it under the table; make up silly words (Presto! Alacazam! Zim, Zam, Zoom!)
- Take a colorful beach towel, spread it on the floor, and declare it to be a flying carpet for the day. Use it as a sitting spot for reading your books today, as they take you to faraway, exciting places.
- Make a string or piece of yarn pick up an ice cube: loop the string over the ice cube, then sprinkle the top with salt. Say, "Hocus Pocus, loop the loop" and pull up the cube by the string (the salt makes the string stick frozen onto the cube).

Music

Sillytime Magic and Dancin' Magic (Joanie Bartels)*; Abracadabra (Joe Scruggs)*

Outdoors

- Take a plastic glass and fill it half-way with water. Put a square of cardboard on top of it, hold it in place, then turn the glass upside down. Let go of the cardboard—it will stay in place! (The air pressure below holds it up.)

Hints for Your Own Situation…

Dress up as a master of surprises: a white shirt, black pants, and suspenders are great (along with your new top hat), but even just a cape will do. Pin a towel, pillow case, or length of knit material either loosely around your neck, or just to each shoulder.

☆ ☆ ☆

Make a paper book cover (see Library Crafts), and decorate it with shiny stars. Put it over any book—presto, your book of amazing instructions (no peeking)!

☆ ☆ ☆

Write an invisible message on paper with a wax candle (white on white, pink on pink, etc.). Make it suddenly appear using a pencil (see directions)!

Snack-time

Make cupcakes or muffins with hidden messages inside (ahead of time, write funny notes on small pieces of paper, wrap them in a square of waxed paper, and put the note in the bottom of each cupcake paper before filling it with batter).

☆ ☆ ☆

Have everyone help make a bowl of Jello. The light-colored powder suddenly changes color when a grown-up pours in the hot water.

- Turn three identical cups upside down; hide a bottle cap under one, and slide them around; where is the cap?
- Buy some sunprint paper (from Edmund Scientific—see Catalog section). Take one sheet at a time (perhaps cut it into four pieces). Choose an item from outdoors (a leaf, a flower, a seed pod, a rock, even a bubble blower) and set it on the paper in the sun. Following the timing suggestions that come with the paper, see the amazing picture appear!

Books

Wizard and Wart by Janice Lee Smith
(Harper Collins Publishers 1994) (4/6)
Mixed-Up Magic by Joanna Cole
(Hastings House 1987) (4/6)
Princess Lullaby and the Magic Word by Martine Osborne
(Random House/Derrydale 1994) (4/6)
Zorah's Magic Carpet by Stefan Czernecki
(Hyperion 1995) (4/6)
The Wizard, the Fairy, and the Magic Chicken by Helen Lester
(Houghton Mifflin 1983) (4/6)
The Magic House by Robyn Harbert Eversole
(Orchard Books 1992) (4/6)
Snuggle Piggy and the Magic Blanket by Michele Stepto
(Dutton/Unicorn 1987) (2/3)
Molly's Magic Carpet by Emma Fischel
(Usborne/EDC 1996) (4/6)
Strega Nona's Magic Lessons by Tomie de Paola
(Scholastic/Harcourt Brace 1993) (4/6)
Tye May and the Magic Brush by Molly Garrett Bang
(Greenwillow 1981) (4/6)

Videos

The Sword in the Stone (Disney)
Aladdin (Disney)

Art/Craft Materials

black construction paper or posterboard
black poster paint
red ribbon (about ½" wide, 2 ft. long)
scissors, tape
white paper
paper towel tube, or a 12" length of a dowel
white candle (unlit)
pencil

Art/Craft Directions

Master of Surprises Top Hat

1) Cut a 12" diameter circle from the black paper or posterboard. Carefully cut an oval (about 5" x 7") from the center, and save it for later.

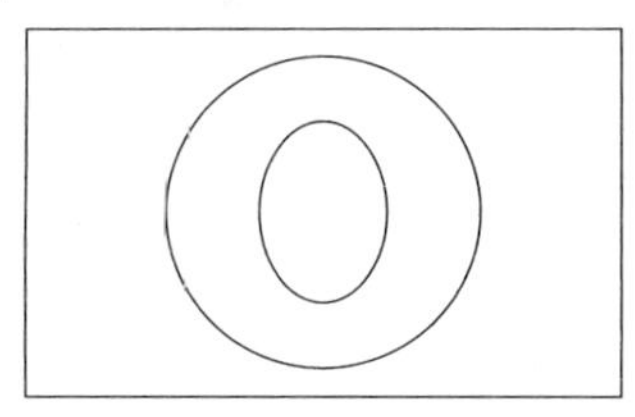

2) Cut a rectangle of black paper, 10" high by 17" wide (or as wide as the child's head measurement plus 1").

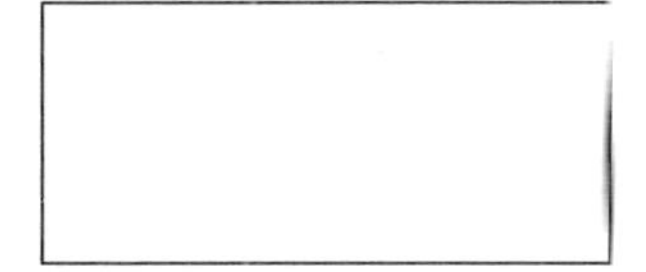

3) Roll the rectangle into the oval until it fits snugly. Tape the overlapped edges of the rectangle, forming a tube.

4) Slide the tube all the way into the oval, stopping it just at the edge. Tape it to the brim all around. Tape the saved oval to the top of the tube.

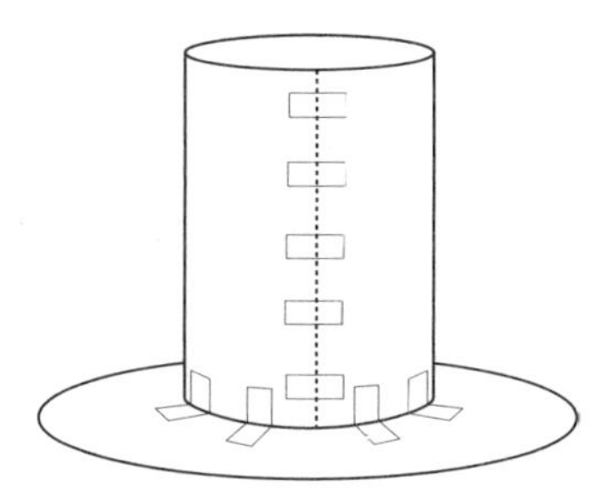

For a Little Something Extra...

Plan ahead to buy some new small toy or craft supply. Wrap it in a small box, then put that box in a bigger one and wrap it again. Keep putting the box into a larger box and wrapping it. Then let the children take turns unwrapping one layer at a time. They will start to wonder when it will ever end, and will be very surprised by the result!

Presto! Wand

1) With younger children (who may try to "bop" each other), make the wand out of a paper towel tube. Older children can work with a section of a wooden dowel.

2) Paint the tube or the dowel black, and let it dry.

3) Wrap a length of ½" red ribbon around the wand, leaving about a ½" wide gap between turns. Adjust the tightness of the wrap until the ribbon lays smoothly, then glue it all in place.

4) Cut 2 strips of white paper about 1"wide and 2" to 3" long. Wrap and glue one strip around each end of the wand.

Secret Message

1) Using a white candle on white paper, a red candle on red paper, etc., write child's name, or a message.

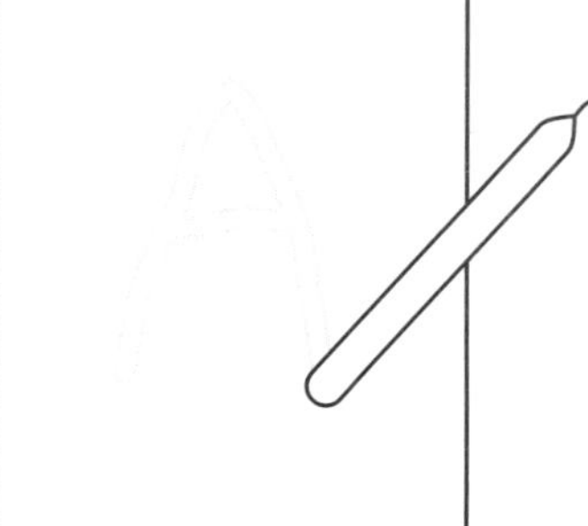

2) Using the side of the pencil, color over the waxed area with broad, dark strokes. The hidden message will suddenly appear!

Theater/Movies

Art/Craft

- Pick favorite stories to act out, depending on the number of children (although they can play many roles). Try Goldilocks and the Three Bears, Jack and the Beanstalk, Red Riding Hood, the Three Little Pigs, etc. Make masks out of construction paper (animal characters are really fun) and use dress-up clothes (see directions).
- Draw and cut out tickets for your production.
- For each child, draw a star shape on cardboard and cover it with foil (or use metallic posterboard). Write their name on a piece of paper to fit the star, and tape it in the center. Tape the stars to their bedroom doors, for their "movie star dressing-rooms" (see directions).
- On large paper rolls, make scenery to go with the plays you've chosen to act out. You may want to draw large trees, a house, etc., for the children to color in themselves.

Indoors

- Set up a theater, with rows of chairs and a stage area. If you can arrange a sheet as a curtain over a length of rope, all the better. Or, set up a puppet theater, using a simple box turned on its side, or a stove/refrigerator box with an opening cut in the front. Decorate with paper or markers.
- Make a TV box, similar to the puppet stage. Have one or two children inside it, then let someone sit in front with a remote control. The viewer says, "I want to watch...," and names a show or videotape they all know. The actors on TV then act out the request, saying well-known lines or singing songs. Take turns.
- Use outfits, makeup, sunglasses to be movie/rock stars.
- Put on music they all know, grab plastic spoons, ice-cream cones (or toy microphones), and sing along.

Music

A Child's Celebration of Showtunes*
A Child's Celebration of Broadway*

Hints for Your Own Situation...

Make movie cameras out of cardboard shoe boxes, a toilet paper tube, and paper plates. Cover them with black paper (see directions). Pretend to "crank away."

☆ ☆ ☆

Have everyone sing favorite songs, together and separately, and record them on a tape player. Listen to how different you sound when you play them back.

☆ ☆ ☆

Make star cutouts to tape over real sunglasses (see directions).

Outdoors

- Are there steps you could use as a stage? Could you tie a rope between some poles or a tree, and throw a tablecloth over it as the curtain? If not, just set up a row of chairs for the audience. Take turns doing an outdoor "talent" show. Let each child do what they want—sing, dance, do somersaults, throw a ball up and catch it, etc.
- Pretend one of you has a movie camera (or use the one you made) and another has a microphone. "Interview" each other about how they liked a movie, what they saw on a trip, or ask them what their favorite cereal is, etc.

Snack-time

Older children could have microwaved popcorn.

☆ ☆ ☆

Decorate star-shaped cookies with canned white frosting, then use colored icing to write each "movie star's" name on them.

☆ ☆ ☆

Serve vanilla/ chocolate ice-cream sandwiches. Draw lines on them with whipped cream, and pretend they are movie "take" blackboards. (Draw a picture to show children what they really are, and use two wooden blocks to make the sound.)

Books

On Stage & Backstage by Ann Hayes
(Harcourt Brace & Co. 1997) (4/6)

Albert's Play by Leslie Tryon
(Antheneum 1992) (4/6)

Angelina on Stage by Katharine Holabird
(Scholastic 1994) (4/6)

Angelina Ice Skates by Katharine Holabird
(Trumpet/Bantam 1993) (4/6)

Opening Night by Rachel Isadora
(Greenwillow 1984) (4/6)

The Berenstain Bears Get Stage Fright by Stan and Jan Berenstain
(Random House 1986) (4/6)

Penny Goes to the Movies by Harriet Ziefert
(Puffin Penguin 1990) (2/3)

Peeping Beauty by Mary Jane Auch
(Holiday House 1993) (4/6)

Lights! Camera! Action! by Gail Gibbons
(Crowell 1985) (4/6)

The Bionic Bunny Show by Marc Brown & Laurene Krasny Brown
(Little, Brown and Co. 1984) (4/6)

Videos

Muppet Masterpiece Theater
Richard Scarry's Best Learning Songs Video Ever!
Sing Yourself Sillier at the Movies (Sesame Street)

Art/Craft Materials

construction paper
yarn scraps
markers, hole punch
scissors, tape
white posterboard
small shoebox
paper plates, foil
toilet paper tube
brass fasteners (optional)
gold posterboard
glasses

Art/Craft Directions

Story Masks

1) Pick your favorite character from a book, and use the pictures to help you draw a half-mask on posterboard. For example, Red Riding could show the red hood, the curly hair, and big eye-lashes.

2) Color in the mask, and cut around the outside. Cut out the eyeholes. Punch holes on sides, and knot lengths of yarn into both of them to make ties.

Star Dressing Room Sign

1) Cut a big star shape (12" to 18" across) from posterboard. Cover it with foil. Print the child's name on a piece of white paper, and tape it to the front of the star.

2) Hang the sign on the child's bedroom door.

For a Little Something Extra...

Go to a community or high school play.

☆ ☆ ☆

If you have a video camera, tape the day's "performances."

Movie Camera

1) Cover a shoebox with black paper. Cover a toilet paper tube with foil. Cut a hole in one end of the shoebox (a rough square will work), large enough to slide the toilet paper tube inside about an inch. Tape it to the box from the inside.

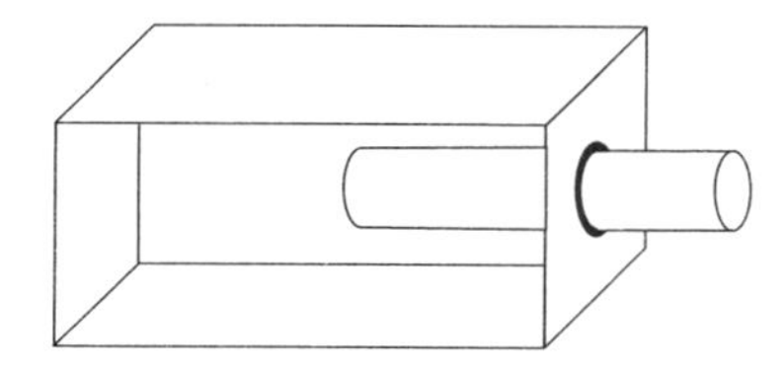

2) Depending on the size of the paper plates and the shoebox, cut the plates to circles that will fit side by side, with a little room to spare, on the side of the box. Use brass fasteners to attach them in the centers or just glue them on. Use black marker to make the plates look like film reels.

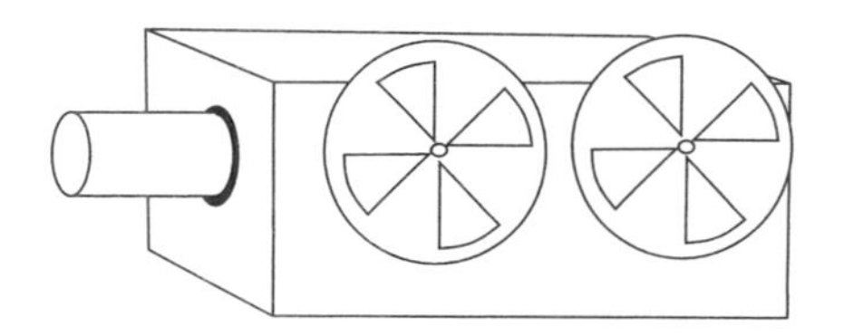

Star Glasses

1) Take any pair of glasses—real, pretend, or sunglasses—and lightly trace around the fronts on the back side of gold posterboard, making two ovals.

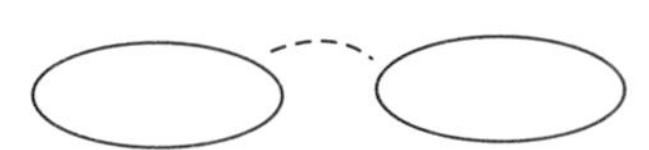

2) On top of each oval, draw a star outline roughly to fit (star cookie cutters of different sizes give you lots of choices to trace), then draw another one about ¼" larger, just outside the first one. Cut on the inside edge and the outside edge. Lightly tape both stars over the fronts of the real frames.

Trains

Art/Craft

- Collect shoe boxes, oatmeal containers, toilet paper tubes, construction paper, pint cartons from heavy cream, milk jug lids, and lids from chip cans. Cover boxes with construction paper (leave some open for cargo, and have some closed as box cars), decorate, and assemble as a train. A small train can be a table decoration, while a large one can carry stuffed animals (see directions).
- Collect different sizes and shapes of empty plastic bottles. Practice blowing across the tops of them to make different train whistle sounds.

Indoors

- Set up chairs as seats on a train, or line up a series of big boxes (moving boxes, book boxes, or copy paper boxes with lids that are very strong). Put stuffed animals on top, and have the children sit on them too. Take turns with one child as engineer, one as conductor, one who shovels the coal, etc. Will the train take you over mountains, by the sea, across fields of wheat or flowers? What do you see?
- If you have a real train set, put it together and take turns being the engineer.
- Use masking tape on carpet to lay out "tracks" big enough to move your boxes along. Carry different cargo.
- Line up, holding onto the waist of the child in front of you. Take turns letting the first person be the leader, and "choo! choo!" your way all around the house, first slowly, then quickly, then slowing down again. Sing away!

Music

Cars, Trucks & Trains (Jane Murphy)*
"I've Been Working on the Railroad"
Choo Choo Boogaloo (Buckwheat Zydeco)*
Come Ride Along With Me (James Coffey)*

Hints for Your Own Situation...

Have everyone wear "bib" overalls (striped, if they have them!)

☆ ☆ ☆

Make a fancier engineer's cap from posterboard (blue or white) and draw white or blue lines all over it (see directions).

"Do the Locomotion"
Songs for Our Kids (SongTrain)*

Outdoors

- Connect a number of sturdy, empty boxes with rope through cut-out holes. Tie the first one to a tricycle, and fill the boxes with bears or other cargo. Take turns pulling them around the driveway.
- Play Simon Says, but call it Conductor Says.
- Have one child be the Station Master in charge of leading a game of Red Light, Green Light while the others are trains trying to come into the station. Take turns.

Books

The Little Engine That Could by Watty Piper
(Platt & Munk/Grosset & Dunlap 1990) (2/3)
Meet Thomas the Tank Engine and His Friends (based on Rev. W. Awdry series)
(Random House Inc. 1989) (4/6)
Richard Scarry's Trains by Richard Scarry
(Golden Books 1992) (2/3)
The Train by David McPhail
(Little Brown & Co. 1977) (4/6)
The Train Ride by June Crebbin
(Candlewick Press 1995) (2/3)
All Aboard ABC by Doug Magee and Robert Newman
(Cobblehill/Dutton 1990) (4/6)
Freight Train by Donald Crews
(Greenwillow Press 1978) (2/3)
Train Song by Diane Siebert
(Harper Collins 1981) (4/6)
Trains: A First Discovery Book
(Scholastic 1998) (4/6)
The Little Red Caboose by Marian Potter
(Golden/Western 1953) (2/3)

Snack-time

Set up a "dining car" with a little table, a tablecloth, a vase of silk flowers, a tiny lamp, small chairs, etc.

☆ ☆ ☆

Make railroad cars out of Twinkies: line them up and put on "wheels" of gumdrop slices or Ritz Bits with a bit of frosting. The engine could be real (from a toy set). Or, take one entire package of graham crackers, held together lightly with frosting and set on its side. Use Oreos for wheels and half a Twinkie for the engineer's cabin.

☆ ☆ ☆

Make a smaller train out of cut-up chunks of cantelope or water-melon. Strawberries cut width-wise can be wheels.

Videos

Thomas the Tank Engine series
Railroaders: What Do You Want to be When You Grow Up?*
I Love Toy Trains #1-5 (Tom McComas)*
The Wee Sing Train*
The Little Engine That Could

Art/Craft Materials

small shoe boxes, any other boxes
baby wipe boxes
toilet paper tubes
1 quart juice or milk carton
empty 13 ounce coffee can (or similar can)
empty film cannister
copy paper boxes (3 or 4, with lids)
½ gallon juice carton
3 pound coffee can (or similar)
white or blue posterboard
scissors, tape, Tacky glue

Art/Craft Directions

Table-Top Train

1) Cover small shoe boxes, check boxes, etc., with construction paper. Or, just tape paper decorations or stickers on the sides of plastic baby wipe boxes.

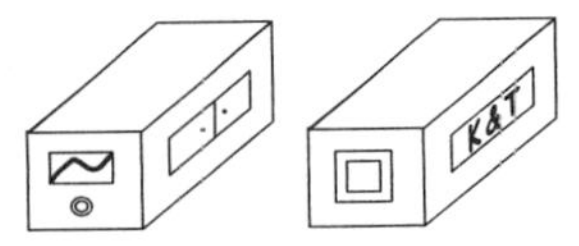

2) Glue and tape 2 toilet paper tubes to the bottom of each box (cut them to shorten them, if the tubes are longer than the box is wide). From the sides, these will look like wheels.

For a Little Something Extra...

Call Amtrak Passenger Railway Service (800) 872-7245 to ask for brochures for some special trips you might want to take.

☆ ☆ ☆

Contact the railroad's Operation LifeSaver for free railroad safety coloring books and a bookmark. Call (800) 537-6224 or check out addresses online: www.oli.org.

3) Cut square holes out of the upper sides of the 1 qt. juice carton, to be the engineer's cab. Cut off the peaked top of the carton. Cover the sides with construction paper.

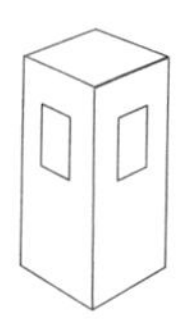

4) Cover the coffee can with construction paper. Tape or glue the juice carton to one end, and glue 2 or more toilet paper tubes along the bottom for wheels. Tape a film canister on top.

5) Connect the engine to the other cars with strips of paper, ribbon or yarn, taping them end to end. Use markers to add details (look at one of the story books for ideas).

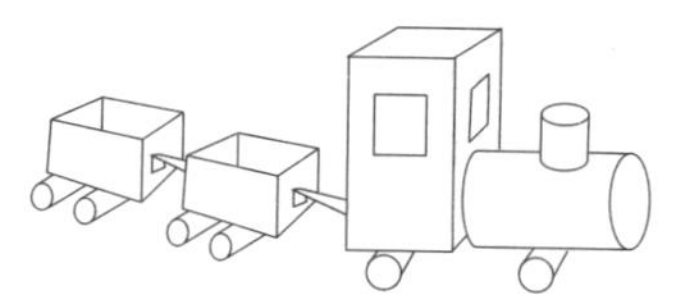

Floor Train

Using big copy paper boxes, covered with wrapping paper, build a large train. Cut cardboard wheels to tape to the sides. Use a ½ gal. juice carton and 3 lb. coffee can to make the same style engine as above. You can either fill the railroad cars with stuffed animals, and take them for a ride, or put the lids back on the boxes and "ride" them yourselves; they'll last at least the day!

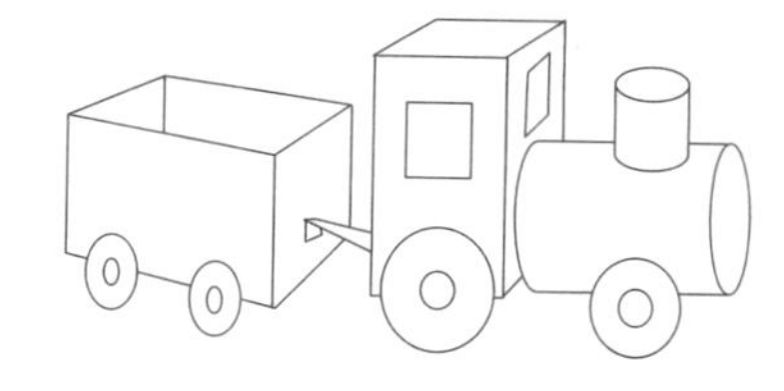

Engineer's Cap

1) Cut a 3" wide strip of posterboard. Bend it into a band to fit the child's head. Tape the edges together. Trace the circle formed by the band, onto another section of posterboard. Cut it out and tape it on top of the band.

2) Cut a brim from the scrap remaining next to the cut-out circle, and tape it in front. Draw on stripes (white on blue, or blue on white).

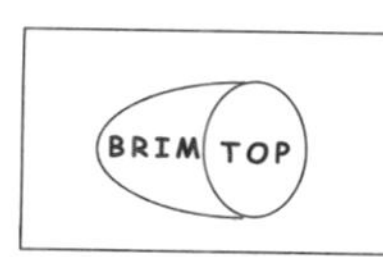

Western Days

Art/Craft

- Make a fringed vest from a brown grocery bag by cutting arm and neck holes and a front opening. Snip a fringe. Also, three lunch bags together make leggings. Decorate with markers, paints, or stickers (see directions).
- Make a small-scale teepee with straws and brown paper. Decorate first with symbols from a book on Native Americans, or with some you've made up.
- Make feathered head bands with strips of construction paper and colored, cut-out feathers (see directions).
- Make a paper "saddle" to wear when you decide to be the horse; give bean-bag animals a ride (see directions).
- Create your own "brand" for labeling your toys, books, etc. Combine the initials in your name or nickname, and turn them upsidedown or sideways until you get an interesting look, then copy it to "claim" your property.

Indoors

- Do you have any toy horses or ponies and building blocks? Set up a fort with the blocks and build stables for the ponies. Will they be riding the ranges today, or just exploring some meadows and hills?
- Buy inexpensive bandanas and see how many ways you can wear them: as a neckerchief, as a headband, around a cowboy hat, or just stuck in a pocket (handy for holding treasures). Wear them tied over plaid shirts and jeans.
- Real hobby horses are fun, but a toy broomstick can work too. Cut out and tape a horsehead to the top of the stick.
- Move like a horse: trot, gallop, run to music. Can you trot on all fours? How and what would you eat? Wear the saddle you made for yourself.

Music

"William Tell Overture" (Rossini—The Lone Ranger)
Horse Sense for Kids and Other People;* "Buffalo Gals"

Hints for Your Own Situation...

Older children can make a slide-tie to wear with their vests. Take a clean lid from a juice can or baking powder, and use it to trace a circle on a piece of colored paper. Decorate the paper with scraps of colored paper, markers, stickers, or yarn. Tape the circle to one side of the lid. Cut two one-inch pieces from a plastic straw. Tape them side-by-side, half an inch apart, on the other side of the lid. Thread a shoelace, yarn (with ends taped), or thin ribbon up through one straw and down through the other. Pull the slide wide open to get it over your head, then slide it up to your collar to wear it.

Outdoors

- Hula hoops make a decent substitute for rope if you want one child to be the "horse" and one to be the "rider." The horse puts the hoop around his waist, and the rider holds on from behind. Have the rider tell the horse to "giddy up," "whoa," and go left or right around the yard. Be sure to have everyone take turns in each role.
- On a hot day, use different shapes and styles of water squirters. Take aim at a tree, or a pie-plate you've hung from a tree limb. Draw, then squirt!
- Tie together three long poles as the frame for a tepee (or build a tepee around a narrow tree). Wrap an old sheet around it, fixed with clothes pins. Read or eat inside it.

Books

Matthew the Cowboy by Ruth Hooker
(Albert Whitman & Co. 1990) (4/6)

Cowboy Country by Ann Herbert Scott
(Clarion 1993) (4/6)

Armadillo Rodeo by Jan Brett
(G.P.Putnam's Sons 1995) (4/6)

Cowboy Baby by Sue Heap
(Candlewick Press 1998) (2/3)

My Little House ABC by Laura Ingalls Wilder
(Harper Collins 1997) (4/6)

Going West by Jean Van Leeuwen
(Dial 1992) (4/6)

Someday Rider by Ann Herbert Scott
(Clarion/Houghton Mifflin 1989) (4/6)

Jalapeno Hal by Jo Harper
(Four Winds Press 1993) (4/6)

Whitefish Will Rides Again! by Arthur Yorinks
(Harper Collins 1994) (4/6)

Do Cowboys Ride Bikes? by Kathy Tucker
(Albert Whitman & Co. 1997) (4/6)

Snack-time

Older children can hit the trail with trail mix (equal parts raisins, sunflower seeds, toasted-oat cereal, chocolate bits, peanuts, other dried fruits, and your own touches).

☆ ☆ ☆

Get out the chuck wagon. Set up metal pots for serving hotdogs (cut up if necessary), beans, corn, and biscuits.

☆ ☆ ☆

If you're feeling more like a horse today, you may want to have grass (lettuce), oats (instant oatmeal or oatmeal cookies), apples, and carrots (younger children can have shredded carrots).

☆ ☆ ☆

Make pancakes in the form of your "brands."

Videos

Cowboy Pooh (Winnie the Pooh Playtime)
Cowboys on the Job*

Art/Craft Materials

brown paper grocery bags
6 brown lunch bags
scissors, tape, glue
markers
ribbon (2 yds., 1" wide)
construction paper or grocery bag
hole punch
yarn (2 yds.)

Art/Craft Directions

Vest

1) Cut holes in the top and sides of a brown paper grocery bag, then cut down the front.

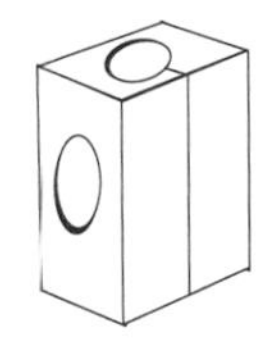

2) Decorate the outside with markers, in western symbols (sun, tree, water, cactus). Snip the bottom edge about 1" deep, to make fringe.

Leggings

1) Cut the bottoms out of the 6 lunch bags, and fringe one end of each. Cut down one side of each bag.

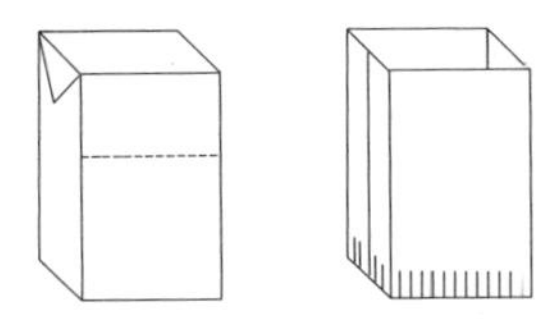

2) Tape 3 bags end to end, overlapping about an inch. Tape or staple 18" of ribbon around the top edge, leaving equal amounts loose to tie around each leg.

For a Little Something Extra...

Take the "brand" you designed to a company that makes custom rubber stamps. It may not be too much of a splurge to have them turn it into your own "branding iron."

Head Bands

1) Cut a strip of black or brown paper (construction paper, or a paper bag) 2" wide by 24" long.

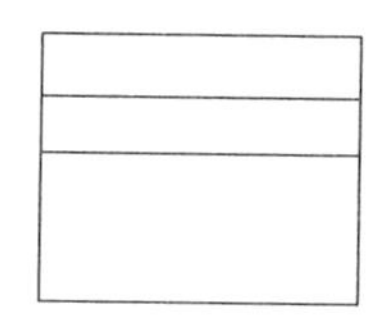

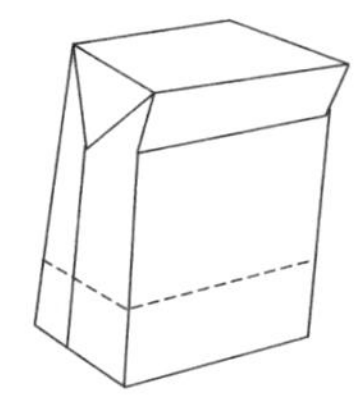

2) Fit the band around child's head and tape the ends together. Cut feather shapes out of different colors of construction paper. Decorate the feathers and the band, then tape the feathers to the inside top of the band.

Saddle for "Horse"

1) Cut 2 saddle shapes from a folded grocery bag. Glue them together, and punch holes about 1" apart all around the edge. (For 4/6-year-olds, make the saddle about 16" x 10"; for younger ones, try about 12" x 8".)

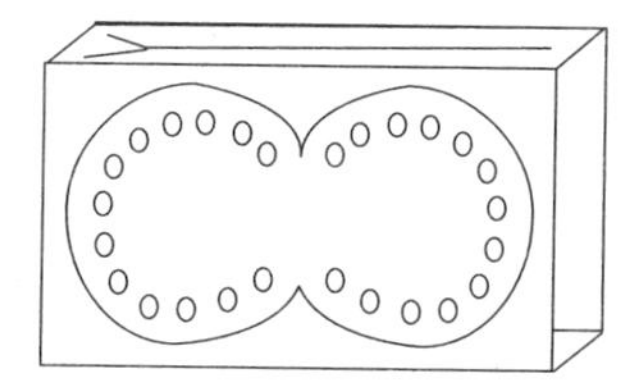

2) Lace the sides with a running stitch (see Sewing) with yarn. Knot off the ends. Staple and tape 18" of wide ribbon to both rounded ends. Tie it around child's back when she goes on all fours, and give those toys a ride! Tuck a folded receiving blanket under the saddle to be authentic.

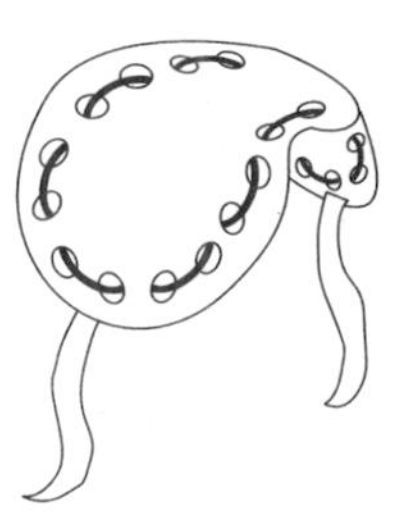

Wheels/Spinning

Art/Craft

- Make pinwheels by cutting paper, and pinning it to the eraser on an unsharpened pencil. The pin is unavoidable, but the point will be hidden. You just have to watch to see if it gets pulled out (see directions).
- Make paper helicopters by folding and cutting white or construction paper and adding a paper-clip (see directions).
- Make a chromatope, an old-fashioned spinning toy, from paper, cardboard, and string. It is a disk like a button that seems to change color when you pull on the attached string (it does take some practice) (see directions).

Indoors

- Clear away the furniture and spin yourself dizzy!
- What spins in your house? Gather toy cars, trucks, tops, an airplane with a propeller, a school-bus, a yo-yo, and a firetruck with a wheel that cranks the ladder up and down.
- Buy a gyroscope and try it out.
- Go hunting for pictures of other spinning things in books or magazines: a fan, helicopter, steering wheel, ship's wheel, paddle wheel boats, and pulleys. (Can you find the big wheel that makes an old-fashioned sewing machine work?)
- See how many spinning things you can find in fairy tales (Cinderella's pumpkin coach wheels, Sleeping Beauty's spinning wheel, the pulley or crank at the well in the Frog Prince, etc.)
- If you have a plastic gear-connecting toy set, such as made by Discovery Toys, take turns connecting different-sized gears in different orders, then turning the crank to see how they move.

Music

"The Wheels on the Bus"
Suzy is a Rocker (Tom Paxton)*
Cars, Trucks & Trains (Jane Murphy)*

Hints for Your Own Situation...

Make a spiral barber shop pole. Wrap an empty paper towel tube in white paper, then wrap it in a spiral with half-inch wide red ribbon. Glue ribbon a few places along the way. Have one person hold it with fingers in each end, then let another one spin it. Or, if you have an old record player, tape it upright over the spindle, and spin it at different speeds.

☆ ☆ ☆

Buy a Spirograph set and help older children use pencils to create different patterns from the spinning stencils.

Snack-time

Make pinwheel sandwiches. Take one slice of white bread and one slice of wheat bread. Remove the crusts and spread with peanut butter, deviled ham, etc. Firmly roll up the sandwich, and secure in four places with toothpicks (be careful). Slice it into four pinwheels and serve.

☆ ☆ ☆

Buy a small wheel of cheese and cut it into tiny wedges. Serve with round crackers.

☆ ☆ ☆

Serve Swiss roll chocolate cake treats.

Outdoors

- Weave crepe paper streamers through tricycle and bicycle wheels, or clip old playing cards to the spokes with clothes-pins, for a wonderful flapping sound. If it's a nice day, get your helmets on and go for a ride.
- On a hot day, turn on a spinning sprinkler.
- Can you find maple-wing seeds? Toss them in the air and see how they spin coming down.
- Try out your paper helicopter and pinwheels outdoors.
- Turn a wheelbarrow upside down and see how fast you can spin its wheel with your hands.

Books

Wheels! by Annie Cobb
(Random House 1996) (2/3)

Curious George Rides a Bike by H. A. Rey
(Houghton Mifflin Co. 1980) (4/6)

Fun on Wheels by Joanna Cole
(William Morrow & Co. 1977) (2/3)

Mama Zooms by Jane Cowen-Fletcher
(Scholastic 1993) (2/3)

Mrs. Peachtree's Bicycle by Erica Silverman
(Simon & Schuster 1996) (4/6)

Roller Skates! by Stephanie Calmenson
(Scholastic Cartwheel 1992) (2/3)

The Bicycle Man by Allen Say
(Parnassus Press/Houghton Mifflin 1982) (4/6)

Wheels Around by Shelley Rotner
(Houghton Mifflin 1995) (2/3)

The Remarkable Riderless Runaway Tricycle by Bruce McMillan
(Houghton Mifflin 1978) (4/6)

The Bear's Bicycle by Emilie Warren McLeod
(Atlantic Monthly/Little, Brown and Co. 1975)

Videos

The Bicycle Man (Reading Rainbow)*
Cro-Adventures in Woolyville (Pulley for You)*
Joe Scruggs in Concert (The Bicycle Song)*

Art/Craft Materials

construction paper
scissors, glue
unsharpened pencil
straight pin with a large head
white paper
big paper clip
posterboard
string or yarn (4 ft.)

Art/Craft Directions

Pinwheel

1) Cut a 6" square from construction paper. Fold it into a triangle, unfold it, and fold it again the other way into a triangle, to make creases. Unfold.

2) Cut along the creases, but leave 1" at the center on each cut.

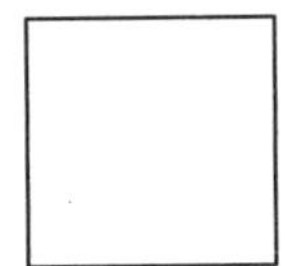
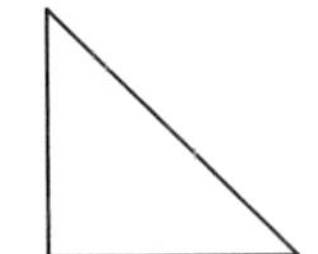
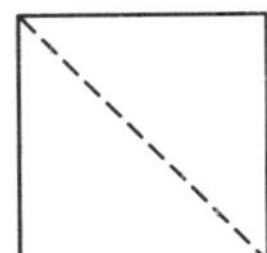
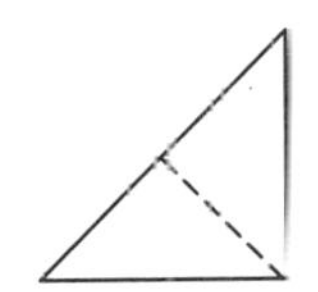
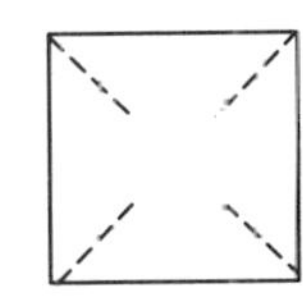

3) Bend every other point in to the center, overlapping them, and push the pin through the middle to catch all 4 points.

4) Push the pin into the eraser of the unsharpened pencil, but not all the way through.

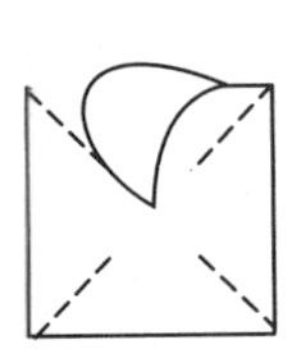

For a Little Something Extra...

Go to a children's science, discovery, or hands-on museum. See how many things they have that use some kind of wheel or spinning motion.

Buy a paddle-wheel toy for the tub.

Helicopter

1) Cut a piece of white paper on the three solid lines shown below.

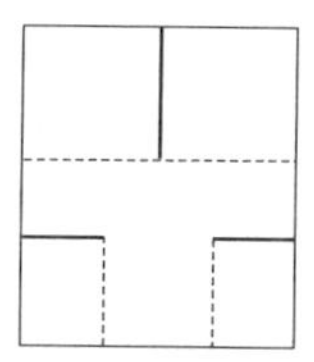

2) Fold in the lower flaps over each other, on the dotted lines, and clip them at the bottom with a large paper clip.

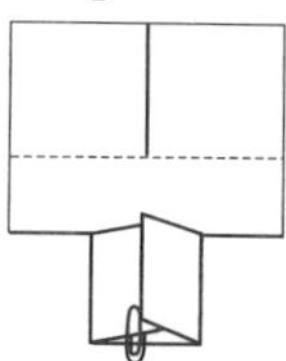

3) Fold one upper flap to the front, and the other upper flap to the back, along the dotted lines.

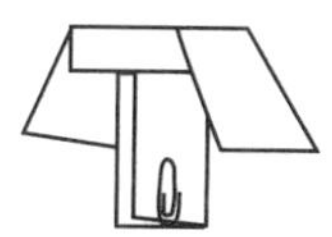

4) Hold the helicopter up high, and let it drop. The wings will open, and the whole helicopter will spin its way down.

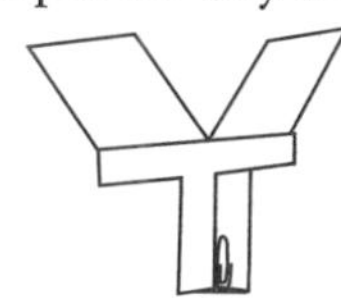

Chromatope Toy

1) Cut one 3" diameter circle out of posterboard, and two 3" diameter circles out of white paper. Glue the paper circles to either side of the posterboard, and divide the circles into four wedges. Color them in opposite, bright colors (blue and yellow, red and green, etc.)

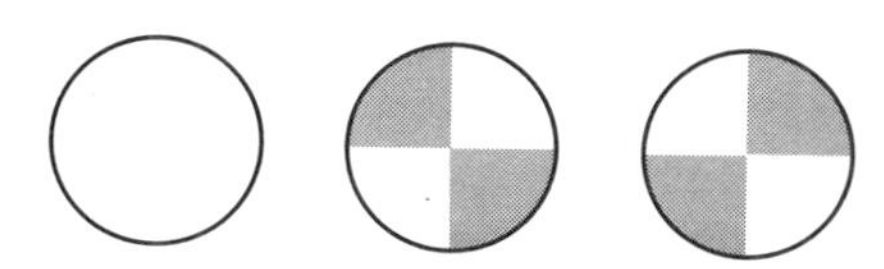

2) Poke 2 holes in the circle opposite each other, about 1" apart. Thread a 4-foot piece of yarn or string in one hole and out the other, then tie it in a square knot. Pull the yarn through so there are loops on either side. Grasp each loop and flip the circle over and over to "wind it up." Pull on both ends to make the colors spin and blend. This can take some practice!

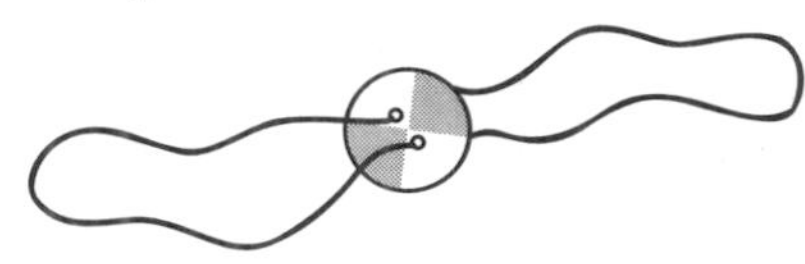

Zoo/Safari

Art/Craft

- Make binoculars from two toilet paper tubes and a length of yarn (see directions under Birds).
- Use finger paints to have the children make "paw" prints of their own design on paper. Make up names for the animals to which they belong.
- Cut up old magazines and catalogs to get pictures of wild animals. Glue them all over a long rolled piece of paper to make a mural. It could either be a zoo scene or a jungle full of wild animals. Draw in trees and ponds.
- Make a snake out of six or more toilet paper tubes strung together on rope. Tie another string to its head, and have fun making it wiggle down the hall or on a sidewalk (see directions).
- Make animal puppets from brown lunch bags.
- Buy tiny plastic animals and have them "walk" through a washable inkpad. Make animal print notepaper or wrapping paper.

Indoors

- Get dressed for safari with shorts, short-sleeved shirts, your binoculars, neckerchiefs, and helmets (especially if you made the "pith" type). Explore from room to room to see how many (stuffed) animals you can find.
- Take turns being different wild animals (lion, tiger, bear, giraffe, monkey, owl, snake, flamingo) and act their movements and the sounds they would make. Have the others guess which one you are.
- Build a zoo out of all your blocks, stacking cups, and tiny animals. Let "action figure" toys be the zoo keepers and visitors.

Music

Goin' on Safari (Annie and the Natural Wonder Band)
Oodles of Animals (Nancy Stewart)*
The Safari*
Enjoy the Zoo (Romper Room)*

Hints for Your Own Situation...

Make pith helmets out of white posterboard. If you can, wrap them with a strip of brown ribbon or fabric (see directions).

☆ ☆ ☆

Ask older children if they can name a type of animal for every letter of the alphabet (ape, bear, cat, dog, elephant, flamingo, giraffe, hippo, ibis, jackal, kangaroo, lion, monkey, nightingale, ostrich, peacock, quail, racoon, seal, tiger, unicorn, vulture, walrus, (e)xtinct animals, yak, zebra—to name a few).

Snack-time

Serve animal crackers. The individual boxes are still the most fun, but one big box is less expensive.

☆ ☆ ☆

Offer bananas to the monkeys, Goldfish crackers to the sea otters, lunch meat to the lions, lettuce to the giraffes, and gummy worms to the robins. Water for everyone!

Outdoors

- Buy a bag of small plastic animals. Ahead of time, hide them all around the yard. Go on a safari "hunting" for all the animals (you might want to count how many you hid, so you know when they've all been found!)
- Go on a photo safari. Take turns with either an inexpensive regular camera, or an instant camera, taking pictures of any "wild creatures" you find: a worm, a grass-hopper, a moth, a robin, a pigeon, a ladybug, a lizard, a spider, your dog, etc.

Books

What Would You Do If You Lived At The Zoo? by Nancy White Carlstrom
(Little, Brown & Co. 1994) (2/3)

At the Zoo by Douglas Florian
(Greenwillow 1992) (2/3)

Is Your Mama A Llama? by Deborah Guarino
(Scholastic 1989) (2/3)

Zoo-Looking by Mem Fox
(Mondo Publishing 1996) (2/3)

Where the Wild Things Are by Maurice Sendak
(Harper & Row 1963) (4/6)

Zoo Dreams by Cor Hazelaar
(Farrar, Straus and Girouz 1997) (2/3)

A Visit to the Sesame Street Zoo by Ellen Weiss
(Random House 1988) (4/6)

1,2,3 to the Zoo by Eric Carle
(Philomel Books 1968) (2/3)

If Anything Ever Goes Wrong at the Zoo by Mary Jean Hendrick
(Harcourt Brace Jovanovich 1993) (4/6)

The Happy Hippopotami by Bill Martin Jr.
(Harcourt Brace Jovanovich 1991) (4/6)

Videos

At the Zoo and At the Zoo 2*; The Jungle Book
See How They Grow: Wild Animals and Jungle Animals (Dorling Kindersley/Sony)*
Zoo Crew: What Do You Want to Be When You Grow Up?*

Art/Craft Materials

8 toilet paper tubes
washable poster paint
clothes-line cord or strong twine
scissors, glue, tape, stapler
red construction paper
white paper
hole punch
brown or yellow ribbon or scarf

Art/Craft Directions

Snake

1) Paint each toilet paper tube. Paint them all in one basic color, let them dry, and then paint designs on them in a second color, all different.

2) Cut a long tongue out of red paper. On one tube, cut out two 1" triangles from one end.

3) Pinch the cut ends together, with part of the tongue stuck in between. Flatten the tube openings and staple it shut. Draw or glue on paper eyes.

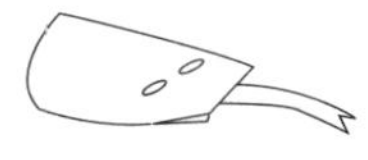

4) Cut about 4 feet of cord. Staple one end inside the open end of the head. Run the cord through all of the 7 other sections, loosely, then staple the cord the inside of the last section. If you want, staple another piece of cord to the top of the head, so you can use it as a handle for pulling the snake.

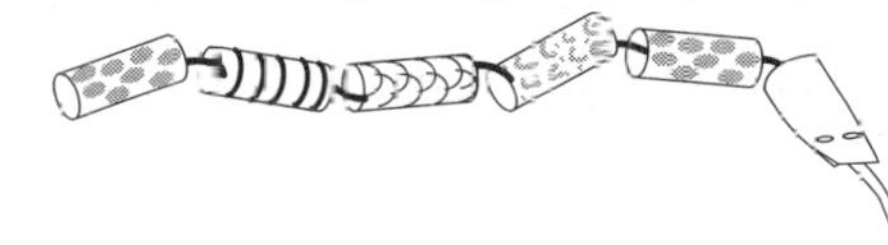

Pith Helmet

1) Fold 3 sheets of white paper in half width-wise and cut them on the crease.

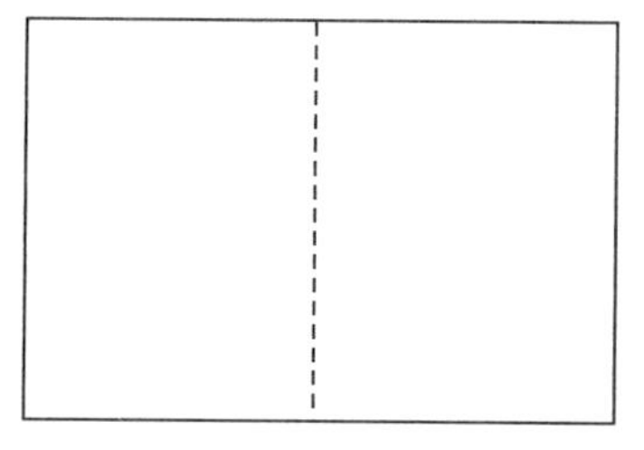

2) Fold the 6 pieces in half, and on each one draw the shape below. Be sure to place the long edge against the fold. Cut out 6 shapes.

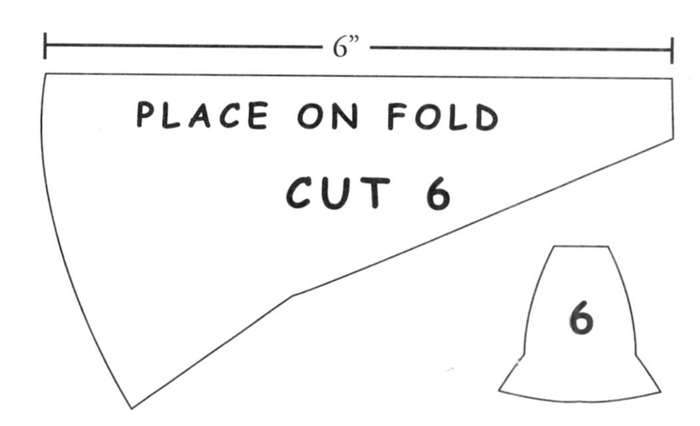

3) Unfold each piece and tape all 6 pieces side by side into a circle (it will be a little lumpy). Let the brim edges overlap before you tape them. Bend the brim up, then curl the edges down a little. Punch or draw 2 air holes on opposite sides.

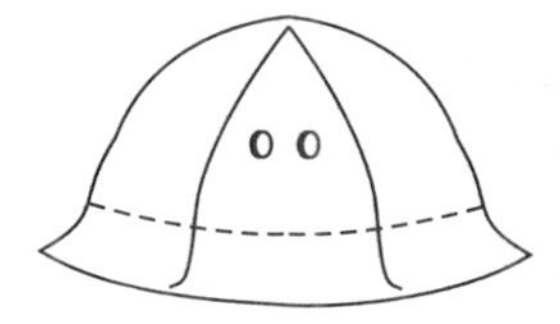

For a Little Something Extra...

Visit a local zoo or pet shop.

☆ ☆ ☆

Try Zookeeper software from Davidson: (800) 545-7677

☆ ☆ ☆

You can buy straw pith helmets ($2.25 each) from Birthday Express: (800) 424-7843

Appendix: Catalogs

For those items you don't have around the house, or for specific theme toys, books, games, materials, song tapes, video tapes, musical instruments, and creative play objects, here are a number of catalogs that carry worthwhile items. There is also a separate list of seed and garden supply catalogs.

Some items are very reasonably priced, some frequently go on sale, and some may be worth an occasional splurge. A few have mostly quite expensive items, yet tucked in here and there are very good buys. If you have the time, check a number of catalogs for the same item; often, the prices will vary greatly, or the same item may be offered for less without an expensive storage box.

Toys, Crafts, Games, Costumes, Music/Videos, Activities

ActiveMinds
One Sportime Way
Atlanta, GA 30340
800-581-6740

Animal Town
P.O. Box 757
Greenland, NH 03840
800-445-8642
www.animaltown.com

Back to Basics Toys
One Memory Lane
Ridgely, MD 21685
800-356-5360

Birthday Express
11220 120th Ave. NE
Kirkland, WA 98033
800-424-7843
www.BirthdayExpress.com

Bits & Pieces
1 Puzzle Place, B8016
Stevens Point, WI 54481
800-544-7297
www.Bits_and_Pieces.com

Childcraft
250 College Park
P.O. Box 1811
Peoria, IL 61656
800-631-5657

Constructive Playthings
1227 East 119th St.
Grandview, MO 64030
800-832-0572
www.constplay.com

Current
The Current Building
Colorado Springs, CO 80941
800-848-2848

Edmund Scientific Co.
Consumer Science Division
101 East Gloucester Pike
Barrington, NJ 08007
800-728-6999
email: scientifics@edsci.com

The Great Kids Company
P.O. Box 609
Lewisville, NC 27023
800-533-2166

Gifts for Grandkids
Genesis Direct
P.O. 1601
Secaucus, NJ 07096
888-472-6354
email: care@genesisdirect.com

Hand in Hand
Genesis Direct
100 Plaza Drive
Secausus, NJ 07094
800-872-9745
email: hinh@genesisdirect.com

HearthSong
6519 N. Galena Rd.
P.O. Box 1773
Peoria, IL 61656
800-325-2502

Just Pretend
104 Challenger Dr.
Portland, TN 37148
800-286-7166
www.justpretend.com

Kids & Things
P.O. Box 14607
Madison, WI 53714
800-243-0464
www.kidsandthings.com

Leaps and Bounds
P.O. Box 517
Lake Bluff, IL 60044
800-477-2189
email: osacatalog@aol.com

Lillian Vernon/Lilly's Kids
Virginia Beach, VA 23479
800-285-5555
email: LVCcustsrv@aol.com

MindWare
2720 Patton Road
Roseville, MN 55113
800-999-0398

Museum Tour
3314 S.E. 16th Avenue
Portland, OR 97202
800-360-9116

PlayFair Toys
P.O. Box 18210
Boulder, CO 80308
800-824-7255

Sensational Beginnings
P.O. Box 2009
987 Stewart Rd.
Monroe, MI 48162
800-444-2147

Stik-EES
1165 Joshua Way
P.O. Box 9630
Vista, CA 92083
800-441-0041

Toys to Grow On
P.O. Box 17
Long Beach, CA 90801
800-542-8338

Troll Learn & Play
45 Curiosity Lane
P.O. Box 1822
Peoria, IL 61656-1822
800-247-6106

U.S.Toy
1227 E. 119th St.
Grandview, MO 64030
800-255-6124
www.ustoyco.com

Worldwide Games
P.O. Box 517
Colchester, CT 06415
800-888-0987
www.worldwidegames.com

Seeds

Burpee Gardens
W. Atlee Burpee & Co.
Warminster, PA 18974
800-487-5530
www.burpee.com

Ferry-Morse Seeds
P.O. Box 488
Fulton, KY 42041
800-283-6400
www.ferry-morse.com

Park Seed
Geo. W. Park Seed Co., Inc.
1 Parkton Ave.
Greenwood, SC 29647
800-845-3369
www.parkseed.com

Videos/Music/Books

Anchor Bay Entertainment
500 Kirts Blvd.
Troy, MI 48084
800-745-1145

Big Kids
1606 Dywer Ave.
Austin, TX 78704
800-477-7811
www.awardvids.com

Dorling Kindersley
DK Family Learning, Inc.
7800 Southland, Ste. 200
Orlando, FL 32809
407-857-5463

Fred Levine Productions
P.O. Box 4010
30 Penhallow Street
Portsmouth, NH 03802
800-843-3686 x497

Goldsholl: Learning Videos
420 Frontage Rd.
Northfield, IL 60093
800-243-8300

Music for Little People
P. O. Box 1460
Redway, CA 95560
800-346-4445

Soundprints
353 Main Avenue
Norwalk, CT 06851
800-577-2413
www.soundprints.com

TM Books Videos
Box 279
New Buffalo, MI 49117
800-892-2822
www.tmbooks-video.com

Appendix: Even More Books

Here are more possible books for you to read out loud. They are just as wonderful as the ones in the theme sections–there just wasn't enough room there for all of them!

After each book title, the numbers indicate a suggested age group. The 2/3-year-old books contain simple words and sentences with lots of pictures. The 4/6-year-old books, although well illustrated, generally have paragraphs and longer stories. However, many three-year-olds will want to hear the long stories, too, so use your own judgement. Early readers also work well as toddler read-out-loud books. A few 6+ year-old books are included simply because they were too good to pass up.

Airports/Planes

Science Fun with Toy Boats and Planes
by Rose Wyler (ref.)
(Simon & Schuster 1986) (4/6)

What's Inside?Planes
ed. by Hilary Hockman
(Dorling Kindersley 1992) (6+)

Astronomy

Aligay Saves the Stars
by Kazuko G. Stone
(Scholastic 1991) (4/6)

Alistair and the Alien Invasion
by Marilyn Sadler
(Simon & Schuster 1994) (4/6)

Big Silver Space Shuttle
by Ken Wilson-Max
(Scholastic Cartwheel 1997) (2/3)

Blue Sun Ben
by Jean & Claudio Marzollo
(Dial/E.P.Dutton 1984) (4/6)

Crafts for Kids Who are Wild about Outer Space
by Kathy Ross (ref.)
(Millbrook Press 1997) (4/6)

The Earth and Sky
by Gallimard Jeunesse and Jean-Pierre Verdet
(Scholastic Cartwheel 1989) (4/6)

The Glow in the Dark Night Sky Book
by Clint Hatchett (ref.)
(Random House 1988)(6+)

It Came From Outer Space
by Tony Bradman
(Dial/Penguin 1992)(4/6)

Magic School Bus Hello Out There
by Joanna Cole
(Scholastic 1995) (4/6)

Papa, Please Get the Moon for Me
by Eric Carle
(Scholastic 1990) (4/6)

Space Case
by Edward Marshall
(Dial Books 1980) (4/6)

Wan Hu is in the Stars
by Jennifer Armstrong
(Tambourine/William Morrow 1995) (4/6)

What Rhymes with Moon?
by Jane Yolen
(Philomel/Putnam & Grosset 1993) (4/6)

Balls

Stop That Ball!
by Mike McClintock
(Random House 1959) (4/6)

Yellow Ball
by Molly Bang
(Morrow Junior Books 1991) (4/6)

Bears

Bea's 4 Bears
by Martha Weston
(Clarion/Houghton Mifflin 1992) (2/3)

Beady Bear
by Don Freeman
(Viking Press 1954) (4/6)

The Bear Next Door
by Ginnie Hofmann
(Random House 1994) (4/6)

Bears
by Isobel Beard
(Wonderbooks/Grosset & Dunlap 1973) (2/3)

Bears at the Beach
by Niki Yektai
(The Millbrook Press 1996) (4/6)

Cully Cully and the Bear
by Wilson Gage
(Greenwillow Books 1983) (4/6)

Moon Bear
by Frank Asch
(Charles Scribner's Sons 1978) (4/6)

This is the Bear and the Scary Night
by Sarah Hayes
(Little Brown & Co. 1992) (2/3)

Birds

Benjy and the Barking Bird
by Margaret Bloy Graham
(Harper & Row 1971) (4/6)

The Bird Alphabet Book
by Jerry Pallotta
(Charlesbridge 1986) (4/6)

Birds
by Esme Eve
(Wonder Books/Grosset & Dunlap 1971) (2/3)

Ride a Purple Pelican
by Jack Prelutsky
(Greenwillow 1986) (4/6)

The Royal Raven
by Hans Wilhelm
(Scholastic 1996)(4/6)

Song of the Swallows
by Leo Politi
(Scribner 1949)(4/6)

The Story about Ping
by Marjorie Flack
(Viking Puffin 1933/1977) (4/6)

Wheel on the Chimney
by Margaret Wise Brown
(J.B.Lippincott 1954) (4/6)

You Silly Goose
by Ellen Stoll Walsh
(Harcourt Brace Jovanovich 1992) (4/6)

Birthdays

Angelina's Birthday Surprise
by Katharine Holabird
(Clarkson N. Potter 1989) (4/6)

Babar: The Best Present in the World
by B. P. Nichol
(Jellybean/Random House 1990) (4/6)

The Birthday Cat
by Lesley Anne Ivory
(Dial/Penguin 1993) (4/6)

Clifford's Birthday Party
by Norman Bridwell
(Scholastic 1988) (2/3)

Happy Birthday (poems)
ed. by Lee Bennett Hopkins
(Simon & Schuster 1990) (4/6)

Jimmy's Boa and the Big Splash Birthday Bash
by Trinka Hakes Noble
(Dial 1989) (4/6)

Miss Flora McFlimsey's Birthday
by Mariana
(Lothrop, Lee & Shepard Books 1952) (4/6)

Nana's Birthday Party
by Amy Hest
(Morrow Jr. Books 1993) (4/6)

The Surprise Party
by Pat Hutchins
(MacMillan 1969) (2/3)

Tomorrow is Daddy's Birthday
by Ginger Wadsworth
(Caroline House/Boyds Mills Press 1994) (4/6)

Wish Upon a Birthday
by Norma Q. Hare
(Garrard Publishing Co. 1979) (4/6)

Boats

Boat Ride with Lillian Two Blossom
by Patricia Polacco
(Philomel Books 1988) (4/6)

Boats: A First Discovery Book
by Gallimard Jeunesse
(Scholastic Cartwheel 1993) (4/6)

The Incredible Year-Round Playbook
by Elin McCoy (ref.)
(Random House 1979) (4/6)

Mr. Bear's Boat
by Thomas Graham
(Unicorn/Dutton 1988) (2/3)

Mr. Little's Noisy Boat
by Richard Fowler
(Grosset & Dunlap 1986) (4/6)

Science Fun with Toy Boats and Planes
by Rose Wyler (ref.)
(Simon & Schuster 1986) (4/6)

Bugs/Butterflies

Butterflies
by John Mousdale
(Wonderbooks/Grosset & Dunlap 1973) (2/3)

The Icky Bug Alphabet Book
by Jerry Palletta
(Charlesbridge 1986) (4/6)

The Ladybug and Other Insects: A First Discovery Book
by Pascal De Bourgoing
(Scholastic 1991) (4/6)

The Magic Schoolbus Gets Ants in its Pants
by Joanna Cole
(Scholastic 1996) (4/6)

Two Bad Ants
by Chris Van Allsburg
(Houghton Mifflin 1988) (4/6)

Camping

A Tent Too Full
by Stephen White
(Barney Publications 1993) (4/6)

Amelia Bedelia Goes Camping
by Peggy Parish
(Avon Camelot 1985) (4/6)

Harry Goes to Day Camp
by James Ziefert
(Puffin/Penguin 1994) (4/6)

Little Critter at Scout Camp
by Mercer Mayer
(Golden/Western 1991) (2/3)

Carpentry

How Things Were Built
by David J. Brown
(Random House 1992) (4/6)

The Perfectly Orderly House
by Ellen Kindt McKenzie
(Henry Holt and Co. Inc. 1994) (4/6)

Tools
by Venice Shone
(Scholastic/Cartwheel 1991) (4/6)

Cars/Trucks

Big Rigs
by Hope Irvin Marston
(Cobblehill/Dutton 1993) (4/6)

Cars and Trucks and Other Vehicles: A First Discovery Book
by Gallimard Jeunesse
(Scholastic Cartwheel 1996) (4/6)

Mr. Little's Noisy Car
by Richard Fowler
(Grosset & Dunlap 1985) (4/6)

Sam Goes Trucking
by Henry Horenstein
(Houghton Mifflin 1989)(4/6)

Truck
by Donald Crews
(Scholastic/Greenwillow 1980) (2/3)

Trucks: Traveling Machines
by Jason Cooper
(Rouke Enterprises Inc.1991) (4/6)

Castles/Royalty

Castles: A First Discovery Book
by Jeunesse, Delafosse & Millet
(Scholastic Cartwheel 1993) (4/6)

If I Were Queen of the World
by Fred Hiatt
(Margaret K. McElderry/
Simon & Schuster 1997) (4/6)

The Knight Who Was Afraid of the Dark
by Barbar Shook Hazen
(Puffin Dial 1989) (4/6)

The Knight Who Was Afraid to Fight
by Barbara Shook Hazen
(Dial 1994) (4/6)

Knights
by John Howe & Sadie Fields (ref.)
(Orchard Books 1995) (4/6)

Knights
by Rachel Wright (ref.)
(Franklin Watts 1991) (4/6)

Knights in Shining Armor
by Gail Gibbons
(Little Brown & Co. 1995) (4/6)

The Princess and the Painter
by Jane Johnson
(Farrar, Straus & Giroux 1994) (4/6)

Princess Horrid
by Erik Christian Haugaard
(Macmillan 1990) 4/6

Circus

Detective Whoo
by Dennis Panek
(Bradbury Press 1981) (2/3)

Ernest and Celestine at the Circus
by Gabrielle Vincent
(Greenwillow 1988) (4/6)

Mirette and Bellini
by Emily Arnold McCully
(G.P.Putnam's Sons 1997) (4/6)

Morris and Boris at the Circus
by B. Wiseman
(Harper Collins 1988) (4/6)

Star of the Circus
by Michael & Mary Beth Sampson
(Henry Holt 1997) (2/3)

Wanda's Circus
by Amy Aitken
(Bradbury Press 1985) (4/6)

Word Bird's Circus Surprise
by Jane Belk Moncure
(Children's Press 1981) (2/3)

Clocks/Time

Clocks and More Clocks
by Pat Hutchins
(MacMillan Publishing Co. 1994) (4/6)

Gumdrop Beats the Clock
by Val Biro
(Gareth Stevens Publishing 1986) (4/6)

My First Look at Time
ed. by Jane Yorke
(Random House/DK 1991) (2/3)

Colors/Light

Color Farm
by Lois Ehlert
(J.P. Lippincott 1990) (2/3)

Colors of the Day
by Ruth Bragg
(Simon & Schuster) (4/6)

Growing Colors
by Bruce McMillan
(Lothrop Lee & Shepard 1988) (4/6)

Gus Was a Gorgeous Ghost
by Jane Thayer
(William Morrow & Co. 1978) (4/6)

Harold and the Purple Crayon
by Crockett Johnson
(Harper 1955) (2/3)

I Love Colors
by Stan & Jan Berenstain
(Random House 1987) (2/3)

Is it Red? Is it Yellow? Is it Blue?
by Tana Hoban
(Greenwillow 1978) (2/3)

Light: A First Discovery Book
by Gallimard Jeunesse
(Scholastic Cartwheel) (4/6)

Mary Wore Her Red Dress &
Henry Wore His Green Sneakers
by Merle Peek
(Houghton Mifflin 1993) (4/6)

Mouse Paint
by Ellen Stoll Walsh
(Harcourt Brace Jovanovich 1989) (2/3)

Red is Best
by Kathy Stinson
(Annick Press Ltd. 1982) (2/3)

Sparky's Rainbow Repair
by Max Haynes
(Lothrop, Lee & Shepard 1992) (4/6)

Dancing/Jumping/Hopping

Dance!
by Ward Schumaker
(Harcourt Brace & Co. 1996) (2/3)

Hen Lake
by Mary Jane Auch
(Holiday House 1995) (4/6)

I Dance in My Red Pajamas
by Edith Thacher Hurd
(Harper & Row 1982) (4/6)

The Little Ballerina
by Katharine Ross
(Random House 1996) (4/6)

Noah's Square Dance
by Rick Walton
(Lothrop, Lee & Shepard 1995) (4/6)

Rosie's Ballet Slippers
by Susan Hampshire
(Harper Collins 1996) (4/6)

Detectives

Clue #2 The Secret Secret Passage
by A.E. Parker
(Scholastic 1992) (4/6)

Encyclopedia Brown series
by Donald Sobol (4/6)

Gumshoe Goose
by Mary Deball Kwitz
(Dial Books 1988) (4/6)

Mr. Sniff and the Motel Mystery
by Thomas P. Lewis
(Harper & Row, 1984) (4/6)

The Mystery at Number Seven, Rue Petite
by Ellen Shire
(Random House 1978) (4/6)

Dinosaurs

Big Old Bones
by Carol Carrick
(Clarion/Houghton Mifflin 1989) (4/6)

The Day of the Dinosaur
by Stan & Jan Berenstain
(Random House 1987) (4/6)

Dinosaur Encore
by Patricia Mullins
(Harper Collins 1993) (4/6)

Dinosaur Roar!
by Paul & Henrietta Stickland
(Dutton Children's Books 1994) (2/3)

Dinosaurs: A First Discovery Book
by Gallimard Jeunesse
(Scholastic Cartwheel 1993) (4/6)

Jethro's Difficult Dinosaur
by Arnold Sundgaard
(Pantheon Books 1977) (4/6)

Mrs. Toggle and the Dinosaur
by Robin Pulver
(MacMillan 1991) (4/6)

Ten Terrible Dinosaurs
by Paul Strickland
(Dutton Children's Books 1997) (2/3)

Doctor/Dentist/Vet

Andrew's Loose Tooth
by Robert Munsch
(Scholastic Cartwheel 1990) (4/6)

Jenny's in the Hospital
by Seymour Reit
(Golden/Western 1984) (4/6)

Just Going to the Dentist
by Mercer Mayer
(Golden/Western 1990) (4/6)

Milo's Toothache
by Ida Luttrell
(Dial 1992) (4/6)

Dragons/Fairies

The Dragon Nanny
by C.L.G. Martin
(MacMillan1988) (4/6)

Everyone Knows What a Dragon Looks Like
by Jay Williams
(Four Winds Press 1976) (4/6)

Farm Life

Farm Alphabet Book
by Jane Miller
(Scholastic 1981) (4/6)

Farms
by Esme Eve
(Wonderbooks/Grosset & Dunlap 1972) (2/3)

The Day Jimmy's Boa Ate the Wash
by Trinka Hakes Noble
(Dial 1980) (4/6)

Pigs from A to Z
by Arthur Geisert
(Houghton Mifflin 1986) (2/3)

Firefighting

Firetrucks
by Peter Brady
(Bridgestone Books/Capstone 1996) (4/6)

Fish/Under the Sea

At the Beach
by Anne & Harlow Rockwell
(Macmillan 1987) (2/3)

Barney's Sand Castle
by Stephanie Calmenson
(Golden/Western 1983) (2/3)

By the Sea
by Mary Hofstrand
(Atheneum 1989) (2/3)

Fish Eyes
by Lois Ehlert
(Harcourt Brace Jovanovich 1990) (2/3)

Fish Fish Fish
by Georgie Adams
(Dial 1993)(4/6)

Fish is Fish
by Leo Lionni
(Alfred A. Knopf 1970) (4/6)

The Ocean Alphabet Book
by Jerry Pallotta
(Charlesbridge 1986) (4/6)

Ocean Day
by Shelley Rotner & Ken Kreisler
(Macmillan 1993) (2/3)

The Runaway Whale
by Keith Faulkner
(Longmeadow Press 1990) (2/3)

The Seashore: A First Discovery Book
by Gallimard Jeunesse & Elisabeth Cohat
(Scholastic Cartwheel 1990) (4/6)

Sun Sand Sea Sail
by Nicki Weiss
(Greenwillow 1989) (2/3)

Whale is Stuck
by Karen Hayles
(Simon & Schuster 1992) (4/6)

What's in the Deep Blue Sea?
by Peter Seymour
(Henry Holt and Co. 1990) (2/3)

Flags/Signs

Flags
by Theodore Rowland-Entwistle (ref.)
(Wayland 1987) (6+)

I Walk and Read
by Tana Hoban
(Greenwillow 1984) (2/3)

Red Light Stop, Green Light Go
by Andrew Kulman
(Simon & Schuster/Young Readers 1993) (2/3)

The World of Flags
by William Crampton (ref.)
(Rand McNally 1994) (6+)

Flowers/Vegetables

An Atlas of Plants
by Gallimard Jeunesse
(Scholastic Cartwheel 1996) (4/6)

Anna in the Garden
by Diane Dawson Hearn
(Silver Moon Press 1994)

The Carrot Seed
by Ruth Krauss
(Harper & Row 1945) (2/3)

The Clover County Carrot Contest
by John Himmelman
(Silver Press/Simon & Schuster 1991) (4/6)

Daisy's Garden
by Mordicai Gerstein
(Hyperion Books for Children 1995)

The Flower Alphabet Book
by Jerry Pallotta
(Charlesbridge 1986) (4/6)

Grandpa's Garden Lunch
by Judith Caseley
(Greenwillow Books 1990) (2/3)

Growing Vegetable Soup
by Lois Ehlert
(Harcourt Brace Jovanovich 1987) (4/6)

The Magic School Bus Plants Seeds
by Patricia Relf/Joanna Cole
(Scholastic 1995) (4/6)

Mr. Pepino's Cabbage
by Diane Wilmer and Anna Currey
(W. H. Smith/Gallery Books 1989)

Paddington's Garden
by Michael Bond
(Harper Festival/Harper Collins 1992) (4/6)

Still-Life Stew
by Helena Clare Pittman
(Hyperion Books 1998) (4/6)

The Surprise Garden
by Zoe Hall
(Blue Sky/Scholastic 1998) (4/6)

Tulips
by Jay O'Callahan
(Picture Book Studio1992) (4/6)

Vegetables in the Garden: A First Discovery Book
by Pascal De Bourgoing
(Scholastic Cartwheel 1994) (4/6)

Fruit/Trees

A Tree is Nice
by Janice Udry
(Harper & Row 1956) (2/3)

I Wish I Had a Big, Big Tree
by Satoru Sato
(William Morrow 1989) (4/6)

The Seed the Squirrel Dropped
by Haris Petie
(Prentice-Hall 1976) (2/3)

Geology

All That Glitters
by Rebecca Magruder
(Scholastic 1996) (4/6)

I am a Rock
by Jean Marzollo
(Scholastic 1998) (2/3)

Hair

Amanda's Perfect Hair
by Linda Milstein
(Tambourine/William Morrow 1993) (4/6)

Hubert's Hair-Raising Adventure
by Bill Peet
(Houghton Mifflin 1987) (4/6)

Rapunzel
by Jacob Grimm/Anthea Bell
(North-South Books 1997) (4/6)

Hats/Shoes

Aunt Flossie's Hats
by Elizabeth Fitzgerald Howard
(Clarion Books 1991) (4/6)

Caps, Hats, Socks and Mittens
by Louise Borden
(Scholastic 1990) (2/3)

The Hat
by Tomi Ungerer
(Four Winds Press 1970) (4/6)

Jennie's Hat
by Ezra Jack Keats
(Harper & Row 1966) (2/3)

Juice the Pig
by Martine Oborne
(Henry Holt & Co. 1996) (4/6)

My Best Shoes
by Marilee Robin Burton
(Tambourine/William Morrow 1994) (2/3)

Olive and the Magic Hat
by Eileen Christelow
(Clarion/Houghton Mifflin 1987) (4/6)

This is the Hat
by Nancy Van Laan
(Little Brown & Co. 1992) (4/6)

Shoes Shoes Shoes
by Ann Morris
(LLothrop, Lee & Shepard 1995) (2/3)

The Witch's Hat
by Tony Johnston
(B. P. Putnam's Sons 1984) (4/6)

Inventions

The Marvelous Toy
by Tom Paxton
(Morrow Junior Books 1996) (2/3)

No Problem
by Eileen Browne
(Candlewick Press 1996) (4/6)

The Way Things Work
by David Macaulay (ref.)
(Houghton Mifflin 1988) (6+)

Kitchen Fun

Chocolate Chip Cookies
by Karen Wagner
(Henry Holt & Co. 1990) (4/6)

Betty Crocker's Cooking with Kids ed.
by Karen Coune (ref.)
(Simon & Schuster/Macmillan 1995) (4/6)

The Duchess Bakes a Cake
by Virginia Kahl
(Charles Scribner's Sons, 1955) (4/6)

Encyclopedia Brown Takes the Cake!
by Donald Sobol
(Scholastic Inc. 1983) (4/6)

Hedgehog Bakes a Cake
by Maryann Macdonald
(Bantam Little Rooster Book 1990) (4/6)

Marcel the Pastery Chef
by Marianna Mayer
(Bantam 1991) (4/6)

My First Cook Book
by Angela Wilkes (ref.)
(Knopf/Dorling Kindersley 1989) (4/6)

Library

Check It Out!
by Gail Gibbons
(Harcourt Brace Jovanovich 1985) (4/6)

The Frog Princess
by Pamela Mann
(Gareth Stevens Publishing 1995) (4/6)

The Inside Outside Book of Libraries
by Roxie Munro
(Dutton Children's Books 1996) (4/6)

Library Bear
by Bob Reese
(ARO Publishing 1995) (2/3)

Molly at the Library
by Ruth Shaw Radlauer
(Simon & Schuster 1988) (2/3)

Sophie and Sammy's Library Sleepover
by Judith Caseley
(Greenwillow 1993) (4/6)

Maps/Traveling

As the Crow Flies
by Gail Hartman
(Bradbury/Macmillan 1991) (4/6)

A Bird's-Eye View: A First Look at Maps
by Harriet Wittels and Joan Greisman
(Scholastic 1995)(4/6)

Barney's Treasure Hunt
by Guy Davis
(The Lyons Group 1997) (2/3)

Be Your Own Map Expert
by Barbara Taylor (ref.)
(Sterling Publishing 1994) (6+)

Magic Carpet
by Pat Brisson
(Bradbury Press 1991) (4/6)

Maps and Mapmaking
by Anita Ganeri (ref.)
(Franklin Watts/Grolier 1995) (6+)

My Map Book
by Sara Fanelli
(Harper Collins1995) (4/6)

My Mom Travels a Lot
by Caroline Feller Bauer
(Puffin/Viking Penguin 1985) (2/3)

Musical Instruments

The Flute Player
by Robyn Eversole
(Orchard Books 1995) (4/6)

Meet the Marching Smithereens
by Ann Hayes
(Harcourt Brace & Co 1995) (4/6)

Musical Instruments: A First Discovery Book
by Claude Delafosse
(Scholastic Cartwheel 1994) (4/6)

Nursery Rhymes

The Discovery Toys Book of Nursery Rhymes
by Julie Lacome
(Discovery Toys/Walker 1989) (2/3)

Marguerite de Angeli's Book of Nursery and Mother Goose Rhymes
(Doubleday 1954)(4/6)

The Nursery Collection
by Shirley Hughes
(Lothrop, Lee & Shepard 1986) (2/3)

Old Mother Hubbard and Her Wonderful Dog
by James Marshall
(Farrar, Straus and Giroux 1991) (4/6)

Richard Scarry's Best Mother Goose Ever
(Golden Press 1970) (4/6)

This Little Piggy
by Nicholas Heller
(Greenwillow 1997) (4/6)

Twinkle Twinkle Little Star
by Jane Taylor/Michael Hague
(Morrow Junior Books 1992)(2/3)

Old-Fashioned Days

The Quilt Story
by Tony Johnston
(Putnam 1985)(4/6)

Yonder
by Tony Johnston
(Dial 1988)(4/6)

Pirates

The Horrendous Hullabaloo
by Margaret Mahy
(Viking Penguin 1992) (4/6)

Look Out For Pirates!
by Iris Vinton
(Random House 1961) (4/6)

Penelope and the Pirates
by James Young
(Arcade/Little, Brown and Co. 1990) (4/6)

The Pirate Who Tried to Capture the Moon
by Dennis Haseley
(Harper & Row 1983)

Pirates
by Gail Gibbons
(Little Brown & Co. 1993) (4/6)

Pirates (Facts, Things to Make, Activities)
by Rachel Wright (ref.)
(Franklin Watts 1991) (4/6)

Post Office

A Letter to the King
by Leong Va
(Harper Collins 1987) (4/6)

The Lettuce Leaf Birthday Letter
by Linda Taylor
(Dial 1995) (4/6)

The Post Office Book
by Gail Gibbons
(Thomas Y. Crowell 1982) (4/6)

Postman Pat and the Mystery Thief
by Jon Cunliffe
(Scholastic/Cartwheel 1993) (4/6)

Writing and Printing
by Chris Oxlade (ref.)
(Franklin Watts 1995) (4/6)

Rain

April Showers
by George Shannon
(Greenwillow Books 1995) (2/3)

Caught in the Rain
by Beatriz Ferro
(Doubleday 1980) (2/3)

Hippo Thunder
by Susan Sussman
(Albert Whitman & Co. 1982) (2/3)

The Magic School Bus Inside a Hurricane
by Joanna Cole
(Scholastic 1995) (4/6)

Rain Song
by Lezlie Evans
(Houghton Mifflin 1995) (2/3)

Peter Speir's Rain
(Doubleday 1982)(4/6)

Puddles
by Jonathan London
(Viking Penguin 1997) (2/3)

Umbrella
by Taro Yashima
(Penguin Books 1985) (2/3)

What Does the Rain Play?
by Nancy White Carlstrom
(Macmillan 1993) (4/6)

Restaurant

Curious George and the Pizza
by H.A. Rey
(Houghton Mifflin 1985) (4/6)

Frog Goes to Dinner
by Mercer Mayer
(Puffin Pied Piper 1974) (2/3)

The Rinky-dink Cafe
by Maggie S. Davis
(Simon & Schuster 1988) (4/6)

School

Arthur's Teacher Trouble
by Marc Brown
(Joy St. Books 1987)(4/6)

Dorrie and the Haunted Schoolhouse
by Patricia Coombs
(Clarion/Houghton Mifflin) (4/6)

First Day of School
by Helen Oxenbury
(Dial 1983) (2/3)

Morris Goes to School
by B. Wiseman
(Harper & Row 1970) (4/6)

My Teacher's My Friend
by P.K. Hallinan
(Ideals Children's Books 1989) (4/6)

Off to School
by Ann Schweninger
(Viking Kestrel 1987) (4/6)

Seven Froggies Went to School
by Kate Duke
(E.P.Dutton 1985) (2/3)

Timothy Goes to School
by Rosemary Wells
(Dial 1981) (4/6)

When Daddy Came to School
by Julie Brillhart
(Albert Whitman & Co. 1995) (2/3)

Will I Have a Friend?
by Miriam Cohen
(Aladdin/Macmillan 1989) (4/6)

Sewing/Knitting/Weaving

Bizzy Bones and the Lost Quilt
by Jacqueline Briggs Martin
(Lothrop, Lee & Shepard Books 1988) (4/6)

Buttons Buttons
by Rosanne Lanczak Williams
(Creative Teacher 1995) (4/6)

Derek the Knitting Dinosaur
by Mary Blackwood
(Carolrhoda Books 1990) (4/6)

The Long Red Scarf
by Nette Hilton
(Carolrhoda Books 1987) (4/6)

The Mountains of Quilt
by Nancy Willard
(Harcourt Brace Jovanovich 1987) (4/6)

The Patchwork Lady
by Mary K. Whittington
(Harcourt Brace Jovanovich 1991) (4/6)

Poppa's New Pants
by Angela Shelf Medearis
(Holiday House 1995) (4/6)

The Rag Coat
by Lauren Mills
(Little Brown & Co. 1991) (4/6)

The Quilt Story
by Tony Johnston
(Putnam 1985)(4/6)

Shapes

Spirals, Curves, Fanshapes and Lines
by Tana Hoban
(Greenwillow 1992) (2/3)

What Shape?
by Debbie MacKinnon
(Dial 1992) (2/3)

Shopping

Bunny Money
by Rosemary Wells
(Dial 1997) (4/6)

George's Store at the Shore
by Francine Bassede
(Orchard Books 1997) (4/6)

Let's Go Shopping
by Steven Lindblom
(Golden/Western 1953) (2/3)

The Rolling Store
by Angela Johnson
(Orchard Books 1997) (4/6)

The Shopping Basket
by John Burningham
(Candlewick Press 1980) (4/6)

The Storekeeper
by Tracey Campbell Pearson
(Dial 1988) (4/6)

Snow

Amy Loves the Snow
by Julia Hoban
(Harper & Row 1989) (2/3)

BRRR!
by James Stevenson
(Greenwillow 1991) (4/6)

Geraldine's Big Snow
by Holly Keller
(Greenwillow 1988) (2/3)

Ice Cream is Falling!
by Shigeo Watanabe
(Philomel Books 1989) (4/6)

In the Snow
by Huy Voun Lee
(Henry & Co. 1995) (4/6)

Katie's Snowman
by Kay Chorao
(E.P.Dutton 1982) (2/3)

Sadie and the Snowman
by Allen Morgan
(Scholastic/Kids Can Press 1985) (4/6)

Sledding
by Elizabeth Winthrop
(Harper & Roe 1989) (2/3)

Snow Day
by Betsy Maestro
(Scholastic 1989) (4/6)

The Snow Speaks
by Nancy White Carlstrom
(Little Brown & Co. 1992) (2/3)

Zoom Away
by Tim Wynne-Jones
(Laura Geringer/Harper Collins 1985) (4/6)

Sound

I Can Hear
by Peter Curry
(Price/Stern/Sloan 1982) (4/6)

It's Too Noisy!
by Joanna Cole
(Thomas Y. Crowell/Newfield 1989) (4/6)

Night in the Country
by Cynthia Rylant
(Aladdin/Macmillan 1991) (2/3)

Noisy books (Country/Winter/Indoor/ Seashore/Quiet/Summer)
by Margaret Wise Brown
(Harper & Row 1942) (2/3)

Splish Splash Bang Crash
by Karen Gundersheimer
(Scholastic Cartwheel 1995) (2/3)

Surprises!

Abracadabra
by Ingrid & Dieter Schubert
(Front Street 1997) (4/6)

The Grolier Kids Crafts Magic Book
by Dennis Patten
(Grolier Educational 1997) (6+)

The Magic Leaf
by Winifred Morris
(Antheneum/Macmillan 1987) (4/6)

Magic Fun
ed. by Marilyn Baillie (ref.)
(Little Brown & Co. 1991) (6+)

My First Kitchen Kaper Magic Tricks
by Stephanie Johnson (ref.)
(Lowell House/Contemporary 1993) (6+)

The Porcelain Cat
by Michael Patric Hearn
(Little Brown & Co. 1987) (4/6)

Rabbit-Cadabra!
by James Howe
(Morrow Junior Books 1993) (4/6)

The Sorcerer's Apprentice
by Don Ferguson
(Golden/Western 1974) (4/6)

Theater/Movies

The Berenstain Bears and Too Much TV
by Stan & Jan Berenstain
(Random House 1984) (4/6)

Pet of the Met
by Lydia and Don Freeman
(Viking Press 1953) (4/6)

Speak Up, Blanche!
by Emily Arnold McCully
(HarperCollins 1991) (4/6)

Trains

Big Blue Engine
by Ken Wilson-Max
(Scholastic Cartwheel 1996) (2/3)

Freight Trains
by Peter Brady
(Bridgestone/Capstone 1996) (4/6)

Teddy Bears Take the Train
by Susanna Gretz
(Four Winds Press 1987) (4/6)

The Train to Lulu's
by Elizabeth Fitzgerald Howard
(Bradbury/Macmillan 1988) (4/6)

Trains
by Ray Broekel
(Childrens Press 1981) (4/6)

Trains
by Angela Royston
(Dorling Kindersley 1992) (4/6)

Steam Train Ride
by Evelyn Clarke Mott
(Walker and Co. 1991) (4/6)

Western Days

Cowboy Ed
by Bill Grossman
(Laura Geringer/Harper Collins 1993) (4/6)

Cowboy Small
by Lois Lenski
(Henry Z. Walck, Inc. 1949) (2/3)

The Golly Sisters Go West
by Betsy Byars
(Harper Collins 1989) (4/6)

How I Spent My Summer Vacation
by Mark Teague
(Crown 1995) (4/6)

Sam's Wild West Show
by Nancy Antle
(Dial/Penguin 1995) (4/6)

Why Cowboys Sleep with Their Boots On
by Laurie Lazzaro Knowlton
(Pelican Publishing 1995) (4/6)

Wheels/Spinning

Bicycle Bear
by Michaela Muntean
(Gareth Stevens Publishing 1994) (4/6)

Bicycle Book
by Gail Gibbons
(Holiday House 1995) (4/6)

Delphine
by Molly Bang
(Morrow Junior Books 1988) (4/6)

Franklin Rides a Bike
by Paulette Bourgeois
(Scholastic 1997) (4/6)

Little Duck's Bicycle Ride
by Dorothy Scott
(Dutton 1991) (4/6)

Motorcycles: Traveling Machines
by Jason Cooper
(Rourke Enterprises 1991) (4/6)

Mrs. Armitage on Wheels
by Quentin Blake
(Alfred A. Knopf 1987) (4/6)

Rabbits on Roller Skates
by Jan Wahl
(Crown Publishing 1986) (2/3)

Wheels
by Shirley Hughes
(Lothrop, Lee & Shepard 1991) (4/6)

Wheels
by Jane Resh Thomas
(Clarion/Houghton Mifflin 1986) (4/6)

Wheels Away!
by Dayle Ann Dodds
(Harper & Row 1989) (2/3)

Wheels Go Round
by Yvonne Hooker
(Grosset & Dunlap 1978) (2/3)

Wheels Go Round
by W. Nikola-Lisa
(Doubleday 1994) (2/3)

Zoo/Safari

Jungle Jack Hanna's Safari Adventure
by Jack Hanna
(Scholastic 1996) (4/6)

'Night, Zoo
by Richard Bernal
(Kipling/Contemporary 1989) (2/3)

What Do You Do at a Petting Zoo?
by Hana Machotka
(Morrow Junior Books 1990) (4/6)

Wipe Your
by Daniel Lehan
Dutton Books 1993) (4/6)

Appendix: Video, Audio, and Internet Sources

This information is as current as possible, but be aware that music and video production companies often come and go, sell out their inventory, or change distribution channels. If you at least have a title, you can go to any video store and ask about video availability. Look for the titles at your library, and ask around to see if friends may have them for borrowing.

Be sure to use your library's Internet connections to search for titles (or subjects) at all the libraries in your area. You may be able to get it delivered to your own library.

A growing source of videos is Internet distributors; see the list at the end of this chaper.

Many children's videos are coming out that are geared to ages six and up, or eight and up, but in some cases younger children can still find them visually entertaining. The Eyewitness series from Dorling Kindersley is recommended in their catalog as being for ages eight and up, but their graphics still work well for the 4/6 group.

Another good video series that may appeal to five or six-year-olds is the "I Wanna Be" set distributed by Simitar (www.simitar.com). They offer very good introductions to various careers, but are primarily aimed at ages seven and up; you would have to try to see if they would hold the interest of your somewhat younger child. Titles include: *I Wanna Be A: Ballet Dancer, Cowboy, Race Car Driver*, and *Ship's Captain*.

Videotapes

All About Boats
Pint Size Prod.
P.O. Box 81412
Mobile, AL 36689

At the Airport!
Pappillon Prod.
P.O. Box 2665
Sausalito, CA 94965
800-227-6548

At the Zoo/At the Zoo 2
Goldsholl: Learning Videos
420 Frontage Rd.
Northfield, IL 60093
800-243-8300

Basil Hears a Noise
(Jim Henson)
Children's Television Workshop
Republic Pictures Corp.
12636 Beatrice St.
Los Angeles, CA 90066

The Big Plane Trip 1994
Little Mammoth Media/
Big Kids Prod.
1606 Dywer Ave.
Austin, TX 78704
800-477-7811
www.awardvids.com

Bugs Don't Bug Us! 1991
Bo Peep Prod.
P.O. Box 982
Eureka, MT 59917

Building Skyscrapers
DAAI David Alpert Assoc
800-265-7744

Cars! Cars! Cars!
Mother's Lode
P.O. Box 325
Liberty Corner, NJ 07938
908-604-2152/ 800-665-9210
www.choicemall/carscarscars

Cleared for Takeoff
Fred Levine Prod.
P.O. Box 4010
30 Penhallow St.
Portsmouth, NH 03802
800-843-3686 x497

Corduroy & Other Bear Stories 1993
Children's Circle
Wood Knapp Video
5900 Wilshire Blvd.
Los Angeles, CA 90036

Cowboys on the Job 1997
On the Job Prod.
310-578-1008

Cro: Adventures in Woolyville 1994
Children's Television Workshop
Republic Pictures
12636 Beatrice St.
Los Angeles, CA 90066

Eyewitness series (DK Vision)
Oregon Public Broadcasting
www.dk.com

Fantastic Journey to the Farm
(Imagine and Discover Series)

Fire & Rescue
Fred Levine Prod.
P.O. Box 4010
30 Penhallow St.
Portsmouth, NH 03802
800-843-3686 x497

GeoKids series
Columbia Tristar Home Video
3400 Riverside Dr.
Burbank, CA 91505

Get Your Teddy Ready 1994
(Shari Lewis)
A&M Records
Children's Division
1416 N. LaBrea Ave.
Hollywood, CA 90028

The Great Inventors 1989
(Charlie Brown)
Paramount Pictures

Happy Snappy Birthdays 1996
Kaplan Video Prod.
Webb Communication Services
Pembroke Pines FL
1606 Dywer Ave.
Austin, TX 78704
800-477-7811
www.awardvids.com

Harriet's Magic Hats series
The Learning Division
2246 Camino Ramon
San Ramon, CA
800-767-4486

Heavy Equipment Operator: What Do You Want to be When You Grow Up?
Big Kids Prod.
1606 Dywer Ave.
Austin TX, 78704
800-477-7811
www.awardvids.com

House Construction Ahead
Fred Levine Prod.
P.O. Box 4010
30 Penhallow St.
Portsmouth, NH 03802
800-843-3686 x497

Household Marching Band! 1996
You Can Prod.
San Francisco, CA

How It's Done 1 & 2 1995
Video Treasures, Inc.
500 Kirts Blvd.
Troy, MI 48084

Hullaballoo series
DK Family Learning, Inc.
7800 Southland Blvd., Ste. 200
Orlando, FL 32809
407- 857-5463
www.dk.com

I Can Build! 1994
(CAN Too! A Div. of Bellman Girls Prod.)

I Love Toy Trains
(Tom McComas)
TM Books Videos
Box 279
New Buffalo, MI 49117
800-892-2822
www.tmbooks-video.com

I Want to Be a Ballerina 1995
Clayton Prod.
P.O. Box 117493
Burlingame, CA 94011
800-700-8622

Joe Scruggs in Concert 1992
Shadow Play Video
Education Graphics Press
P.O. Box 180476
Austin, TX 78718

Johnny Appleseed 1989
(Shelley Duvall)
Tall Tales and Legends
Platypus/Playhouse Video

Learning the ABC's 1992
(Learning Can Be Fun)
The Little Red Schoolhouse
Learning Center
Freehold, NJ 07728

Let's Go to the Farm
Big Kids Prod.
1606 Dywer Ave.
Austin TX, 78704
800-477-7811
www.awardvids.com

The Magic Schoolbus series
Scholastic/KidVision
Warner Vision Entertainment

Mary Had a Little Lamb 1995
Jim Henson's Preschool Collection
Buena Vista Home Video

Milk & Cookies 1997
Kid Vids Educational
Entertainment
1606 Dywer Ave.
Austin, TX 78704
800-477-7811
www.awardvids.com

Miss Christy's Dance Adventure
Distr: Kid's First!
www.cybersuperstores.com/cgi-bin/dbsearch.cgi
Kids Club
84 Broadway
Taunton, MA 02780
FAX: 508-880-0468

Mister Roger's Neighborhood: Making Music; Circus Fun
Fox Video/Family Com.

The Mother Goose Video Treasury:
Vol.1 *Humpty Dumpty*
Vol.2 *Little Miss Muffet*
Vol.3 *Little Bo Peep*
Vol.4 *Old Mother Hubbard*
(additional stories included on tapes)
J2 Communications 1987
10850 Wilshire Blvd., Ste. 1000
Los Angeles, CA 90024

My Visit to the Doctor
Kids In Daily Situations, (KIDS)
20900 St. Clair Ave.
Cleveland, OH 44117
216-360-0240/800-282-3466

The Olden Days Coat 1981
Atlantis Films

The Orchestra 1990
(Peter Ustinov)
Mark Rubin Prod.
Distr: Alcazar Inc.
P.O. Box 429
Waterbury, VT 05676

Patrick's Dinosaurs/ What Happened to Patrick's Dinosaurs?
MCA 1992
Shelley Duvall's Bedtime Stories

Postman Pat 1992
(Fisher-Price)
GoodTimes Home Video
16 East 40th St.
New York, NY 10016

Railroaders: What Do You Want to be When You Grow Up?
Big Kids Prod.
1606 Dywer Ave.
Austin, TX 78704
800-477-7811
www.awardvids.com

Rainy Day Adventure
Joanie Bartels
Discovery Music
5554 Calhoun Ave.
Van Nuys, CA 91401

Ramona: The Great Hair Argument
Warner Bros.
4000 Warner Blvd.
Burbank, CA 91522

Road Construction Ahead
Fred Levine Prod.
P.O. Box 4010
30 Penhallow St.
Portsmouth, NH 03802
800-843-3686 x 497

See How They Grow series
Dorling Kindersley/Sony
Sony Music Entertainment
550 Madison Ave.
New York, NY 10022

Sesame Street Visits the Firehouse 1990
Random House/
Children's Television Workshop

Sesame Street Visits the Hospital
Random House/
Children's Television Workshop

Shamu & You series
Edutainment Resources./
Video Treasures Inc.
500 Kirts Blvd.
Troy, MI 48084

Star Scouts Discover NASA series
Gateways to Space
5976 W. Las Positas Blvd., Ste. 122
Pleasanton, CA 94588

Sunken Treasure
(Reading Rainbow)
Great Plains National
P.O. Box 80669
Lincoln, NE 69501
800-228-4630
www.pbs.org/readingrainbow/

The Teddy Bear Factory
Premier Images
217 Acadia St.
San Francisco, CA 94131
888-858-8433
www.video11.com

There Goes a Boat / There Goes the Mail
Vision Entertainment/
Power to Create Inc.
KidVision/Warner Music
Group Co.

The Video Guide to Stamp Collecting 1988
Premiere Home Video
Hollywood, CA 90038

Walk, Ride, Fly! 1994
Goldsholl: Learning Videos
420 Frontage Rd.
Northfield, IL 60093
800-243-8300

Wee Sing:
- *In the Big Rock Candy Mountain* 1995
- *In the Marvelous Musical Mansion* 1995
- *Grandpa's Magical Toys* 1988
- *King Cole's Party* 1987
- *Train* 1993
- *Under the Sea* 1994

Price Stern Sloan
MCA Home Video

Winter Tales
(Little Bear/Maurice Sendak)
Paramount Video
213-956-5907

Zoo Crew: What Do You Want to Be When You Grow Up?
Big Kids Prod.
1606 Dywer Ave.
Austin, TX 78704
800-477-7811
www.awardvids.com

Audio Cassettes/CDs

Abracadabra (Joe Scruggs) 1986

Ants (Joe Scruggs) 1994

Shadow Play Records
Educational Graphics Press
P.O. Box 180476
Austin, TX 78718
800-274-8804

Back to School Again 1996
(Mr. Al & Stephen Fite)
Melody House
819 NW 92nd St.
Oklahoma City, OK 73114
800-234-9228

Bananaphone 1994
(Raffi)
Shoreline Troubadour Records
1075 Cambie St.
Vancouver, B.C., Canada V6B 5L7

Bear-Robics 1990
(The Teddy Bear Band)
Distr: ActiveMinds
One Sportime Way
Atlanta, GA 30340
800-581-6740

Busytown Radio:
The Big Traffic Jam 1994
Richard Scarry
Rockin' Horse Records
500 Kirts Blvd.
Troy, MI 48084

A Car Full of Songs 1989
(Tom Paxton)
Pax Records
78 Park Place
East Hampton, NY 11937

Cars, Trucks & Trains 1997
(Jane Murphy)
Kimbo
Box 477
Long Branch, NJ 07740

A Child's Celebration
of Broadway 1995
Music for Little People
P.O. Box 1460
Redway, CA 95560
800-346-4445

A Child's Celebration
of Showtunes 1992
Music for Little People
P.O. Box 1460
Redway, CA 95560
800-346-4445

The Circus 1978
Clarus Music
340 Bellevue Ave.
Yonkers, NY 10703

Classic Nursery Rhymes 1991
(Hap Palmer)
Educational Activities
P.O. Box 392
Freeport, NY 11520

Come Ride Along With Me 1997
(James Coffey)
TM Books and Videos/
Blue Vision Music
P.O. Box 15118
Ft. Wayne, IN 46885

Corner Grocery Store 1979
(Raffi)
MCA Records
70 Universal City Plaza
Universal City, CA 91608

Dancin' Magic
(Joanie Bartels)
Discovery Music
5554 Calhoun Ave.
Van Nuys, CA 91401

The Dinosaur Album: A Musical
Adventure Through the Jurassic Age 1993
Kid Rhino/ Rhino Records
10635 Santa Monica Blvd.
Los Angeles, CA 90025

Dinosaur Choir 1992
(Bonnie Phipps)
Children's Music Connection
Denver, CO

Dinosaurs, Dragons, and
other children's songs 1990
Kevin Roth Music
Marlboro Records
P.O. Box 808
Unionville, PA 19375

Dirt Made My Lunch 1989
(Banana Slug String Band)
Music for Little People
P.O. Box 1460
Redway, CA 95560
800-346-4445

Disney Children's Favorites Vol. 3-4
-*With Apologies to Mother Goose*
-*Why Do They Make Things*
Like They Do?
-*The Marvelous Toy* 1986/1990
Walt Disney Records
Burbank, CA

Enjoy the Zoo 1984
Romper Room Songbook
of Musical Adventures

Family Garden 1993
(John McCutcheon)
Appalseed Prod.
1025 Locust Ave.
Charlottesville, VA 22901
804-977-6321
www.folkmusic.com

Folk Dance Fun 1984
Kimbo
Box 477
Long Branch, NJ 07740
Distr: ActiveMinds
One Sportime Way
Atlanta, GA 30340
800-581-6740

Happiness Cake 1989
(Linda Arnold)
A&M Records

Happy Birthday 1988
(Sharon, Lois & Bram)
Elephant Records
P.O. Box 101
Station Z
Toronto, Canada M5N 2Z3

Hello Sun, Goodnight Moon (SongSisters)
SongSisters
P.O. Box 7477
Ann Arbor, MI 48107

Homemade Band 1973
(Hap Palmer)
Educational Activities
P.O. Box 392
Freeport, NY 11520

Hop Like a Bunny, Waddle Like a Duck 1987
Golden Books
Western Publishing

Horse Sense for Kids and Other People 1992
(was Music for Little People)
Attn: Justin Bishop
P.O. Box 160525
Sacramento, CA 95816

I Love a Parade 1991
(Boston Pops/John Williams)
Sony Music Inc.

I'm a Happy Pirate 1989
(Doug & Gary)
Play Time Music
Bob Marini Doug & Gary

Insects, Bugs & Squiggly Things 1993
(Jane Murphy)
Kimbo
Box 477
Long Branch, NJ 07740

Mail Myself to You 1988
(John McCutcheon)
Appalseed Prod.
1025 Locust Ave.
Charlottesville, VA 22901
804-977-6321
www.folkmusic.com

Mainly Mother Goose 1984
(Sharon, Lois & Bram)
A&M Records

Oldies for Kool Kiddies
Re-Bop Records
Box 985
Marshfield, VT 05658
(802) 426-3558

On the Move with Greg & Steve 1983
Youngheart Records
P.O. Box 27784
Los Angeles, Ca 90027

Oodles of Animals
(Nancy Stewart)
Friends St. Music/BMI, S.E. 28th
Mercer Island, WA 98040

Peppermint Wings 1990
(Linda Arnold)
Children's Music Division
A&M Records
1416 North Labrea Ave.
Hollywood, CA 90028

Play Ball! 1998
(Cincinnati Pops)
Eric Kunzel
Telarc

Rainbow Palace 1991
(Linda Arnold)
Children's Music Division
A&M Records
1416 North Labrea Ave.
Hollywood, CA 90028

Rhinoceros Tap 1996
(Boynton & Ford)
Boynton! Recordings
Workman Publishing Co.
708 Broadway
New York, NY 10003

Rhythm of the Rocks 1993
(Marylee Sunseri & Nancy Stewart)
Friends St. Music/BMI, S.E. 28th
Mercer Island, WA 98040

Rhythms on Parade 1995
(Hap Palmer)
Hap-Pal Music
Box 323
Topanga, CA 90290

The Safari 1979
Clarus Music
340 Bellevue Ave.
Yonkers, NY 10703

Sailor Moon 1996
Kid Rhino/ Rhino Records
10635 Santa Monica Blvd.
Los Angeles, CA 90025

Shining Time Station:
Birthday Party Singsongs 1994
Quality Family Music
Video Treasures
500 Kirts Blvd.
Troy, MI 48084
800-745-1145

Sillytime Magic
(Joanie Bartels)
Discovery Music
5554 Calhoun Ave.
Van Nuys, CA 91401

Sing Around the Campfire 1995
(Sharon, Lois & Bram)
Drive Entertainment
10351 Santa Monica Blvd.
Los Angeles, CA 90025

Slugs at Sea 1991
(Banana Slug String Band)
Music for Little People
P.O. Box 1460
Redway, CA 95560
800-346-4445

Songs for Our Kids
(Song Train)
Song Train Music
1601 Glen Keiph Blvd.
Baltimore, MD 21286

Suzy is a Rocker
(Tom Paxton) 1992
Sony Music Video
666 Fifth Ave.
P.O. Box 4455
New York, NY 10101-4455

Swinging on a Rainbow 1990
(Cheryl Kirking)
Mill Pond Records
P.O. Box 525
Lake Mills, WI

Totally Teddy
(Derrie Frost)
Melody House
819 NW 92nd St.
Oklahoma City, OK 73114
800-234-9228

Trees, Trees, Trees:
Environment and Nature Songs
(Rainbow)

Unbearable Bears 1986
Marboro Records
845 Marlboro Spring Rd.
Kennett Square, PA 19348

Under the Big Top 1991
(Stephen Fite)
Melody House
819 NW 92nd St.
Oklahoma City, OK 73114
800-234-9228

What's That Sound? 1987
Living and Learning
Discovery Toys
P.O. Box 232008
Pleasant Hill, CA 94523

Where are the Dinosaurs?
(Diane Batchelor)
The Learning Line
P.O. Box 1406
University, AL 35486

Your Birthday Party 1986
(Oscar Brand and Friends)
Caedmon
1995 Broadway
New York, NY 10023

Internet Web Sites for Children's Videos

(reviews and purchase information)

www.awardvids.com

www.cybersuperstores.com/kidsfirst/list.html

www.greattapes.com

www.kidscore.com

www.kiwivideo.com

www.newkidhomevideo.com

www.newreleasesvideo.com/cgi-local/frontpag.cgi

www.pbs.org/readingrainbow/

www.sonywonder.com

About the Author

Pamela Waterman is a professional writer and mother of three children currently under the age of ten. She is a contributing author to *JumpStart 5th Grade Activities*, an educational book jointly produced by Knowledge Adventure Software and EPI. She is a teacher's aide and volunteer in preschool and elementary classrooms, in addition to being a leader and workshop designer for Brownies and Girl Scouts with a special emphasis on science and engineering. Waterman has published numerous articles on parenting, home renovation, and business, and is a Contributing Editor to Desktop Engineering magazine.

Index

A

Note: Headings in boldface refer to theme sections. Page numbers in italics refer to project directions.

B

N

O

P

Q

R

S